Ernest Ingersoll

Down East Latch Strings

Seashore, lakes and mountains by the Boston & Maine railroad - Descriptive of the tourist region of New England

Ernest Ingersoll

Down East Latch Strings

Seashore, lakes and mountains by the Boston & Maine railroad - Descriptive of the tourist region of New England

ISBN/EAN: 9783337193683

Printed in Europe, USA, Canada, Australia, Japan

Cover: Foto ©Andreas Hilbeck / pixelio.de

More available books at **www.hansebooks.com**

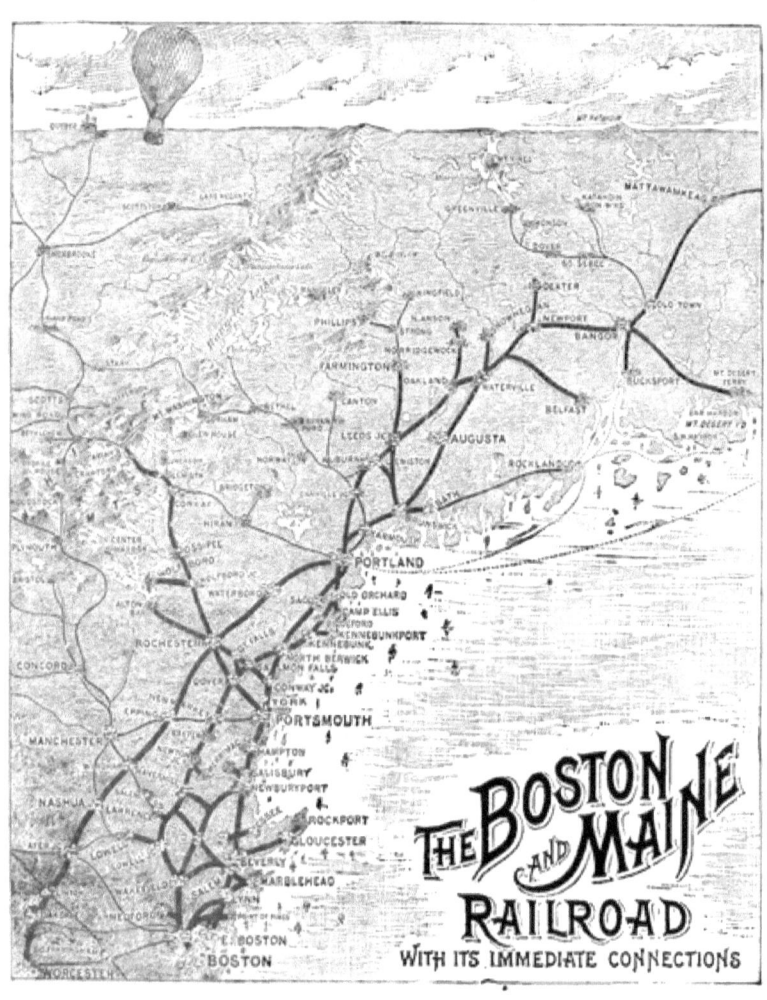

Down East Latch Strings;

OR

SEASHORE, LAKES AND MOUNTAINS

BY THE

Boston & Maine Railroad.

DESCRIPTIVE OF THE TOURIST REGION OF
NEW ENGLAND.

BY ERNEST INGERSOLL.

ILLUSTRATED
BY
H. B. COLBY AND F. H. TAYLOR.

PUBLISHED BY
PASSENGER DEPARTMENT BOSTON & MAINE RAILROAD.
1887.

RAND AVERY SUPPLY CO., BOSTON.

OFFICERS

Boston & Maine Railroad.

George C. Lord, President . . . . . Boston.
James T. Furber, General Manager . . . . "
Dana J. Flanders, Gen'l Passenger and Ticket Agent . "
Charles E. Lord, Ass't Gen'l Passenger and Ticket Agent. "
Charles A. Waite, Div. Pass'r Agent, Worcester, Nashua
    & Portland Division . . . . . . Worcester.
William Merritt, Jr., Sup't Western Division . . Boston.
Daniel W. Sanborn, Superintendent Eastern Division . "
John W. Sanborn, Sup't Northern Division, Wolfeboro' Junct.
George W. Hurlburt, Superintendent Worcester, Nashua
    & Portland Division . . . . . . Worcester.
Frank D. Gourley, Travelling Passenger Agent . . Boston.

TICKET AGENTS OF THE BOSTON & MAINE RAILROAD OF WHOM EXCURSION TICKETS MAY BE OBTAINED.

Samuel Gray .	306 Washington Street, Boston.
J. M. French .	Station, Haymarket Square, Boston.
J. C. Hiltz .	Station, Causeway Street, Boston.
C. M. Ruggles	Union Station, Worcester.
L. W. Marden .	" Salem.
A. A. Davis . .	" Lynn.
J. Clark .	" So. Lawrence.
A. C. Tapley . .	" Haverhill.
F. J. Clark .	" Lowell.
F. W. Pope .	" Clinton.
C. H. Kinney	" Ayer Junction.
F. Barr .	" Nashua.

ALSO, AT THE

PRINCIPAL TICKET OFFICES IN NEW YORK, PHILADELPHIA, BALTIMORE, WASHINGTON, AND IN ALL THE PRINCIPAL CITIES THROUGHOUT THE COUNTRY.

Publisher's Preface.

In presenting to the intending summer tourist a description of the scenery along the line of, and reached by the Boston & Maine Railroad and its immediate connections, the first difficulty, and in fact the only one, is in knowing where to commence and where to leave off.

The almost impossibility of condensing into a volume of two hundred and seventy pages the contents of innumerable volumes of historical and descriptive matter, all of which may be of interest and value to the pleasure seeker and the sportsman, is fully appreciated by the publishers of this little work.

There is no section of our country which furnishes so much of historical interest to the American as New England, and the constant streams of tourists through the summer months sufficiently evidence its popularity from a scenic or a medicinal point of view.

Here along its beaches or among its rocky promontories, with the broad Atlantic's breezes cooling the heated air, its piney woods and lakes furnishing health and sport to the Nimrods and Isaak Waltons of our land, or its pastoral valleys and "cloud-capped granite hills," may be found entertainment, health and pleasure for all tastes, however developed or inclined.

In presenting the attractions of this region to the *people*, no attempt has been made to more than touch upon its history or its beauties, but simply to extend the Latch Strings, having confidence that an acceptance of the invitation to pull, will open the door to an unlimited field of research into the history or the scenic beauty of New England's seashore, lakes and mountains.

It has been asserted that too much of a good thing is worse than none at all, and with this belief the author has sought to break up the monotony of description by interspersing the comments of a trio during their trip through some of the most interesting portions of this section, and the reader will accept this as an apology, if apology be needed, for devoting to romance, space that might easily have been devoted to dry facts.

The author's name alone, is a sufficient guarantee that the different subjects have been well handled, and the artistic work speaks for itself in the illustrations and maps.

As to the expense of a trip through, or a sojourn in this part of New England, the individual tastes must be consulted, and upon a reference to the list of excursions, hotels and boarding-houses accompanying the book, will, no doubt, answer any inquiries in that direction.

In regard to the facilities for reaching the points and places of interest referred to, it need only be said that the Boston and Maine, having its pecuniary interests in view, is bound to furnish the best there is in the way of road-bed, train service and rolling stock, and at rates to meet the necessities or desires of the public.

CONTENTS.

CHAPTER.		PAGE.
I.	OUTWARD BOUND	1
II.	ALONG THE OLD BOSTON & MAINE	3
III.	THE NASHUA VALLEY	11
IV.	LAKE WINNIPESAUKEE	17
V.	PORTLAND AND THE MAINE BEACHES	31
VI.	ALONG THE MAINE COAST	44
VII.	MOUNT DESERT	53
VIII.	THE PISCATAQUIS VALLEY	71
IX.	MOOSEHEAD LAKE	76
X.	BANGOR AND THE MARITIME PROVINCES	92
XI.	THE VALLEY OF THE KENNEBEC	104
XII.	KENNEBEC TO THE ANDROSCOGGIN	112
XIII.	ON THE RANGELEY LAKES	117
XIV.	UMBAGOG AND THE MAGALLOWAY	130
XV.	BETHEL AND GORHAM	145
XVI.	THE GLEN	155
XVII.	MOUNT WASHINGTON	164
XVIII.	AT FABYAN'S	178
XIX.	FRANCONIA NOTCH AND THE PROFILE	182
XX.	THE CONNECTICUT VALLEY	193
XXI.	THROUGH THE CRAWFORD NOTCH	198
XXII.	AT NORTH CONWAY	215
XXIII.	HOMEWARD BY THE NORTH SHORE	231

ILLUSTRATIONS.

	PAGE
AROUND LANCASTER,—B. & M. R.R. BRIDGE, THE BIG ELM	13
A BIT OF MEADOW	15
A PASSING SHOWER, LAKE WINNIPESAUKEE	18
LAKE WINNIPESAUKEE FROM LONG ISLAND	21
BLACK MOUNTAIN FROM MOULTONBOROUGH BAY, LAKE WINNIPESAUKEE	23
A GLIMPSE AT LAKE WINNIPESAUKEE	24
RED HILL FROM MOULTONBOROUGH BAY	26
GREAT FALLS STATION	31
EARLY MORNING,—THE NUBBLE, YORK BEACH	33
STORM AT BALD HEAD CLIFF	35
OCEAN VIEW FROM CAPE ARUNDEL, KENNEBUNKPORT	37
SPOUTING ROCK, KENNEBUNKPORT	38
OLD ORCHARD BEACH	39
OLD HOUSE ON CAPE ELIZABETH	40
SOMES' SOUND, MT. DESERT	54
BAR HARBOR, MT. DESERT	57
AROUND MT. DESERT,—ALONG SHORE, OUT TO SEA FROM TOP OF GREEN MOUNTAIN, SARGENT'S MOUNTAIN, MILL AT SOMESVILLE	61
COTTAGE AT BAR HARBOR	64
OTTER CLIFF	66
MT. KINEO, MOOSEHEAD LAKE	79
MOOSEHEAD LAKE FROM MT. KINEO	81
SQUAW MOUNTAINS, BIG AND LITTLE SPENCER MOUNTAINS	82
KATAHDIN FROM NORTH BAY, MOOSEHEAD LAKE	90
CANTILEVER BRIDGE, ST. JOHN, N. B.	94
GRAND FALLS, N. B.	95
A BIG TROUT	119
VIEWS FROM RANGELEY LAKES, BALD MOUNTAIN, DEAD RIVER MOUNTAINS	121
BEMIS STREAM, WEST KENNEBAGO MOUNTAIN	123
AZISCOOS MOUNTAIN FROM MOOSELUCMAGUNTIC	124
DEER MOUNTAIN, RANGELEY LAKES	126
ON THE MAGALLOWAY RIVER	131
IN DIXVILLE NOTCH, MOSS GLEN	133

	PAGE
White Mountains from Umbagog Lake	134
Aziscoos Falls, Magalloway River	135
Upper Magalloway	137
Diamond Peaks	138
On the Magalloway River	139
On Lake Parmachenee	141
A Glimpse of Saddle Back Mountain	143
Screw-Auger Falls, Grafton Notch	144
Entrance to Carter Notch from Gorham	146
A By-Road at Bethel	148
Near the Glen House, Peabody River	156
Glen Ellis Falls	159
Jacob's Ladder, Mt. Washington	176
A Gray-Day in Crawford Notch	199
A Lonely bit of Meadow, Crawford Notch	201
Through the Notch	203
The Mountains from Upper Bartlett	211
Peak of Moat Mountain, North Conway	212
Mts. Bartlett and Kiarsarge, North Conway	216
Pitman's Arch, North Conway	217
The Ledges, North Conway	218
Cathedral Ledge and Echo Lake, North Conway	219
One of North Conway's Cascades	221
A Glimpse of White Face	223
Entrance to Albany Intervale	224
The Pinnacles	225
Mt. Washington from Conway Meadows	229
Old Wentworth House	234
Church Point, Portsmouth	236
Cottage at Jaffrey Point	238
Hampton Marshes	241
Old Wharves at Gloucester	250
Tail-Piece,—Diana's Baths, North Conway	256

MAPS.

Bird's-Eye View Boston & Maine System	Frontispiece.
Boston & Maine Railroad and Connections	4
Boston & Maine Railroad	14
Lake Winnipesaukee	24
Mount Desert	56
Hunting and Fishing Resorts of Maine	80
White Mountains	180

Gems of the Northland, never yet
Were lakes in lovelier valleys set
Glassing the granite and the pines
That mark New Hampshire's mountain lines.
And not less fair the winding ways
Of Casco and Penobscot bays.
They seek for happier shores in vain
Who leave the summer isles of Maine!

                            John G. Whittier

Danvers
1st mo. 26 1882

CHAPTER I.

OUTWARD BOUND.

And for to see, and eke for to be seye. —CHAUCER.

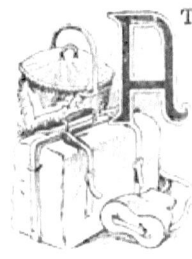AT last I had some good news for Prue — and for myself, too. It had looked for a time as though there was to be no vacation this year, when it seemed more than usually needful to both of us; though we were by no means broken in health — only a little strained. But that is just the point when one wants to stop and recuperate, partly because it costs the system less energy to recover than after the breaking-down is complete, and partly because a pretty well man can enjoy his vacation so much more than a pretty ill one can.

So I rode home that evening in a hurry, but curbed my spirits before I went into the house, and made no sign until the roast was out of the way, and I had a little cup of coffee and my after-dinner cigar well a-light. Then I suppose my satisfaction began to come to the surface for my wife spoke out, rather sharply, —

"Can't you tell me the joke? If there's anything especially disagreeable in you, Theo, it's that way you have of hugging a good story to yourself and not telling it to me. If you knew how lonesome and hot it has been out here all day, you wouldn't be so careless of my pleasure. *Do* stop that furious grin!"

Furious grin! Of all the mixtures of terms I ever heard, that was the worst; yet it seemed to have a certain appropriateness. Evidently we were in need of a change of scene.

"Oh, it's nothing," I answered mildly; "at least nothing much. Only I've a chance for a very pretty vacation trip to the northward that I was going to tell you about presently."

My wife's half-tearful eyes opened wide. She sprang up, rushed round the table and — but no matter. These domestic incidents are neither here nor there.

"Now tell me all about it," she demanded, when peace had been fully restored.

"Well, that bothersome business that I feared was going to keep me in town all summer has at last come to an end, and in a few days I can get away for a good long trip."

"'Whither, Oh whither, Oh whither, away,'" sang my *vis-a-vis* ecstatically.

"I've been longing to see the White Mountains again, and you've been wishing you could go down to Maine. So we will do both, if you'll promise not to make too long a stay in any one place."

"Oh, I'll promise anything, and go anywhere. And I wonder whether we couldn't get Mr. Baily to go with us? You know he said in his last letter that he hadn't been out of town yet, and was undecided about it. I dare say he'd jump at this chance."

"Very likely. I'll write him to-night."

Baily was a friend of ours in New York, who had been a companion on more than one trip before. Though a bachelor he was not cranky, — only orderly, statistical and nice. He had more money than Prue and I together, twice over; was large-minded, serene of temper and an eager sportsman. This trip would undoubtedly suit him, we judged, and judged rightly, for he promptly replied that he would gladly go with us.

So we arranged our journey, with an eye to an enjoyable alternation of scenes and amusements,—now inland scenery and country fare, now hotel life and social gayety by the "loud-resounding sea", and anon some fishing and shooting; and this was the result:—

Boston via Haverhill to Lake Winnipesaukee; thence by rail to Old Orchard and Portland, Maine, and steamer to Mount Desert; thence to Moosehead lake and the Rangeley lakes in succession; and finally to the White Mountains. Several side-trips were suggested in addition, as possible.

Everybody thought this an admirable tour; and Baily telegraphed that he would come up from New York by the way of Worcester and Nashua, and overtake us at Rochester, N.H., at a certain time.

The General Passenger Agent of the Boston & Maine Railroad pinned us together a little book of tickets which should carry us all the way round: the appointed day came and we started, with a look of expectant enjoyment on Prue's somewhat wan face, that it did me good to see, for I knew the color would come into her cheeks fast enough when we got a taste of the balsamic breezes blowing straight from the cool northern hills.

CHAPTER II.

ALONG THE OLD BOSTON & MAINE.

When things are once come to the execution, there is no secrecy comparable to celerity.—BACON.

IN Haymarket Square, the Boston & Maine Railroad has the advantage of possessing the station nearest to the business centre of the city, of all the passenger depots in Boston. Fifty years ago sloops and barges, bringing rural produce, used to float up to the place where it now stands and deliver their merchandise on the adjacent wharves. So large a part of this trade was in hay, that the locality became known as the hay-market. Oyster boats from Wellfleet were accustomed to land here, too. Then the canal was replaced by the railway, and filling went on until it had gone beyond the old causeway (now Causeway street) which formerly bounded the river-front at the edge of the flats.

Now, as we leave the station and cross the Charles river, through a wilderness of tracks and drawbridges, we find it impossible to realize how the Charles must have looked two centuries ago, when spacious meadows lined its current on each side, and boats might be rowed almost to the centre of what is now the Common.

On the right, as we cross the river, the heights of Charlestown and Bunker Hill monument are in full view, while at the left, and ahead, are East Cambridge and Somerville, rising into Winter Hill, where Burgoyne's captive troops viewed the scenery over the muskets of their guards a good deal longer than they cared to. Somerville does not show to good advantage from the cars nor does Chelsea; but when we get past, and out upon the meadows of the Mystic and can look backward to the left at the hills of West Somerville and Medford (the latter crowned by the clustered buildings of Tuft's College), we begin to enjoy the real country. In Medford, is a two-storied, low-roofed brick house, built by Gov. Matthew Craddock, in 1634, and said to be the oldest edifice in New England. The town contains the homes of many prominent business men of Boston. A more general repute belongs to Medford in connection with the rum made there ever since colonial days, when the odor of sanctity was hardly distinguishable from an odor of rum on all occasions of hospitality or celebration.

On the high bank beyond these meadows (in whose colors an artist must always take delight) is old "Mystic-side," now called Malden,—

one of the favorite suburbs of Boston, and the residence of many persons doing business in the city. It was one of the first settling-places of the Puritan pioneers, and its annals are unusually interesting. One of the churches near the station was organized on that site in 1649. Little of the flavor of antiquity lingers about Malden, however. In the grounds cultivated first so long ago, and under aged shade trees, have risen long streets of handsome suburban homes, in the centre of which has lately been opened one of the finest buildings in the state as a public library and art gallery. Malden has several factories and some 17,000 inhabitants, who are wide-awake.

"If mother were here," remarks Prue, "she would tell us that the most noteworthy thing about Malden is, that it was the home of Judson, the famous missionary to Burmah, whose 'Memoir' was one of the very few books I was allowed to read on Sunday, when I was a girl."

Beyond Malden the train carries us into a region of rocky hills, which arrange themselves and the openings between them,—often filled with small ponds, or occupied by some neat cottage or hamlet,— into a constant succession of charming landscapes. In such a region is Melrose, and its pleasantly scattered neighbor, The Middlesex Fells. This district, only seven to ten miles from the city, has retained its wildness so long because it was of little use to the farmer or market gardener. But this was a great boon to the city men; and among its broken hills, crags, and prairie nooks, beside its dancing streams and under the shade of its oaks and chestnuts, have now been built scores of beautiful country homes, picturesque in outward appearance and luxurious within, while magnificent roads have replaced in all directions the old cart-tracks and country highways. We were looking over a collection of photographs, the other day, made among these rugged little hills,—none of which are too high for a child to climb, yet big enough to make imposing features in the limited views afforded to any one house set in their midst,—and we were astonished at the wildness and the artistic charm shown in every direction. Among all the justly admired environs of Boston, I know of none likely to grow into greater beauty than The Middlesex Fells.

Next, we pass through Melrose and Melrose Highlands, where a street railroad connects for Stoneham, a shoe-making town; then Wakefield, which derives its name and a part of its prosperity from the family of that name, whose rattan furniture is seen all over the world, and whose tasteful munificence has adorned a factory town with elegant public and private buildings. One branch railroad diverges near here (at Wakefield Junction) and runs through Lynnfield to Peabody and Salem; while another crosses the hills northward to Newburyport. Its principal stations are Danvers, Topsfield, Boxford, and Georgetown,—situated on one or other of the old turnpikes through Essex county, and as full of traditions of Puritan and Revolutionary days as their fields are full of rocks. In Danvers, first sprang up that fatal delusion of witchcraft, in 1692, which desolated Salem. Oak Knoll in this town is now the residence of the poet, Whittier. Here crosses the Lawrence branch, connecting Lawrence and Salem through Middleton and North Andover; and from Georgetown a branch runs through Groveland to Bradford and Haverhill.

The main line of the "Western," or inland division of the Boston & Maine, by which the through trains are sent northward, bends westward from Wakefield and passes through the farming towns of Reading and Wilmington to Lowell Junction, whence a short branch-road carries passengers to Lowell, on the Merrimac river.

The Merrimac valley was of great renown among the aborigines. Their weirs and fishing stations occurred all along its banks, from the headwaters down, and upon its tributaries. The warm bottom-lands along these streams afforded choice farming places, and the French in Canada were told of it as early as 1604. Lying on the boundary between the possessions of the Laconia company and those allotted to the Massachusetts colony, it was entered by representatives of both. Haverhill was settled about 1635, and other towns were founded a little later along the Merrimac and its tributaries. By 1674, Gookin and Eliot were preaching missionary sermons to the Indians. On one May Sunday they met in Wamesit, at the wigwam of one called Wannalancet, about two miles from the village, near Pawtucket falls in the Merrimac river. The step to this year of grace, 1887, is long, but the story is rapid. "Pawtucket and Wamesit, where the Indians resorted in the fishing season, are now Lowell, the city of spindles and Manchester of America, which sends its cotton cloth around the globe."

But this gigantic weaver is a youth among the towns he has so outstripped in size. A canal was made around Pawtucket falls a century or more ago; but the water-power was not utilized until 1821, when some Boston men set up a factory here. In 1823 the "Merrimac" cotton mills were started. Now, Lowell's textile factories employ a capital of nearly $20,000,000, running 25,000 looms and almost a million spindles. "They produce annually 240,000,000 yards of cotton cloth, 10,000,000 yards of woolens, 3,500,000 yards of carpetings, 120,000 shawls, 16,500,000 pairs of hose; and 100,000,000 yards of cloth are dyed and printed." In addition to this, many other branches of machine industry are followed in this busy city, whose demands have outgrown, twice over, the power afforded by its river, even when conserved by the great dam at the outlet of its Winnipesaukee reservoir. Lowell now contains about 70,000 inhabitants, the larger half of whom are foreign born, and employed in the mills. The best residences are on the hill encircling the city. From Lowell went that 6th Massachusetts regiment which was mobbed in Baltimore on April 19, 1861; and a marble monument to the two young citizens killed at that time stands on Merrimac street, in the busiest quarter of the town.

A few miles beyond is Andover,—than which no rural name in New England is more widely known. "This ancient academic town was settled about 1643, on the Indian domain of Cochickewick, which was bought from the natives for $26.64 and a coat. Andover has some manufactures but is chiefly famed for its schools. The Punchard High School is a local institution of high standing. Phillips' Academy (distinct from that at Exeter, N. H.) occupies a fine building on the hill, and is of wide reputation. It was endowed by the Phillips' family in 1778, with $85,000 and considerable landed estates, and has since occupied a prominent position. The Abbott Female Seminary is an old and famous school for young ladies. The Theological Seminary of the Congregational Church was founded about 1808, and soon after received liberal endowments. . . . This institution has long been the 'school of the prophets' for the sect to which it belongs, and has prepared its ablest divines for their work. . . . Its buildings are very plain, causing the visitor to wonder 'if orthodox angels have not lifted up old Harvard and Massachusetts' halls, and carried them by night from Cambridge to Andover hill.' But the situation is one of extreme beauty, and the grounds are quiet and abounding in trees. . . . A beautiful chapel has lately been built."

There are pretty ponds in Andover, and the valley of the Shawsheen river has the well-known Shawsheen grove and some pleasant rural scenery, while the view from Andover hill (at sunset, especially,) is highly praised. Many summer visitors stay here, partly attracted by the fine society.

This society has, in the past, included many persons of intellectual superiority and fame, and is similarly enriched at present. The names of some of these are "familiar as household words." The husband of Harriet Beecher Stowe was a professor of Hebrew at the Theological school, and the house in which Mrs. Stowe wrote *Uncle Tom's Cabin*, is still standing. Elizabeth Stuart Phelps, author of *Gates Ajar* and other books, is still a resident of the village, where her mother, also an authoress, lived and wrote. The list might be extended.

Just beyond Andover, Lawrence comes into view, located upon both sides of the Merrimac river. A short branch road extends across the river and connects with the Manchester & Lawrence railroad for Manchester and Concord, N. H., and other towns in northern New Hampshire and Vermont.

Lawrence was selected as a factory site half a century ago by the Essex company, who built a great dam across the Merrimac and thus secured an immense water power. This dam is 28 feet high, and 1,000 feet long, so that were it a natural cataract the fall of water over it would be thought a sight worthy of a long pilgrimage. Lawrence has now about 40,000 inhabitants and great wealth. One of its cotton mills alone, runs 150,000 spindles and employs nearly 5,000 operatives; several others employ from 500 to 3,000 people each. Besides the cotton mills there are extensive factories for woolen goods, paper, machinery, woodenware, etc. The mills and the populous community of tenements and boarding houses in which an army of working-people dwells, is separated from the main part of the city by a canal and a park. This leaves the town proper unvitiated by the presence of noisy and unsightly factories, and its wealth has made it into the handsomest city of its class in the state. It received its name from the Lawrence family of Boston, who were early identified with its industries.

The country all along this part of the line is rolling and agricultural, though seeming to a person accustomed to such regions as the Connecticut valley, less thoroughly cultivated than it ought to be. But the irregularity and rockiness of the land, and the many ponds, which render complete cultivation impracticable, add to its interest for us who are merely lookers on, having neither to till it, nor pay its taxes.

After leaving Lawrence, the railroad follows the bright and swift Merrimac for some distance, passes through the village of North Andover, enters Bradford, and crosses the river into Haverhill,—a big town and a busy one, devoted principally to shoemaking, the chief industry of all the Essex towns outside of Lawrence.

This Merrimac river is worth a moment's pause. Bubbling out of the snow-fed springs in the White Mountains, and reinforced by the steady flow of Lake Winnipesaukee, it is pure and vigorous from its birth. " At first it comes on murmuring to itself by the base of stately and retired mountains, through moist primitive woods whose juices it receives, where the bear still drinks it, and the cabins of settlers are far between, and there are few to cross its stream; enjoying in solitude its cascades still unknown to fame; by long ranges of mountains of Sandwich and of Squam, slumbering like tumuli of Titans, with the peaks of Moosehillock, the Haystack, and Kiarsarge reflected in its waters; where the maple and raspberry, those lovers of the hills, flourish amid temperate dews,—flowing long and full of meaning, but untranslatable as its name, *Pemigewasset*, by many a pastured Pelion and Ossa, where unnamed muses haunt, tended by Oreads, Dryads, Naiads, and receiving the tribute of many an untasted Hippocrene. There are earth, air, fire, and water,—very well, this is water, and down it comes. . . . Falling all the way, and yet not discouraged by the lowest fall. By the law of its birth never to become stagnant, for it has come out of the clouds, and down the sides of precipices worn in the flood, through beaver-dams broke loose, not splitting but splicing and mending itself, until it found a breathing-place in this low land. So it flows on down by Lowell, Lawrence and Haverhill, at which last place it first suffers a sea change, and a few masts betray the vicinity of the ocean. Between the towns of Amesbury and Newbury it is a broad commercial river, from a third to half a mile in width, no longer skirted with yellow and crumbling banks, but backed by high green hills and pastures, with frequent white beaches on which the fishermen draw up their nets; . . . until, at last, you glide under the famous Chain Bridge, and are landed at Newburyport. Thus she who at first was 'poore of waters, naked of renowne,' having received so many fair tributaries, as was said of the Forth,

> 'Doth grow the greater still, the further downe;
> Till that abounding both in power and fame,
> She long doth strive to give the sea her name.'"

Here, almost two centuries ago, happened that thrilling incident of colonial history of which the heroic Hannah Dustan was the central figure. Every schoolboy knows it,—how, one bitter March night, Hannah had been dragged from a sick-bed by the Indians and been compelled to march, half-dressed and barefooted through the snowy wilderness far to the northward. "She had seen her seven elder children flee with their father, but knew not of their fate. She had seen her infant's brains dashed out against an apple-tree, and had left her own and her neighbors' dwellings in ashes. When she reached the wigwam of her captor, situated on an island in the Merrimac, more than fifty miles above where we now are, she had been told that she and her nurse were soon to be taken to a distant Indian settlement, and there made to run the gauntlet, naked. The family of this Indian consisted of two men, three women, and seven children, besides an English boy whom she found a prisoner among them. Having determined to attempt her escape, she instructed the boy to inquire of one of the men, how he should despatch an enemy in the quickest manner, and take his scalp. 'Strike 'em there,' said he, placing his finger on his temple, and he also showed him how to take off the scalp. On the morning of the 31st she arose before daybreak, and awoke her nurse and the boy, and taking the Indians' tomahawks, they killed them all in their sleep, excepting one favorite boy and one squaw who fled wounded with him to the woods. The English boy struck the Indian who had given him the information, on the temple as he had been directed. They then collected all the provisions they could find, and took their master's tomahawk and gun, and scuttling all the canoes but one, commenced their flight to Haverhill, distant about sixty miles by the river. But, after having proceeded a short distance, fearing that her story would not be believed if she should escape to tell it, they returned to the silent wigwam, and taking off the scalps of the dead, put them into a bag as proofs of what they had done, and then retracing their steps to the shore in the twilight, recommenced their voyage. . . . Ice is floating in the river,—the spring is opening; the muskrat and beaver are driven out of their holes by the flood; deer gaze at them from the banks; a few faint-singing forest birds, perchance, fly across the river to the northernmost shore; the fish-hawk sails and screams overhead, and geese fly over with a startling clangor; but they do not observe these things, or they speedily forget them. They do not smile or chat all day. Sometimes they pass an Indian grave surrounded by its paling on the bank, or the frame of a wigwam, with a few coals left behind, or the withered stalks still rustling in the Indian's solitary cornfield on the intervale. The birch stripped of its bark, or the charred stump where a tree has been burned down to be made into a canoe, these are the only traces of man,—a fabulous wild man to us. On either side, the primeval forest stretches away uninterrupted to Canada, or to the 'South Sea'; . . . While two sleep, one will manage the canoe, and the swift stream bear them onward to the settlements, it may be, even to old John Lovewell's house on Salmon brook to-night. According to the historian, they escaped as by a miracle all roving bands of Indians, and reached their homes in safety, with their trophies, for which the General Court paid them fifty pounds. The family of Hannah Dustan all assembled alive once more, except the infant whose brains were dashed out against the apple-tree, and there have been many who, in later times, have lived to say that they had eaten of the fruit of that apple-tree. This seems a long while ago, and yet it happened since Milton wrote his *Paradise Lost.*" (*Thoreau.*)

Haverhill has now some 25,000 inhabitants, and the high eminence which it covers gives a wonderful picture of the teeming valley. Certain parts of the town have an appearance of venerable age and picturesqueness. The *new* look of the dozens of factories and business blocks in the midst of which the railroad station stands, is due to the fact that the whole riverside was leveled by fire a few years ago, and has been rebuilt.

"Shall we *never* get away from the city!" cries Prue, impatiently, as we roll out between brick walls and bustling business streets.

"Very soon, now. It is real country beyond here, all the way to Exeter, in New Hampshire, where I can console you, my dear, with a piece of pie baked in a farmer-wife's oven and a glass of new milk."

"Nonsense! I knew a youngster at Phillips' Academy who told me that one of the 'larks' was to get out and have a 'feed' at the station restaurant, because they got *city* things to eat there."

"Well, I'll yield the pie, but I stick to the fresh milk."

The academy of which Prue spoke is the pride of Exeter, which, otherwise, is a most attractive village of about 3,500 people, in the midst of a farming region. It was founded in 1781, by the Hon. John Phillips, who endowed it, and it has since attained to great wealth and the highest rank as a preparatory school, so that it has been called the Eton of America. A long list of famous men are among its alumni,— famous in almost every walk of life,—and include Daniel Webster, Lewis Cass (who was born in the village), Edward Everett, Jared Sparks, and many at present in public prominence. More than 4,000 have been graduated from it, and 200 boys are annually taught there. The buildings are attractive and occupy an elm-shaded campus. There is also a large school for young ladies in the village, but the bars are not often down between the two institutions.

Exeter is at the head of Exeter river, which flows into Great bay, a curious expansion of the Piscataqua, admitting the tide. South Newmarket Junction (where the Concord Railroad crosses) and Newmarket, just beyond, are also on arms of this bay. At Durham, again, we strike it, crossing Oyster river, which takes its name from the oysters found living there by the earliest settlers (more or less native oysters are still gathered at the mouth of this river), and then comes Dover,—the oldest settlement in New Hampshire. Only three years later than the coming of the Mayflower, the Laconia company of commercial speculators to whom this whole region had been granted, sent colonists who settled (1623) where Dover now stands, at the confluence of the Bellamy and Cocheco rivers,—the head of sloop navigation. They belonged to the Church of England, were not seeking religious liberty, but gold and furs, and were greatly annoyed by the intolerant Puritans. In 1641, the colony was forcibly annexed to Massachusetts, but was given back to New Hampshire in 1679. The Indians soon became hostile, and during the first half-century of their history, the Dover people were incessantly in terror of the redskins. A trick by which (in time of peace) they disarmed and captured a large number of savages, several of whom were hung, was avenged in 1689 by a massacre of nearly the whole settlement, and the death under torture of the aged governor who had directed the previous outrage. War did not cease until after the long French-and-Indian struggle in which the redmen exhausted themselves; but Dover was never abandoned. The town now is one of the most interesting and prosperous of the old centres of colonial life. It numbers about 10,000 inhabitants, and has extensive cotton mills and other manufactories.

Here the Northern Division of the Boston & Maine Railroad diverges toward Lake Winnipesaukee and the White Mountains, while the main line keeps on to Portland. We are bound to Lake Winnipesaukee, but are not required to change cars, since we took the precaution in Boston to find seats in a car labeled "Alton Bay," which is detached here and re-attached to the north-bound train. After a brief delay, therefore, we are again under way, in an augmented company of merry holidaymakers, and half an hour later get sight of Rochester, across a broad and level tract long ago called the Norway plain, on account of the prevalence of Norway pines in its forest.

CHAPTER III.

THE NASHUA VALLEY

Not unconcerned, Wachusett rears his head
Above the field, so late from nature won,
With patient brow reserved, as one who read
New annals in the history of man. — THOREAU.

THE first person we saw on the station platform, at Rochester, was our own Baily — light overcoat across his arm, rose in his button-hole, every inch a New York broker, from his high white hat to his low white gaiters.

"Now give an account of yourself," Prue demanded, when the greetings were over and our *confrère* had seated himself beside us.

"Why, there isn't much to tell. I left New York yesterday morning and spent the afternoon and night at Worcester, Mass., in visiting an old chum of mine in Wall Street who was settled down there."

"Tell us something about Worcester?"

"Well, Worcester's an interesting city, both for its antiquity and its modernity. It was settled, they told me, as long ago as 1669, and it was one of the hot-beds of political free-thinking before and throughout the Revolution. Now it has some 70,000 inhabitants, which makes it second only to Boston among Massachusetts towns. My friend drove me all over the place, and I thought it one of the finest towns I was ever in. The main street is a fine wide avenue two miles long, with the business blocks in its centre shading off into elegant residences: 'shading off' is a happy expression, too, since the elms and maples along the sidewalks are continuous. And the number of public institutions and schools pointed out to me is amazing — it's a great town for education, and libraries, museums and that sort of thing. I don't know when I've been more entertained than I was in the rooms of the Antiquarian Society. Worcester is a manufacturing town — makes all sorts of things. My friend thought it must be its central situation in relation to lines of transportation (half a dozen railroads converge there) which made it prosper so well. The wealth of its old families and energy of its new ones is a better reason — one which lies behind the other in my opinion. Anyhow, Worcester is one of the most prosperous and most agreeable towns in New England to spend a day in, and I should say it would be a fine place to live.

"This morning I took a Boston and Maine train on the Worcester, Nashua and Portland Division, for Rochester, via Nashua, and here I am."

"Gracious!" Prue cried, "how did you remember the way?"

"I wrote it down."

"That was wise of you — but tell us some more. What did you see along the road? That is an interesting country, isn't it?"

"Decidedly so. The railroad leads down the Nashua River valley, at first through a lot of manufacturing villages like West Boylston, Sterling Junction and Clinton. Sterling Junction they told me, is an important place in the eyes of the Methodist Church, which sustains an annual camp-meeting there. Close by is a more worldly, and, I fear, more popular, resort in the picnic grounds at Washacum lake. At Clinton, Madame, carpets, — Brussels and Wilton — and also wire netting for window screens, etc., are prominent articles of manufacture; then comes a string of lovely old villages, like Lancaster, Harvard, Groton and Pepperell. There was something to interest me all the way."

The valley of the Nashua was one of the earliest reclaimed by the Puritans; and its devious roads and ancient homesteads, surrounded by spacious meadows or sheltered under the verdant hills, are shaded by aged elms — some of extraordinary girth.

Mt. Wachusett is rather too far away to be counted as belonging to Lancaster (it and the village of Princeton may be reached from Oakdale) but it is conspicuous and beautiful from there, and for a long distance along the railway northward, presiding over wide-rolling uplands. "The roving eye still rests inevitably on her hills, and she still holds up the skirts of the sky on that side."

Since Thoreau went there, described the view from its bold summit, and wrote his poem, Wachusett has become one of the literary shrines. But the view itself is noteworthy as something quite different from "the sublimity and grandeur which belong to mountain scenery" in general — a fact due to the isolation and height (1,900 feet) above the plain. It is a picture of civilization and industry. "On every side," Thoreau writes, "the eye ranged over successive circles of towns rising one above another, like the terraces of a vineyard, till they were lost in the horizon."

The historical incidents of the region are those connected with savage warfare. The earliest explorers were Indian traders, and in 1657 the trade of "Nashuway river" was sold for £8. The region was thickly populated by red men, divided into many small bands, each under its own leader, but all, from the Merrimac to the Connecticut, acknowledging the general supremacy of Passaconaway, sachem of the Pennacook confederacy. This man owed his power not only to his exploits as a warrior, and his skill as a sorcerer, but to his strong native sagacity. He died in 1670, at the reputed age of 120, and his name is preserved not only by the noble mountain north of Lake Winnipesaukee, but in many a tradition. Nasawock (Lancaster) was repeatedly attacked by King Phillip previous to that frightful February day in 1676 marked by Mrs. Rowlandson's capture.

"She herself wrote a most pathetic account of it, and of her captivity." Prue reminds us. "I remember how she speaks of it as 'the dolefullest day that mine eyes ever saw.' It must have been, poor thing."

But that was not all the "doleful" history of this vale. A few miles further north is Groton, where old Monoco's band destroyed everything except the blockhouses. "This same sachem boasted to the besieged that he was marching on Concord and Boston, to destroy those towns. Within a year he was indeed in Boston, but as a captive, led through the

AROUND LANCASTER, MASS.

streets with a rope round his neck, and afterwards hung on the Common." Pepperell is a dear old fashioned town, distinguished as the home of the Prescotts, whose antiquated mansion-house is near the village. Here Wm. Hickling Prescott, the father of the present owner, wrote many of his splendid histories. His father was a circuit judge; and his grandfather that hero of Bunker Hill — Col. Wm. Prescott, who led the Cambridge Minute-men.

These settlements, and Dunstable (now Nashua) at the mouth of the Nashua river, were on the extreme frontier at that time, and remained so through many years, always harassed by Indian raids, of which every town can tell its traditions, and give a hero's name. No name, however, is so notorious as that of John Lovewell, of Dunstable, who, after the uprisings of 1724, raised a company of Indian fighters under an offer of the government to pay £10 for every scalp. Lovewell was a hunter and Indian scout, and the son of one of Cromwell's old Roundheads. His band were men of the same stamp and experience. They trailed the redskins to their retreats, around and beyond Winnipesaukee, and fought them in darkness and ambush, by surprise and strategy, after their own style; and they cleared away from the whole frontier the dread of the ferocious Pequawkets, who had been a menace by day and a terror by night to every farmer and fisherman along the Merrimac; but finally Lovewell lost his life in a fight near Fryeburg, Me., where Paugus, chief of the Pequawkets, was also killed.

> With footsteps slow shall travellers go
> Where Lovewell's pond shines clear and bright.
> And mark the place where those are laid
> Who fell in Lovewell's bloody fight.
>
> Old men shall shake their heads and say,
> 'Sad was the hour and terrible,
> When Lovewell brave 'gainst Paugus went,
> With fifty men from Dunstable.'

As the men of the Nashua valley had defended their homes against the Indians so were they ready to defend them against the French, one company of the famous New Hampshire Rangers going into Queen Anne's war from here. When the Revolution began, Dunstable names were common in the volunteers under Stark who hastened to Bunker Hill, or, later, followed Washington's lead; and here General Blanchard is buried. In 1800 the little settlement "Indian Head," at the mouth of the river, became Nashua Village, and began to flourish as a mercantile point in the boating on the river, for locks had just been built around the Pawtucket falls, where Lowell now stands, so that sloops and barges could come up. In 1823 a dam, canal and factory were erected, whereupon the manufacturing industry, which has made Nashua so prosperous, began, and twenty years later the town had railway connection with Boston.

The city now embraces about 16,000 inhabitants, and is of attractive appearance. The largest manufacturing concerns are the cotton mills, which employ between two and three thousand persons. Cards and glazed paper, locks, cotton-milling machines, edged tools and sundry

fancy articles, besides an immense quantity of iron and steel, and 30,000 yards a year of ingrain carpets, form other sources of wealth to her citizens. Several railways concentrate here, and the Merrimac is handsomely bridged.

Nearly 50 miles remained to Baily between Nashua and Rochester, and he found himself with less notes in his big Russia note book of this half of the journey than of the earlier part. The first twenty-five miles traverse the level farming districts of Hudson and Windham — a region venerable with traditions of the Scotch-Irish Presbyterians who were the first to clear away its primeval forest. Not much of interest attaches to the region beyond, except in the towns of Epping and Lee (the former noted for its Methodist camp-meetings) whose history goes back 250 years and is filled with Indian warfare and

A BIT OF MEADOW.

Revolutionary incidents. Then some mountains and ponds in Nottingham and Barrington arouse curiosity, and Rochester is reached — a town of eight or ten thousand people, set on the banks of the Cocheco river in the midst of the Norway plains, surrounded by a large agricultural region, and devoted to making blankets, bricks, boots and shoes. It is connected with Portland by two lines of railroad, one of which offers two routes. Thus you may go by the Boston and Maine to Dover, and its Western Division to Portland; or to Great Falls and onward by either Western or Eastern divisions; or by the Portland and Rochester R.R., which runs through the historically interesting villages of Springvale, Alfred and Buxton, (one of those towns granted to the victorious soldiers of King Phillip's war, who by their settlement there formed a bulwark defending the neighboring coast-villages); Gorham (named after a hero of the fight at the Narragansett fort, in 1675, and settled by the veterans of that sore campaign); lumber and paper making Sacarappa; and finally Westbrook, a suburb of Portland. Fine views are caught from the train of the hills and ponds in the northward, lying on the outskirts of the White Mountains.

You must understand that while my book has made this side-trip the author and his friends were rolling swiftly on into the heaven of our expectation. Just beyond Rochester we entered the town of Farmington, a shoe-manufacturing village near the Blue hills, or Frost mountains, from the loftiest of which, we are told, the ocean, Monadnock and the White Mountains, are all visible.

"Do you remember?" I ask my companion, "the one great shoemaker who belonged here half a century ago?"

"Oh, yes," says Baily. "Vice-president Henry Wilson; but it was after he had earned money enough to get some education, and had gone to Natick, Massachusetts, that he began to become famous."

A low pyramid — in shape, — but far taller than any hill we have yet seen, comes into view at intervals on the right, which we know to be Copple Crown; certain rugged heights fire our eager interest on the left, and presently we slow up at Alton Bay, on the southern extremity of Lake Winnipesaukee, — the "pleasant water in a high place" which ends the first stage of our vacation pilgrimage.

CHAPTER IV.

LAKE WINNIPESAUKEE.

Till death the tide of thought may stem,
There's little chance of our forgetting,
The highland lake, the water-gem
With all its rugged mountain-setting. — MILNES.

A FLAVOR of the high lands and all the pleasure country in advance, was caught in the very name of the handsome steamer awaiting us beside the wharf-station at Alton Bay, for it was the *Mt. Washington* — the largest boat on the lake.

"Why it's just like a river," Prue exclaimed, with a shade of disappointment in her tone, as she looked down the narrow inlet leading to the lake, five miles distant.

This was a highway for the French and Indian raiders, who came in canoes; and in the troublous old times a stockade and garrison were placed on one of its boldest headlands, still known as Fort point. Near it another promontory bears the name of Gerrish, and recalls the Cocheco massacre of 1689, when Sarah Gerrish and other miserable captives were dragged bleeding along these shores. Cotton Mather has told the story with a full sense of its horror.

When, after dinner, we returned to the upper deck, we had emerged from Alton bay, and Prue found her "river" expanded into a broad irregular sheet of ruffled water, where tiny white caps were sparkling in the sunlight, and the breeze blew stiff and cool. How refreshing was that wind, chilled by the frosty crags, and fragrant with the vast spruce woods of the north! What promises of joy and vigor it held out to us jaded ones; and how richly were those promises afterward fulfilled!

This western wind hath Lethean powers,
Yon noonday cloud Nepenthe showers,
The lake is white with lotus-flowers! *

---

* Prue, happening to look over my shoulder at this page of manuscript, warns me that if I don't put quotation marks about this stanza, readers who don't happen to recall the verses will think they're mine instead of Mr. Whittier's! This is rather hard on the supreme poet of New England landscape; and I may as well declare, once for all, that I shall in no case enter into competition with him, or any lesser rhymer, and therefore can safely omit the unsightly marks from all quotations of poetry.

A PASSING SHOWER—LAKE WINNIPESAUKEE.

After touching at Wolfeborough (of which more anon), the prow was headed straight up the lake, and our trip really began. On our left was the rough elevation of Rattlesnake island, — to which the snakes are welcome, as Baily remarked — and behind it rose the dark and handsome mass of Belknap mountain, with its regular twin peaks dominating the lateral heights and foothills in Gilford and Alton. The higher of the two peaks reaches 2,394 feet * and is an important station in the service of the Coast Survey, upon whose maps it is designated Mt. Gunstock. The view from this summit, pronounced "one of the richest and most fascinating in New England," embraces not only the whole of the lake region and a host of mountains beyond, but a vast area southward between the sea coast and Wachusett. The regular ascent is made from Laconia by a drive of seven miles to Morrill's farmhouse, whence there is a plain path 1½ miles long to the summit; or one can drive twelve miles from Alton Bay.

Though there was little sign of humanity on the hills, the shores of the lake, especially on the right, showed many a prosperous farm. One of these homesteads, on a knoll, struck Prue's eye particularly, because of its antique appearance, intensified by the dismantled old windmill, with domed top and shingled sides, which stood near it. (Any means of "raising the wind," it may be whispered aside, interests that young woman — "a creature not too fair and good for human nature's daily" expenses).

"The windmill is played out," Baily observes. "It has been completely beaten by the steam engine."

"This one at least seems to have succumbed," says Prue, demurely, "for it has laid down its arms."

On the whole, however, less cultivation was to be seen than I had anticipated. "The surroundings are scarcely less wild than they were when, in 1652, Captains Edward Johnson and Simon Willard carved their initials, which are still visible, on the 'Endicott rock' near its outlet." This outlet is on the western shore where Long bay and a series of tributary ponds narrow down to the swift current of the Winnipesaukee river, which a few miles southward unites with the wild Pemigewassett, coming from the heart of the Crystal Hills, to form the Merrimac.

At the first narrows of the outlet is The Weirs — keeping in the name the recollection of the fish-weirs which the red men built there every spring. Further down, at the foot of Long Bay, stands Lake Village. These landings are reached by a daily steamboat, and the neighborhood of each is attractive.

Johnson and Willard were the first men to explore the upper part of the Merrimac valley, which early tempted the cupidity of the English, and members of this expedition took up lands in the vicinity

---

* All the heights given are reckoned as above mean sea-level, unless otherwise stated.

that have come down to their descendants. The celebrated million-acre purchase from Mason bordered on the lake (his explorers had a "merry meeting" commemorated in the old name of Alton Bay), but settlement was forbidden by the fact that these sheltered nooks and fishing-waters were overpopulous with Indians, who for more than a century kept their ancient camping-places and *namkeeks* inviolate.

The shore Indians themselves belonged to the Winnipesaukee tribe on the west and to the Ossipee on the east; but the lake was neutral-ground and rendezvous for all the natives of the region. Along its shores passed the main trails to the valleys of the Connecticut and upper St. Lawrence; its waters formed an unfailing base of supplies; and its hills were watch-towers, whence the savage sentinel could warn his people against hostile approach, or the sachems could easily plan a raid. Many a wild tale lingers yet of fights between the red man and white, or between "heathens" and "praying Indians," up to the time when in 1722 the authorities cut a road through the woods from the Merrimac settlements to its shores, and erected block-houses. In 1726 three townships were surveyed on its eastern side, where settlers soon became numerous, and after the conquest of Canada (in 1760) the lake shore was settled rapidly.

We were now fairly out into the lake, yet seemed in a maze of islands and low capes, which opened and shut, changing position and appearance with every rod of advance. Behind us were Copple Crown and the rounded hills along the Alton shore, with the double pyramid of Belknap towering behind them. On the right, and somewhat ahead, the Ossipee range lay in full view, and ahead the whole north was filled with the peaks of Sandwich and the mountains toward Moosilauke. Few of the islands had shown any life, but now we approached one, at the mouth of Moultonborough bay, where plenty of it appeared — a crowd of people, indeed, waiting upon a wharf. This was Long Island, upon which are farms and several hotels. It is connected by a bridge with the mainland, and is a pretty place.

Among those on the wharf was an aged man, who was so long in bidding farewell to his friends that we had cast off our lines before he got through. Everybody shouted "Don't!" but he crooked his rheumatic knees and hurled himself aboard, amid the plaudits of the spectators. I was sure he'd fall short, and Prue says she *knew* he'd fly to pieces when he struck the deck. The old fellow did neither, but presently toddled upstairs and sat among us with his knees drawn up and his antiquated silk hat on the back of his head, smoking a short clay pipe and oblivious of the notice he had attracted.

It was after we had swung out from Long Island and were moving straight northwestward toward Centre Harbor, that we began to appreciate the peculiar loveliness of this many-armed, islet-studded, hill-guarded lake of the north. The scene shifted with every turn of the paddle-wheels, now opening to view a long lane of water through

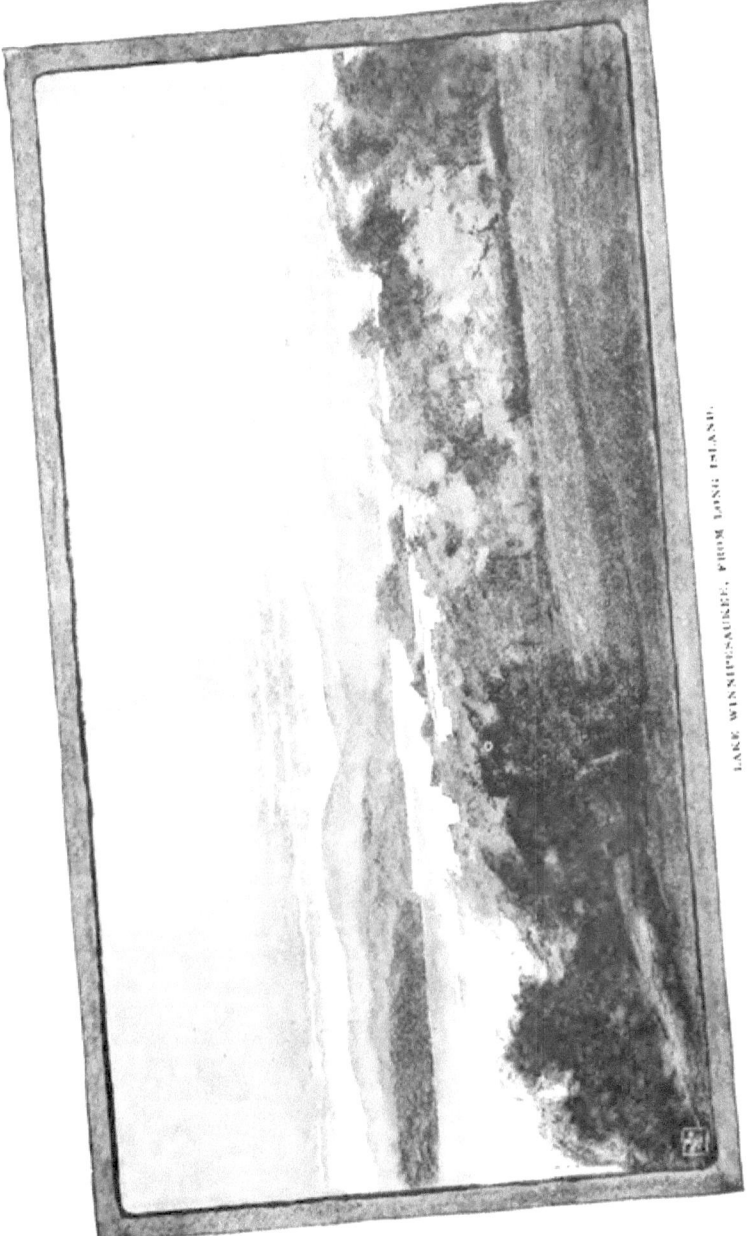

LAKE WINNIPESAUKEE, FROM LONG ISLAND.

the trees, anon shutting it off as some island slipped in between. There are 274 of these scattered green islands, most of them mere knobs of rock densely overgrown with trees, which thrust their branches low down and far out over the water, like boarding-pikes, to resist a landing. Only a few are inhabited or find any utility, except in the charming way they diversify what otherwise would be simply a great plain of water. Some of the largest, whose names are given on the map, support cattle or hayfields, and the farmers bring off the produce in scows called "horse-boats," moved by unwieldy side-wheels revolved by the tramping of a horse in a treadmill amidships.

From watching one of these slow and comical craft we turned to meet, with exclamations of surprise, a most glorious picture in the north. Across a long vista of bushy islets, in a silver setting of placid water, the eye penetrated past dark Ossipee — beyond the fields and fiords of Moultonborough — up to the grand White Hills! Towering over the heads of giants bowing before him, and wearing the radiant crown of royalty, stood Mt. Washington, with Adams, Jefferson and Pleasant by his side.

It was a brief audience, and had we not been on the look out the moment we left the Long Island pier, we might have missed it; but how impressive was this our first sight of the monarchs of the range!

Then come into full view, one after another, the long file of noble mountains in the north, of which we have already caught glimpses, — Chocorua, Paugus, Wannalancet, Passaconaway, Whiteface and many more, enticing in their names alone, recalling legend and the heroic age of New England! Look at Chocorua, on the extreme right, overtopping his fellows with that peak, as clean-cut and sharp as the tip-top spray of one of his own pines; Paugus with his sinuous scar; Passaconaway, tallest of the line, rugged and massive, hiding Washington behind him! Every artist and poet who knows the lake insists upon the supreme beauty of this picture. The gifted Starr King is never tired of extolling it, and makes it a text for an eloquent sermon upon the reality of the charm we find in landscape, and the duty of training one's eye and opening his heart to appreciate nature's beauty in such a treasure-house of it as this lake really is. "If half a dozen pictures," he exclaims, "could be seen in an Art Gallery of New York or Boston, with perspective as accurate, with tints as tender, with hues as vivid and modest, with reflections as cunningly caught, with mountain slopes as delicately pencilled, as the lake exhibits in reality, fifty times in the summer weeks, what pride there would be in the artistic ability, and what interest and joy there would be in seeing such master-pieces from mortal hands!"

The "Crystal hills," as the early men happily called them, were cut off somewhat as we approached Centre Harbor; but pleasure enough remained. Read what numberless encomiums have been bestowed by men of taste upon this bit of inland water. Dr. Timothy Dwight ex-

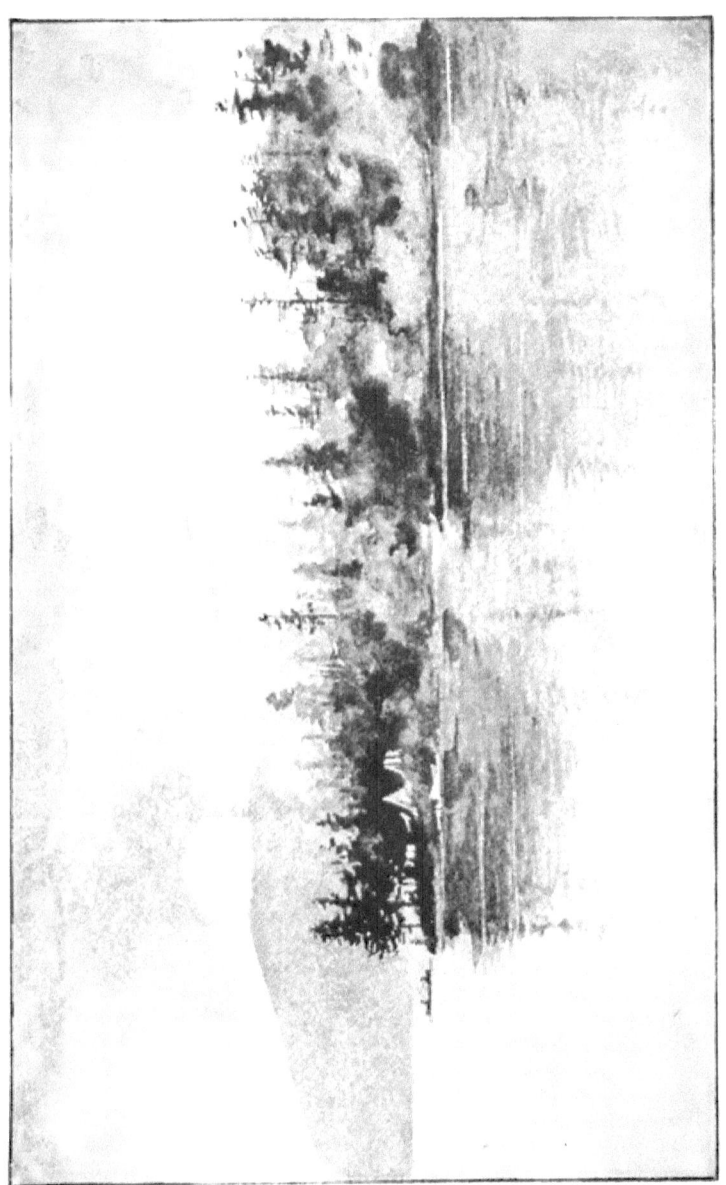

BLACK MOUNTAIN, FROM MOULTONBOROUGH BAY, LAKE WINNIPESAUKEE.

pressed just surprise, that in his day, Lake George was annually visited by people from the coast of New England while "Winnipesaukee, notwithstanding all its accumulation of splendor and elegance, is almost as much unknown to the inhabitants of this country, as if it lay on the eastern side of the Caspian."

The excuse for that, in 1813, lay in its comparative inaccessibility, but this has been corrected, and "the most exquisite jewel in the lake-necklace of New England," as Oakes styles it, is now not only within easy reach, but maintains abundant means for comfort and amusement on its shores.

It was with deep satisfaction that we landed at Centre Harbor, the village at the northern extremity of the lake, and walked up to one of the hotels, where we lost no time in removing the dust of travel and making ready to enjoy ourselves.

A GLIMPSE AT LAKE WINNIPESAUKEE.

There was yet time for a drive, and the direction mattered little, for it would be difficult to go amiss in this region,

> Where your chambers ope to sunrise,
> The mountains and the lake.

One drive follows the historic old Conway stage-road into the Notch, as far as West Ossipee, a station on the Boston and Maine Railroad, and affords "one of the finest panoramic views in this region," the main feature of which is the bristling Sandwich mountains, best visible

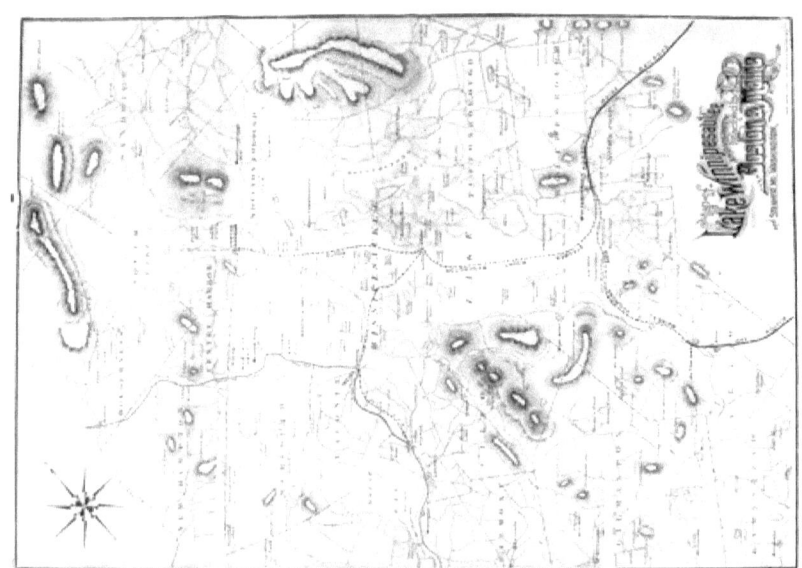

about eight miles from Centre Harbor, where they stand in the order Israel, Sandwich Dome, Whiteface, Passaconaway, Paugus, Chocorua, with Mt. Whittier near at hand on the right. This is a daily stage-route, and is, in fact, an old-established line of travel to the White Mountains, now, of course little used, compared with the railways, but still taken by knowing ones, and excursion tickets can be arranged in Boston which shall include it as a part of the round tour.

Another impressive view of the same nobly modeled range — one of the most muscular, so to speak, in all New Hampshire, — is gained from Shepard hill, (on the road to Plymouth) where the Asquam House overlooks its labyrinthine lake. Stages also run daily up to Ossipee Park, — a modern hotel and cottage-station high upon the shoulders of that fine central height so conspicuous from every part of the lake country.

But the drive of drives, to which a whole day should be given, is that passing around Squam lake, — a small body of water, northeast of Winnipesaukee, — which comes as near to lacustrine perfection as anything in New England.

The road followed is that to Centre Sandwich. It traverses a pleasant series of valleys for four or five miles before "the bright waters of Squam lake are seen, and the road soon descends towards their level, running near a thicket-fringed strand, with wooded islets off-shore."

> Before me, stretched for glistening miles,
> Lay mountain-girdled Squam;
> Like green-winged birds, the leafy isles
> Upon its bosom swam.

After a time, the highway is left for a road which takes you to Chick's Corners, an elevated hamlet fifteen miles (by this route) from Centre Harbor, and thence returns (7 miles) along the purple ridges of the Squam hills, through the notch between the main range and a double-headed spur called Rattlesnake mountain, and thence either over or around Shephard hill. The latter part of this drive is hilly, and at every rise gives some new modification of the amazingly pretty mixture of water, meadow-land and "peaked towers," which composes the landscape.

That great critic of White Mountain scenery, the Rev. Thomas Starr King, took especial delight in the Squam (or properly Asquam) lakes, for there are really two of them; and speaks of "Great Squam, singularly striped with long, narrow, crinkling islands, and, like Wordsworth's river, winding in the landscape 'at its own sweet will,' — and Little Squam, unbroken by islands, fringed and shadowed by thickets of the richest foliage, that are disposed around its western shore in a long sweeping curve-line which will be remembered as a delightful melody of the eye." "The larger one," he remarks in another place, "though not a fourth part so large as Winnipesaukee, is doubtless the most beautiful of all the small sheets of water in New

England; and it has been pronounced by one gentleman, no less careful in his words than cultivated in his tastes, more charmingly embosomed in the landscape than any lake of equal size he had ever seen in Europe or America."

A little steamboat runs upon both lakes, and there are several boarding houses in the vicinity. Squam is renowned for its spring fishing.

Of course we walked up Sunset hill to indolently watch the dolphin-colors of the dying day reflected in the mirror of Winnipesaukee, and had much pleasant chat (possibly a trifle sentimental) over the scene and the cigars.

"No doubt," I say (to quote a specimen of our talk), "one can see just as radiant beauty in the sunsets that blaze over the Brighton hills and dye the tide of the classic Charles; or that set Hoboken against a wall of fire and paint the ferry boats of Weehawken in cloud-reflected colors never thought of by their owners; nevertheless, there remains

RED HILL, FROM MOULTONBOROUGH BAY, LAKE WINNIPESAUKEE.

truth in the paradox that a really much less fine sunset is really a great deal finer up here."

"Well," Prue exclaims, hearing this, "if you're as far gone as that, I think it's time to go in!"

So we saunter back to the hotel, and dress for a hop; but the music has hard work to keep the dancers in out of the moonlight and the balmy air, which are just fit for *tete à têtes*.

The final excursion is a sort of summary of the whole — a trip to the top of Red Hill. This was left to Prue and me, however, for Baily hired a boat and went a-fishing.

Red Hill is really a ridge, but has a summit at the northern end over 2,000 feet high, the picture visible from which, as many men who have gazed upon the noted landscapes of the world will tell you, is unequalled in either continent, for that endearing quality which we call loveliness, and which makes us long to return to the place possessing it, as we do not always care to do where scenes of wild, yet desolate, grandeur have stunned our minds by their magnitude and sublimity.

This trip involved a pleasant ride of four miles (but there is a shorter cut for pedestrians), after which, we walked for a mile up the good bridle-path that tourists may ascend on horseback if they choose, noticing, as we went, the moraines and other glacial marks at the base which interested Agassiz so much.

The top is cleared, and forms a coigne of vantage for taking in a prospect that cannot be over-praised. Its *extent*, alone, is worth noting. Kiarsarge and Monadnock are plainly visible at the southwest; Laconia and the other manufacturing villages smoke beyond Belknap, and in the west, the eye reaches far over the hills toward the Connecticut. Turning to the right, where Squam lake, "with its beautiful green islands fringed with beaches of white sand," is glittering in the foreground of the west, Mt. Cardigan, the hills along the Connecticut, and more to the northward, the immense mass of Moosilauke are seen; then the Franconia mountains, far away over nearer ranges whose names we found on our map. The huge dome of Sandwich cuts off the north for a space, hiding the White Mountains, and their neighbors as far as Carrigain, of which a portion only is revealed, with a part of the slide-marked Tripyramid at its right.

A very circumstantial description of this noble panorama was open to us in Ticknor's excellent *Guide to the White Mountains*. "The beautiful valley of Sandwich," says this account, "fills the foreground to the north and northeast with its peaceful farms and pretty hamlets. The long white village of Centre Sandwich is close at hand, with its two church towers and clustering houses. Over this point are the noble peaks of Whiteface, with its marble-like cliffs and deep ravines, and Passaconaway, of about the same height but throwing out its blackish hues in vivid contrast. To the right of the latter, and below, is the symmetrical green cone of Mt. Wannalancet, on whose right are the bare white ledges of Mt. Paugus, over North Sandwich village. . . . . In the foreground, to the right of Centre Sandwich, is the island-gemmed Red-Hill pond, over which is the superb white peak of Chocorua, with a profound ravine running from the west to the base of its northern peaks. To the right of the main peak is a white spur, whence a long ridge runs out to the plains of Tamworth. Over the spur, about quarter of the way from the spur to the end, and over the islands in Red-Hill pond, is the crest of Kiarsarge. To the right of Chocorua are certain of the Green hills of Conway, above the Saco."

And so the eye is led around to the shapely broadside of the Ossipee, and the circle is complete. What fills this circle as you rest your gaze in the southward? Winnipesaukee — " fashioned with every elegance of figure, bordered with the most beautiful winding shores, and studded with a multitude of islands," as Dr. Dwight expressed it; "liquid silver run into a vessel of unequal surface," as Isaacs fancied it to be; "islands and shores [that] fringe the water with winding lines and long narrow capes of green," as Starr King describes. Then Prue recites softly some lines from Perceval, beginning: —

> Embosomed low
> Mid shadowy hills and misty mountains, all
> Covered with showery light as with a veil
> Of airy gauze. Beautiful were thy shores,
> And manifold their outlines.

Baily had a good report to make of his fishing when we met in the evening; and told us that he had made up his mind to return about the time of the first snow, and go fox-hunting on the Ossipee with the rugged old man who had been his boatman, and had taken him to the right spot in "the basin" to catch pickerel. Our bachelor has the happy faculty of thinking the place he occupies at the moment, the best of all, and will make more serious plans and honest promises about settling there, or at least returning for some special amusement at a later date, than he can remember, for he never carries them out.

"But I thought you'd get some trout," said Prue.

"August is not a favorable month for trout in this part of the lake. By the way, did you know that Winnipesaukee has a species all to itself? It is called the 'symmetrical' in the books, and resembles the lake trout, but is more slender. They are caught through the ice in winter in great numbers, and I mean to have a try at them."

"Then you didn't have as good sport as you expected?"

"Oh, yes I did — had a jolly time. Good sport? Why there's nothing in the world to equal the delight of sailing or a row, fishing or no fishing, on this lake. I'll bet I saw more exquisite pictures down here, glancing out from among the little tufts of islands up at the great sunny mountains, than you did with your eyes wandering over half the state. And when you add a trolling-line or a rod — well —"

"It's just too sweet for anything," exclaims Prue, making a school-girl's simper, and the young man subsides, with half a scowl, for he doesn't like to be made fun of, any better than the rest of us.

Next morning, we boarded the *Mt. Washington* and went back to Wolfeborough, enjoying every mile of the way. A friend, who though a lawyer is nevertheless a good fellow, packed us into his carriage and drove us off over the hills and through the woods of Wolfeborough and Tuftonborough, telling interesting things by the way. What remains sharpest in my memory is the number of small private cemeteries we saw; and we were told that they were to be met with on the back-roads, and even in the heart of the dense second-growth woods, all over the country, startling the hunter and plaguing the antiquary, for in many cases no trace remains of the families whose names appear upon the rude and fallen headstones.

The legend of Wentworth was repeated for us at the site of his mansion on Lake Wentworth, as the older books call what now is simply Smith's pond,—a reservoir of power for the mills at its outlet. Wentworth's story is the elegant romance of the region. The family was one of quality and heroic valor in England, and one of its scions came to America as early as 1638, seeking adventures. He found them, and honor and wealth to boot, in the New Hampshire Colony, and it was his descendant (that famous John Wentworth, whose mansion we shall see by and by in Portsmouth, and who was governor of the Province from 1766 to 1775) by whom this country-house was built. It was 100 feet long by 45 broad and had five large barns. Here he entertained like a feudal baron, and among his guests was the young Massachusetts man who afterward became the great Count Rumford of Bavaria. When the war for independence began, the loyal old governor stood by his king and his colors, and was driven out, none too gently, by the colonists. He was given the ruling of Nova Scotia as a reward, and allowed to add to his coat of arms, two keys, in remembrance of his fidelity.

Wolfeborough (named after the hero of Quebec), began to be settled, here in the heart of the "king's woods," about 1770; but the next year the Province cut a road thence along the western shore of the lake and through Plymouth to Dartmouth college. In 1774 the people attacked Wentworth House, which was so badly abused after its seizure that it fell into decay, and in 1820 was burned.

Besides the fishing and shooting (in their proper seasons) which attract many to Wolfeborough, there is much here at all times for the tourist to enjoy, and excellent hotels for his accomodation. Beyond the main village of some 3,000 people, there are a number of closely neighboring hamlets, the most important of which is Mill Village on Smith's pond, where half a million dollars' worth of blankets and woolen yarns are made annually.

The view from the higher points of the village is always fine. Ossipee and Belknap lose none of their majesty by being close at hand, while a score of entrancing lake-pictures present themselves. Two lesser mountains are within easy reach, Tumble Down Dick and Copple Crown, the latter of which we climbed. We heard the usual yarn about the origin of the first name, and listened politely, but incredulously, owing to the fact that there are half a dozen Tumble-down-dicks in New England. More novel and interesting was the history of Copple Crown, wherein it appears that a generation or more ago a wealthy man of the neighborhood built at his own expense a carriage road to the summit, which was partly cleared. He bequeathed this road and the summit park to the public, on condition that it should be kept in repair, and for a time the injunction was attended to, but lately nothing has been done upon the road, which is fast disappearing.

Six or seven miles of interesting driving take you to the mountain, after which it is an easy walk of a mile, along a good forest-path, to the top. Though only 2,100 feet high, Copple Crown, by its isolation, is not only itself splendidly conspicuous throughout this whole region, but commands a wide and notable view. Even the Isles of Shoals can be seen on the southeastern horizon, if the day be very clear; and in the south, over Merrymeeting pond and the "Twin Breasts" (as the Indians called Uncanunucs), Wachusett and Monadnock sit low upon the horizon.

"Why!" exclaims Prue, as we pick these out. "From Monadnock you can almost see the State House; so that it's only about two looks from here to Boston!"

"Just about."

"And those three mountains — Monadnock, Wachusett, and Uncanunucs — though they don't amount to a great deal in size and can hardly be seen from Concord, have inspired more good poetry in the sages of that wonderful settlement — Emerson, Thoreau and those fellows, you know — than any other hills in the whole Union."

It was the New Yorker, of course, who made these disrespectful allusions, and his remark started talk about bigness and nearness not being necessary, but perhaps even objectionable, in poetic subjects, all of which interested us, but don't belong here.

Westward the eye catches far-away glimpses of the Green mountains, and finds the true Kiarsarge near at hand over the rough shoulders of Belknap. Coming round to the shining plain of the lake, we reverse the view we got from Red hill and duplicate its loveliness, with the irregular spires and domes of the Sandwich range, and many a dim, nameless crest behind them.

> Where the gray rocks strike
> Their javelins up the azure.

Moat mountain, opposite North Conway, is seen just at the right of Chocorua, who is —

> The pioneer of a great company
> That wait behind him, gazing toward the east, —
> Mighty ones all, down to the nameless least.

And over Moat, "fifty miles away on the horizon, a little west of north, is the stately cone of Mt. Washington, with parts of Adams and Madison, Monroe and Pleasant, flanked on the right with all the heights between them and Kiarsarge. Far to the north can be seen even the hills that look upon the Rangely lakes, and westward the upland sloping down to Sebago. We were like Moses upon Pisgah, looking over upon the promised land of our journeys to come; but with this advantage over the weary patriarch, that we crossed *our* Jordan, went into this Canaan, and possessed it for you, gentle readers.

CHAPTER V.

PORTLAND AND THE MAINE BEACHES.

And now her talk was of the East,
And next her talk was of the sea.—OLD SONG.

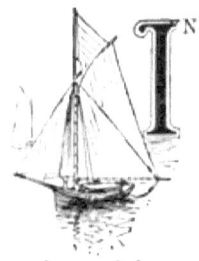

IN THE morning the train out of Wolfeborough took us through the wild woods along the base of Copple Crown, down to Wolfeborough Junction on the main line (Northern Division of the Boston and Maine Railroad). There, after time for luncheon in a neat station-restaurant, we boarded a train going south, filled with tourists returning from the White Mountains, bearing sheaves of alpenstocks, rustic canes and rusty umbrellas, and accompanied them as far as Salmon Falls, where we met a northward bound train filled (for the most part) with pleasure-seekers outward bound, innocent as yet of trophies or rust. At Great Falls we change cars, for the train

GREAT FALLS STATION.

we leave goes on to Conway Junction, and then by the Eastern Division to Boston. We, on the contrary, intend to take the Western Division, or coast line, eastward to Portland. At North Berwick, half-a-dozen miles farther, the two Divisions cross — that which has been the coast line, from Boston, through Salem and Portsmouth, now taking an inland route through a series of farming villages which have nothing very striking to show us; while the Western Division, by which a few days ago we travelled from Boston through Lawrence and Haverhill to Dover, now seeks the coast and follows it closely to the outskirts of Portland.

How interesting would it have been, could we have spared the time,— as some day we mean to do,— to ride or walk along that coast by the old road and beaches at the ocean's edge which runs from Kittery to Kennebunk! Kittery Point is the oldest settlement in Maine, dating back to 1623. The next town above is old York, where the colonists of Sir Fernando Gorges established themselves in 1624; then comes Wells, "not a town, but a street, stretching for five or six miles along the shore, and everywhere commanding an extensive and unbroken ocean view." Then Kennebunk. The villages now are quiet enough, but each contains relics of the earliest colonial history, and coast scenery of the rarest beauty. Who has not heard of the beaches of York and Wells, with their hard, wide sands entombing hidden wrecks, that start from forgotten graves after storms to frighten the beholder? Who that has seen the surf flying against Bald Head Cliff, or overlooked the offing from the top of Mt. Agamenticus (of whose bulky green dome we catch glimpses from the car-windows between North Berwick and Kennebunk), or scrambled over the rocks of Ogunquit, will forget it?

York beach was the highway for the scattered colonists 250 years ago, when they were afraid to trust themselves among the "lyons" and "salvages" of the forests. To-day it is lined with summer hotels, and its sands bear the imprint of carriage wheels and the heel-marks of tiny boots and parasol-tips. Standing in front of the old church at York, with its quaintly-carpentered steeple, one can feel that he is on ground as nearly classic as any in America; for this is the centre of the first incorporated city in New England,— Gorgeana. In 1623-4, Englishmen, sent out by Gorges and led by Norton, had made their home on the York river. The Pilgrims had already settled in "Agawam;" disputes as to relative rights were ended by the setting apart of the whole region between the Merrimac and Kennebec rivers. for 120 miles inland, as a grant to Gorges, styled the Province of Maine. He arranged for it an elaborate system of sub-divisions and government, and united the "plantations at Agamenticus" into the city of Gorgeana, incorporated in 1642. This cumbrous machinery and the immorality of the community were both disadvantageous, and union with the Massachusetts Bay colonists was out of the question. Still, they increased, organized churches, had trade and fishing as well as farming industries, and prospered fairly until they were immersed in the Indian conflicts that followed King Phillip's war. In February of 1692, the town was attacked at dawn by three or four hundred Indians and Frenchmen, marching from Canada and the Abnaki country on snowshoes, who destroyed all of the houses and killed or took captive everybody outside of the two garrison houses, which are still standing, though much decayed. From that time, until the peace of 1744, the

District was in a constant state of seige, and during Queen Anne's war (1702-12) spy-boats patrolled the coast. A large part of the men in the Louisburg expedition were recruited here, and its contingent was among the earliest enlisted in the army and navy of the Revolution.

The old village of York is now most easily reached by a branch railroad from Portsmouth, which has been built the present year.

York beach is a mile north of York village, and is two miles long; it probably has no superior on the coast of Maine. It stops abruptly on the north at the rocky promontory of Cape Neddick, with its group of summer cottages, and the Nubble, an islet lying off the extreme point, in deep water. This is the nearest land to Boon island, whose

EARLY MORNING — THE NUBBLE, YORK BEACH.

light-house can be seen rising like a tall mast above the waves. Grim legends of shipwreck belong to both this island and the stern headland, and poems and pictures have been made to embody their thrilling tale.

To reach the next headland, six miles up the coast, one must pass through the pretty little village of Cape Neddick, whose inn (now destroyed by fire) used to be famous in the old staging days. It was here, that in 1676, one of the worst of the massacres occurred; and this is the point from which to reach Mt. Agamenticus, about four miles distant. It is a rough road thither, and the mountain, which is surrounded and covered with rocky, almost useless lands supporting a tangled forest, where a few rude woodsmen and basket-makers dwell, affords little reward for the exertion of climbing it, until its top has been reached — a naked, rocky platform. The outlook seaward is a very long one, and this mountain is a landmark to sailors for a great distance. "Large ships," says a recent observer, "resembled toys, except that the blue space grasped by the eye was too vast for playthings. Cape Elizabeth in the north and Cape Ann in the south, stretched far out into the sea, as if seeking to draw tribute of all passing ships into the ports between. Here were the Isles of Shoals, lying in a heap together. That luminous, misty belt was Rye Beach. And here was the Piscataqua, and here Portsmouth, Kittery and Old York, with all the sea-shore villages." Inland vision reaches to the White Mountains, of which Agamenticus is the seaward picket, and the spires and factory chimnies of many a village can be identified.

The headland north of Cape Neddick, to which I started at the beginning of the last paragraph, is Bald Head Cliff, the nearest village to which is Ogunquit, of which Samuel Drake, author of *Nooks and Corners of the New England Coast*, has given a graphic sketch; let me quote a part of it:—

"From the village of Ogunquit there are two roads. I chose the one which kept the shore, in order to take my way to Bald Head Cliff, a natural curiosity well worth going some distance to see. The road so winds across the rocky waste on which the village is in part built, that in some places you almost double on your own footsteps. Occasionally a narrow lane issues from among the ledges, tumbling, rather than descending, to some little cove, where you catch a glimpse of brown-roofed cottages and a fishing-boat or two, snugly moored. . . . Literally, the houses are built upon rocks, encrusted with yellow lichens in room of grass. Wherever a dip occurs, through which a little patch of blue sea peeps out, a house is posted, and I saw a few carefully tended garden-spots, among hollows of the rock, in which a handful of mould had accumulated. . . . A native directed me by a short cut ‘how to take another ox-bow out of the road,’ and in a few minutes I stood on the brow of the cliff. What a sight! The eye spans twenty miles of sea-horizon. Wells, with its white meeting-houses and shore-hotels, was behind me (northward). Far up in the bight of the bay, Great Hill headland. Lord's, Hart's and Gooch's beaches — the latter mere ribbons of white sand — gleamed in the sunlight. Kennebunkport and its shipyards lay beneath yonder smoky cloud, with Cape Porpoise light beyond. There below us, looking as if it had floated off from the main, was the barren rock called The Nubble, the farthest land in this direction, with Cape Neddick harbor in full view. All the rest was ocean. The mackerel fleet that I had seen all day — fifty sail, sixty, yes, and more — was off Boon island, with their jibs down, the solitary gray shaft of the light-house standing grimly up among the white sails, a mile-stone of the sea.

"There are very few who would be able to approach the farthest edge of the precipice called The Pulpit, and bend over its sheer face. . . . Here is a perpendicular wall of rock, 90 feet in height (as well as I could estimate it) and about 150 feet in length, with a greater than Niagara raging at its foot — a rock buttress, with its foundations deeply rooted in the earth, breasting off the Atlantic; and the mossy fragments lying splintered at its base, or heaved loosely about the summit, told of many a desperate wrestling-match, with a constant gain for the old athlete. . . . The strata of rock lie in perpendicular masses, welded together as if by fire, and injected with crystal quartz-seams, knotted like veins in a Titan's forehead. Blocks of granite

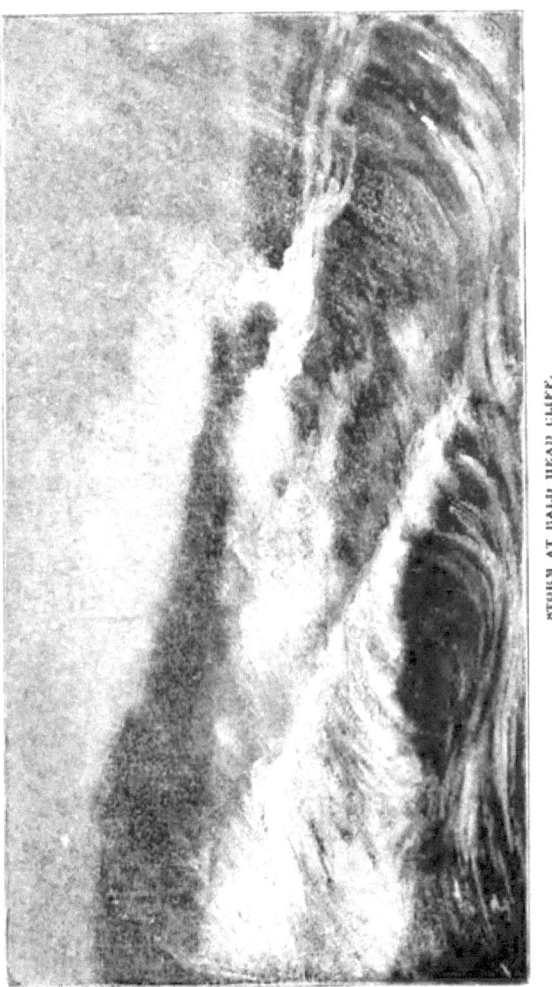

STORM AT BALD HEAD CLIFF.

weighing many tons, honeycombed by the action of the water, are loosely piled where the cliff overhangs the waves, and you may descend by regular steps to the verge of the abyss."

It was with reading and talking thus, about this historic, grandly picturesque, sombre-storied old shore, that we beguiled the time as we sped along through the woodlands and farms of York, Wells, and Kennebunk, to the twin cities, Biddeford and Saco.

From Kennebunk, a branch railway, five miles long, runs down to Kennebunkport, at the mouth of the Kennebunkport river, once a shipbuilding and fishing port of great importance to Maine. Years ago, large and important vessels were built there, and the reputation of its yards was high for staunchness and good "lines;" but the decay of this industry, and the retreat of cod, mackerel and menhaden, would have left the quaint old port desolate, had not the good taste and wealth of interior cities found the locality and chosen it for a summering place. The huge old homesteads of rich skippers and shipwrights were opened to summer boarders, and upon the beaches that face the sea at the river's mouth great hotels were erected, like the well-known Ocean Bluff House and others. Beside them, little groups of private cottages and semi-private boarding houses were built, employing labor and spending money which have given the coast people a new era of prosperity. Of all the many charming summering places along this noble coast, none excels Kennebunkport in artistic value, or the opportunity for healthful and varied pleasures. New England cannot show a more interesting region for walking or driving than these beaches and shore roads between the Piscataqua and the mouth of the Saco, at Biddeford Pool and its curious rock-hollowed "basin."

Biddeford and Saco are large and flourishing towns at the falls of the Saco, where a magnificent water power drives a group of immense cotton mills and machine shops. On the Saco side, many summer residents dwell in cottages and hotels near the mouth of the river, or along the fine beaches eastward. The fishing in tributary brooks, and the shooting in the coniferous woods and old pastures of the neighborhood, add a powerful attraction.

Three miles beyond Saco the railroad reaches the ocean itself at Old Orchard beach, where lines of hotels, great and small, "pavilions," amusement places, bathing houses and summer shops extend compactly along both sides of the railroad tracks, and the sand is alive with visitors, making holiday. The name is derived from a traditional orchard, the last tree of which disappeared before the Revolution; and the Old Orchard House, now one of the largest and most fashionable of New England seaside hotels, grew out of a single farmhouse which a few years ago stood upon its site. In 1875 a fire swept the shore clean of houses; but the people had become too fond of the place to abandon it, and there has arisen since an almost continuous village of hotels and cottages between here and the mouth of the Saco at Camp Ellis, grouped about Ocean Park, Ferry beach and other centres, and connected by a branch railroad which runs hourly trains back and forth through all the warmer half of the year. Its admirers think that no beaches in New England are equal to this ten miles at Old Orchard, and

the almost equally long stretch in front of Scarborough a little way to
the eastward. In a fine grove just back of the station, an immense re-

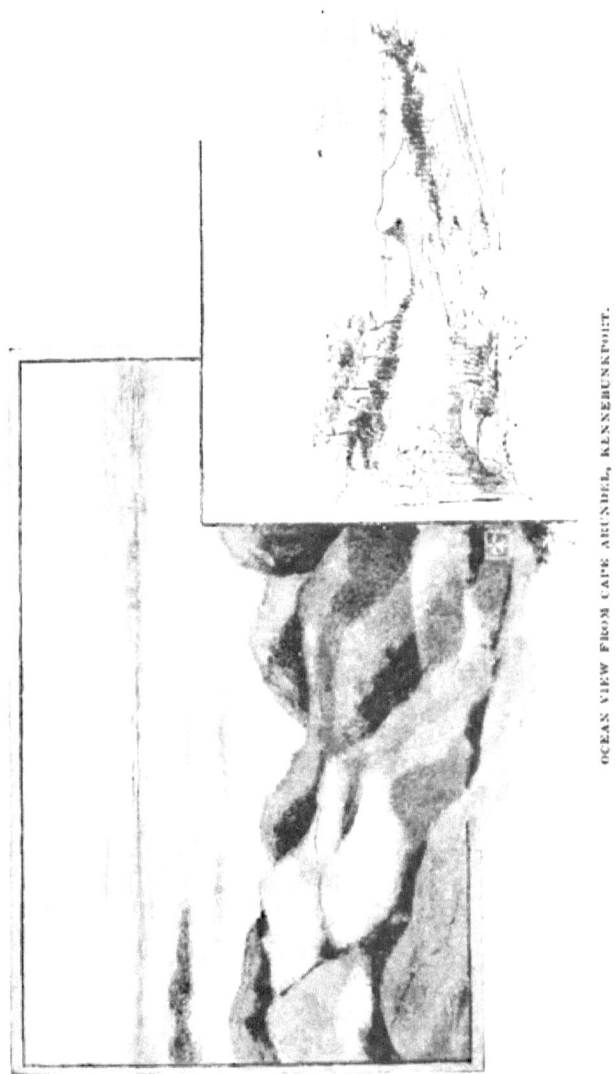

OCEAN VIEW FROM CAPE ARUNDEL, KENNEBUNKPORT.

ligious camp-meeting is held every summer. In short, Old Orchard is
to Northern New England and Canada, what Ocean Grove and Asbury

Park together, are to the Middle States; and the relation which these latter bear to Long Branch or Cape May is very much that between Old Orchard and Newport and Mt. Desert. The station for Scarborough beach is three miles eastward, and the whole road in this part runs along the edge of the sea, whose cool breezes blow against our faces,

SPOUTING ROCK, KENNEBUNKPORT, ME.

while the surf delights our eyes. Scarborough, and in fact, all this country-side has an eventful story, in which well-remembered names and incidents appear, going back to the advent of the 18th century, while its very beginnings belong to the earliest discoveries in America. The Boston colonists of 1630 were boarded when entering Salem by a

OLD ORCHARD BEACH.

Plymouth man going about his business at Pemaquid. English fishing ships hovered about the island for a dozen years before the *Mayflower* swung to her anchorage in the 'ice-rimmed' bay.

Beyond Scarborough the train runs across Cape Elizabeth, upon whose breezy headlands are other favorite summer resorts, crosses the long and expensive bridge that spans Fore river, halts at the animated Maine Central Junction, where those going to the interior of Maine, change cars, and then enters the city of Portland, rising in terraces of architecture upon the bluffs at our left, as we skirt the harbor front to the Union Station. Here we intended to spend Sunday, as it was now Saturday afternoon; and we therefore lost no time in betaking ourselves and our baggage to the hotel.

In Portland, the "regular thing" to do, and in this case a most satisfactory thing, is to ascend the Observatory on Munjoy hill, and scan the whole city, harbor and outer country. This we did immediately after tea, and in time for the sunset.

OLD HOUSE ON CAPE ELIZABETH.

Horse-cars pass the Observatory, which is an octagonal wooden tower surmounted by a lantern, like a light-house. It was built by merchants early in the present century as a watch-tower for incoming ships,—ships running up and down the coast with fish and fruit and merchandise, not only, but weather-beaten craft that had circumnavigated the globe.

> And the homeward vessels which long have sped,
> Through tempest, and spray, and foam,
> Catch first a glimmer of old White Head,
> And are sure they are almost home.

The moment a ship is sighted, one of the signal flags, or burgees, which fill rows of pigeon-holes in the top of the tower, is flung to the breeze by the watchman, and its coming is announced in the shipping-exchanges of Boston and New York, before it has cast anchor.

The telescope with which this keen-eyed sentinel of the sea scans the offing, is placed at our disposal, and we turn it hither and thither upon the landscape, while we chat with him.

Munjoy hill, he tells us, is named after one of the early settlers, who was an important man in the new colony, though not the first. The earliest white men (to stay) were Cleaves and Tucker, two men from Plymouth, England, who settled near the shore at the base of this hill. The spring by which they placed their cabins still flows, at the foot of India street. "When was this?" In 1632, and in 1637 they received a grant of the ridgy peninsula upon which the city now healthfully stands, and induced settlers to come in by generous gifts of land. In 1658, however, Massachusetts asserted her control over the region, and named the locality Falmouth,—a name which has survived in the suburbs, among several other designations going back to the 17th century. A very superior class of persons now arrived, among whom the most prominent was the owner of this hill—George Munjoy, an educated man from Boston.

"Of course," Baily, the envious New Yorker, interrupts spitefully, "Where else in the world *could* an 'educated' man come from?"

Thus affairs were flourishing, when a fearful interruption was caused by the Indian massacre of 1676. For two years the town remained desolate, after which a few persons returned, and that other hill over there in the western part of the town, now perpetuating his name, was bought as a part of his farm by George Bramhall, of Portsmouth. Not long afterward a party of educated Huguenot immigrants was welcomed; Fort Loyal was built, and the town was again progressing spiritedly, when the terrible French-and-Indian campaigns of 1689 caused its ruin a second time, nor did it revive until after the peace-treaties of 1713. At the time of the breaking out of the Revolution the town numbered 2,000 citizens, Boston having less than 15,000 at the same date.

As usual in the seaports, the parties of revolution and loyalty were each strong; and here the more than ordinary wealth and intelligence made excitement run higher than elsewhere. Political street-rows were frequent enough; and once, when Mowatt, the commander of the British fleet, and his surgeon, were walking with a well-known Tory on this very hill-top, all three were seized by a hot-headed captain of militia and locked up. Though the officers of the ships gave the town short grace to release their superior or else take a cannonade, it was no easy task to persuade the eager Continentals to set him free.

"That officer must have remembered this town," we remarked.

"Remember it? Indeed, he did, sir. He never forgave it, and the next October, on the 18th,—I've heard my grand-father tell of it often,—he came back with five men-of-war and bombarded the town till he'd laid it in ashes. Almost the only building left standing, in the thick part of the town, was the old wooden meeting-house, which stood down there where the First Parish church is now."

As we look down over the beautiful bay, with its many islands dotted with farm-houses and summer hotels, and completely sheltering the deep and spacious harbor, we do not wonder that when the war was over, Portland (as it came to be called, after the incorporation act of 1785), was quick to revive, and grew steadily in commercial prosperity. It was a port not only for its own merchants, but the ocean-doorway to all that great region in New Hampshire, Vermont and western Maine, which so rapidly filled up when liberty was ensured to all Americans; and though the Embargo measures of 1812 did the city great harm, yet she has gone on steadily until now,—would have gone faster, of late, in fact, had not the war of the Rebellion been so disastrous to the merchant marine in which lay the foundation of her wealth. And then came the great fire of July 4th, 1866, which for fifteen hours swept diagonally across the wealthiest and busiest portion of the city; and with such swiftness that people knew not where to fly for safety. In a few hours it had destroyed 1,500 buildings, laid in ashes eight miles of thoroughfare closely built, thrown 10,000 of the inhabitants houseless and homeless upon the charity of others, and consumed ten millions of property.

There had been a certain obscurity in the west, which had almost hid the long notched line of the New Hampshire hills, but as the sun neared the horizon its rays dissipated or rendered this transparent, and we could pick out scores of peaks with which a few weeks later we were to make an intimate and joyful acquaintance. Then the rich sunset effect began around and over the sierra; and while we watch it. Prue repeats for us those verses of Whittier's, made for this very scene,—perhaps on this very hill:—

> You should have seen that long hill-range,
> With gaps of brightness riven,—
> How through each pass and hollow streamed
> The purpling lights of heaven,—
>
> Rivers of gold-mist flowing down
> From far celestial fountains,—
> The great sun flaming through the rifts
> Beyond the wall of mountains.

The next day was Sunday. In the afternoon we hired a carriage and took a long and delightful ride about the city not only, but outside of it. I do not propose to describe Portland,—that would be superfluous,—further than to say that her public buildings, and especially the City Hall, are stately, and her streets beautiful and interesting. All those in the older part of the city, spared by the fire, are shaded by elms and maples of mature and graceful growth, and one street has four rows of these great elms, so that its long colonnades of leafage are like a continuous park.

Portland was the early home of the poet Longfellow, and every tourist takes interest in seeing his birth-place, and identifying Deering's Oaks and the other localities which he mentions in his local poem, *My Lost Youth*. "At the corner of Hancock and Fore streets is the 'old, square, wooden house, upon the edge of the sea,' where the poet was born in 1807. The dwelling next to the Preble House, on Congress street, and known as the 'Longfellow House,' was not occupied by Stephen Longfellow until after his son Henry's birth."

Only a few miles away, on the shore of Lake Sebago (Portland and Ogdensburg Railway, 17 miles), Nathaniel Hawthorne lived when a boy. This lake is now one of the pleasure resorts of the city, especially for fishing parties. A steamer runs upon it, and the scenery, with Kiarsarge and the White Mountains for a dim, blue background, is said to be very charming. The steamer crosses the lake, and wriggles its way up the tortuous Songo river, through ever-varying scenes, until admitted by locks to the upper part of the Songo, the Bay of Naples and finally to Long lake. Bridgeton and Harrison are villages near this farthest water, and in summer both are filled with city boarders, anglers and excursionists. Lovewell's pond is not far away.

On Monday we devoted ourselves to the bay, going the rounds of the excursion boats that run to the various headland and island pleasure-resorts, and enjoying the day immensely. Baily had picked up a forgotten book, which we read, a bit at a time, and agreed to be one of the brightest tales of summer-travel ever penned. It was styled *A Summer Cruise on the Coast of New England*. The date was 1858 and the author, Robert Carter. The voyage was made in a fishing-sloop from Boston to Mount Desert, and this is what the writer (who is not inclined to gush) records of Casco bay : —

"Scarcely anywhere in the world can you find a more varied or more lovely commingling of land and water. The shores of the islands and the promontories are mostly covered with woods of maple, oak, beech, pine and fir, growing nearly to the water's edge and throwing their shadows over many a deep inlet and winding channel. It is impossible to conceive of scenery more charming, more romantic, more captivating to the eye or more suggestive to the imagination. No element of beauty is wanting. Many of the islands are wildly picturesque in form,—and from their woodland summits you behold on the one hand the surges of the Atlantic, breaking almost at your feet, and on the other the placid waters of the bay, spangled by multitudinous gems of emerald, while in the dim distance you discern on the horizon the sublime peaks of the White Mountains."

From Portland, the Grand Trunk Railway runs to Gorham, N. H., one of the portals of the White Mountains; and to several interesting manufacturing and summering-places in Maine, such as Lewiston, South Paris, Bryant's Pond and Bethel. At the distance of only twenty-five miles, and reached by either the Grand Trunk or the Maine Central Railways, is Poland Springs. This is the source of the celebrated Poland mineral and medicinal water, and the springs have become a fashionable resort, not only of invalids, but of pleasure-seekers. A great hotel, with cottages, baths and all the modern appurtenances of such a place, has been built, and during the warm months a gay crowd makes it the centre of every species of midsummer recreation.

CHAPTER VI.

ALONG THE MAINE COAST.

*The lights begin to twinkle from the rocks;
The long day wanes; the slow moon climbs; the deep
Moans round with many voices. Come, my friends,
'Tis not too late to seek a newer world.*—TENNYSON.

"WHAT route shall we take to Mount Desert?" was Baily's question, in a general way, at breakfast on Tuesday morning.

"There are two or three ways overland," I explained, "or we can go by steamer. Which shall it be?"

"By the steamboat, of course," said our imperious lady-member with an air of astonishment over any possible indecision, "for our tickets read that way."

I departed forthwith to the office of the Portland, Mt. Desert and Machias Steamboat Company, and bought stateroom tickets for that evening's boat. It was to be the "City of Richmond." She would sail at 11 P.M., when the train leaving Boston at 7 o'clock arrived, and would reach Mt. Desert about noon on the next day, by a devious route through the beautiful islands of Penobscot bay.

The overland routes I had indicated were two: chiefly the Maine Central railroad, by the way of Bangor and Mt. Desert ferry; and, secondarily, the Maine Central and Knox and Lincoln railroads, by the way of Brunswick and Bath to Rockland, and thence by steamboat. The former of these is very popular with pleasure-seekers, while many take the Rockland route, either going or coming.

It was a very interesting coast we were passing all that restful night,—one identified with the very birth of New England, and as interesting for its scenery and geology, as for its history and present population. It is a coast gashed with deep fiords—long, irregular inlets of the ocean reaching up into the land and admitting vessels to the salt meadows and farmer's doors.

Into the largest of these fiords, empties the Kennebec, and on the most spacious of the ridgy promontories, at the eastern limit of Booth (the Kennebec's) bay, stood Pemaquid fortress. Its story is best told in Drake's *Nooks and Corners of the New England Coast* : "The Kennebec," says Drake, "was known to the French earlier than the English, and by its proper name. Champlain's voyage in the autumn of 1604, extended, it is believed, as far as Monhegan, as he names an isle ten leagues from 'Quinebeque.' . . . De Monts followed Champlain in 1605 . . . visiting and observing the Kennebec, of which a straightforward story is told. Even then, the river was known as a thoroughfare to Canada.

"The mouth of the Kennebec is interesting as the scene of the third attempt to obtain a foothold on New England's soil. This was the colony of Chief Justice Popham, which arrived off Monhegan in August, 1607."

This settlement, though well begun, proved a failure, and was abandoned in less than a year, though fifty houses within a fortification had been built, and a "prytty pynnace" framed and launched. This was the origin of Maine ship-building, the principal centres of which are still at Bath and Boothbay, in the same estuary.

There has been a tendency toward romancing as to the next half-century; but it appears that only a few families of white people inhabited the coast, engaged in fishing. A stockade existed on Pemaquid point, in 1630, and was rifled in 1632 by the freebooter, Dixy Bull; but previous to 1677, when Andros mounted five guns in his little Fort Charles, the place had not been of any account. This lasted until 1689, when it was destroyed by Indians. By this time, however, the strategic importance of this point had been impressed upon the minds of the Massachusetts colonists, and in 1692 the erection of Fort William Henry was begun by trained engineers. This became the strongest fortress in America at that date. It was of stone and earthworks, had a great round tower, and mounted fourteen guns, six of which were eighteen-pounders.

"The importance of Pemaquid, as a check to French aggression, was very great. It covered the approaches to the Kennebec, the Sheepscot, Damariscotta and Pemaquid rivers. It was, also, being at their doors, a standing menace against the Indian allies of the French, with a garrison ready to launch against their villages or intercept the advance of war parties toward the New England settlements. . . . On the other hand the remoteness of Pemaquid rendered it impracticable to relieve it when once invested by an enemy. Only a few feeble settlements skirted the coast between it and Casco bay, so the same causes combined to make it both weak and formidable. Old Pentagoët, which the reader knows for Castine, and Pemaquid, were the mailed hands of each nationality, always clinched, ready to strike." (*Drake.*)

French and Indians schemed together against it, and in 1696, the naval captains D'Iberville and Bonaventure, accompanied by 200 Indians in canoes, under St. Castin, sailed into the harbor and summoned the fort to surrender, which it speedily did. Plunder and massacre followed. Charlevoix gives an account of it, and the Indian story of the fight is detailed in Father Vetromile's *History of the*

Abnaki's. Two days were spent in demolishing the fortress, so well built but so ingloriously defended; and then the French departed.

The Indians, however, were allied to the French,—and I don't blame them! The English voyagers and settlers uniformly outraged the natives, while the buoyant, adaptive French conciliated them. By 1730, however, the French wars were over, and on the ruins of the old fortress, Massachusetts erected at Pemaquid point a new one named Fort Frederick, the remains of which are yet plainly visible; but only fish-oil factories, and a few shore-people occupy the ground where, 250 years ago, Dunbar laid out the squares of a great city-to-be.

The islands at the mouth of the Kennebec are fervidly recommended by a recent reporter, for reasons apart from antiquarian interest. "We shall find," is his promise, "the islands gleaming with white tents and parti-colored cottages, clean and neat hotels and boarding-houses. The two-hours' sail down the river, among the islands, without the least fear of sea-sickness, is a most delightful one. Do you enjoy deep-sea fishing, with never a care or thought of the pains and penalties of sea-sickness? Then this is the place to visit. Do you relish fresh fish, just drawn from the coolest depths of old ocean, and do you wish your fevered cheeks to be fanned by the sea-breezes in their purity? Then come here." A steamboat runs daily from Bath to these cooling-places for fevered cheeks.

Opposite Bath begins the track of the Knox and Lincoln Railroad that connects all the coast villages together. Its scenery is a rapid alternation of hills and waves, seaports and farm hamlets. The tidal rivers swirl about the rocks, or wander lazily among black-edged flatlands, their waters here lost in the maze of a fish-trap made of brush, and intricate enough to puzzle a fox, there hidden in the jetty shadow of some tall-limbed, broken-backed bridge which goes straddling across the muddy flats as if on stilts. Then the traveler rushes through a deep trench in the rocks; whisks by a sunny road, where, perhaps, a farmer stands leaning indolently on the neck of one of his oxen; or is charmed by the sight of some still pond, blue as the sky, whose granite shores are bordered with the gay decoration of raspberry, vaccinium, and woodbine, quick to feel the autumn.

Wiscasset (scene of *One Summer*); Damariscotta (the station for New Castle and Pemaquid, and renowned for the immense Indian shell-heaps described in Ingersoll's *Oyster Industries of the United States*); and Thomaston (the former home of the lordly Knox, soldier of the Revolution, and patron-saint of this part of the world), are passed in quick succession,—each a storehouse of entertaining legend, enchanting scenery, health and sport. Finally the Penobscot mouth comes into sight and Rockland is reached.

Rockland and its vicinity are devoted to the quarrying of the peculiar lime-rock, which, when calcined, becomes "Portland" cement. There are nearly 100 kilns, which make a million and a half barrels of hydraulic lime every year; and on a dark night, when these great kilns are blazing in all directions, the river-banks and outskirts of the town present a strange and somewhat infernal appearance.

As a village, Rockland is not unlike any of the other coast villages, but its surroundings are a delightful combination of hill and coast scenery. This is attracting the attention of people who are in search of agreeable summering places, for they find here a variety of pleasure and a bracing climate within easy reach of the business and social world. The shores of Penobscot bay, not only, but the whole western half of this cool, rocky, picturesque, historic, old shore-line of Maine, is rapidly being appropriated to the genial purposes of midsummer recreation. Camden and Belfast, above Rockland, are favorite localities.

For a large part of this coast, in both directions, Rockland is the supply point. The islands near town sustain quarries of a fine-grained gray granite, greatly in demand as building stone. "Dix island is a vast mass of granite where the vessels load directly from the sides of the ledges. It furnished the stone for the New York and Philadelphia post-offices, and the huge monolithic columns for the United States treasury at Washington. The Bodwell company at Vinal Haven and Sprucehead, furnished the material for the new government buildings at Cincinnati, and the state, war and navy departments at Washington." Rockland now has direct communication by railroad and steamers with Portland, Bangor, and all the adjacent landings; and it possesses at least one good hotel.

I was in no haste to get up that morning, as early as I was urged to do; and when finally I reached the deck, whither my room-mate had preceded me, the boat had already been made fast to the wharf at Rockland, and the port rail was lined with passengers, while others were coming aboard, all fresh and loquacious.

Baily and Prue were full of enthusiasm, but otherwise, apparently, an aching void, for "breakfast! breakfast!!" was all the word I could get out of either of them. I wasn't so indecently ravenous as this, though the nipping salt air was fast stimulating appetite, and I made some sharp remark intended to rebuke these two youngsters for their lack of patience and dignity.

"Well, what of it!" was Prue's retort,—there is a certain person to whom she is not always as duly respectful as I could wish,—"'Dost thou think, because thou art virtuous, there shall be no more cakes and ale?' No wonder you're not hungry,—*you* haven't been on a sea voyage, like us."

"And where, then, your majesty, have I been?"

"You've just been sound asleep!"

Manifestly it was idle to argue anything with a young woman who would look you straight in the eye and say such a thing as that. I therefore wasted no reply, but turned my attention to the shore.

The sun was just rising. The foreground of high-perched warehouses and wharves, lifted far above the fallen tide, where craft, large and small, trim and slovenly, were moored upon the smooth water, had hardly yet rid itself of the lurking shadows of night; and the clustered roofs and spires of the city were only half revealed in the still, gray light. Behind the town, the jagged masses of the Camden hills rose dark against the flushed sky, where, as we looked, they were suddenly veiled in silver mist, which lifted them into a sort of mirage of reflected white light, wonderful to behold. Then as we left the wharves behind and crept out into the bay, this gauzy veil was shot through and through with threads of gold, beyond which every pinnacle became sharply defined, then rimmed with molten gold, then fused in the ineffable blaze and glory of the sunrise, as the orb of light came slowly above Megunticook, and bid the world give worship.

"Look!" I cried. "Behold with what pomp—"

"Do you think it will be long?" said my wife, plaintively,— she was gazing toward the cabin, not into "the purple window of the east."

"*What* will be long?" I asked with some impatience at this stolid interruption.

"Why, to wait for breakfast. Talk not to me of the sun's bright rays till I've had my coffee! *Then* you shall see that my soul will glow with—"

I never heard *what* it would "glow with," for a gong sounded afar off, and faintly, yet we heard it, and fled as one man.

Half an hour later we were prepared to enjoy the devious channel into Castine.

"The voyager approaching these shores," wrote Mr. Noah Brooks, whose boyhood was spent upon them, "beholds a wonderful panorama of sea and land. The bay of the Penobscot is studded with unnumbered islands. These are covered, for the most part, with fir, spruce and larch. The shores are bold and rocky, and rich tones of brown, gray and purple, are reflected in the silvery tide. Far up the Penobscot, as one rounds the eastern end of Long island, stretches a lovely vista of tender blue, melting into more positive hues in the middle distance where old Fort Point, once Fort Pownal, stands like a sentinel at the entrance to the river. To the right and eastward, the bluffy and well-wooded extremity of the peninsula of ancient Pentagoët dominates the scene, its light-house marking, like a white finger, the highest point of that section of the shore. To the right of the light-house opens another vista where the Bagaduce, with the shores of Brooksville mirrored in its tide, leads the eye up into a tangle of hills and dales, over which rises the azure peak of Blue hill. Still farther to the eastward, over the hills, and resting like a cloud on the horizon, are the heroic lines of the ridges of Mount Desert."

"It's a little one," remarked Baily, casting his eye over the peninsula before us, "but it has grown more romance to the acre than any other in Maine. It seems like going back a good ways in this new world, when an American can connect his local history with the machinations of the great Cardinal Richelieu."

"Can Castine do that?"

"Yes. The Plymouth colony had set up a trading post here, called Pentagoët, as early as 1629. But Louis XIII. and Richelieu, Razilly and the rest of the French masters, thought English aggression toward Acadia better be nipped in the bud, and so sent a fleet under D'Aulnay de Charnisay to oust the Pilgrims and set up a French station. Having succeeded (1635), to him was given control of all that is now Maine, while east of the St. Croix the French crown was represented by Charles St. Estienne, Lord of La Tour, another titled cut-throat. Both of 'em were sent out here, I fancy, because too ungovernable to remain comfortably at home.

"Having nobody else to fight they pitched into one another on the score of religion, — a fragment of the bloody contest of Jesuit versus Huguenot which convulsed and was presently to decimate France; for D'Aulnay was a Roman Catholic, while La Tour was a Protestant; here was material for 'a very pretty quarrel,' and they utilized it to the full. The Indians not only, but the Massachusetts colonists were dragged into the feud, and battles by sea and land, sieges and counter-sieges (in one of which Miles Standish figures), marked year after year with bloody incidents. Through all, stands the figure of Madame La Tour, — sharp, expedient, courageous, saucy — a worthy mate for such a man. Finally, in 1643, La Tour, having left his fort on the St. John imperfectly guarded, while he went off on a cruise to Boston, D'Aulnay suprised it, took ten thousand dollars worth of plunder, and brought La Tour's wife to Pentagoët as a prisoner. That is the subject of Whittier's fine poem *St. John*. The Puritans of Boston of course favored the Huguenot, loading his vessel with the supplies he so sorely needed, whereupon he hastened homeward to find his fortress overthrown and his colony in ashes. A priest is there to tell him the story."

And opening his Whittier, Baily read to us, grandly: —

> Pentagoët's dark vessels
> Were moored in the bay,
> Grim sea-lions roaring
> Aloud for their prey.
> "But what of my lady?"
> Cried Charles of Estienne:
> "On the shot-crumbled turret
> Thy lady was seen:
> Half veiled in the smoke-cloud
> Her hand grasped thy pennon,
> While her dark tresses were swayed
> In the hot breath of cannon!"

"How terrible!" Prue exclaims.

"Yes, — terrible. It killed the proud-spirited captive, after a very few weeks, and a little later D'Aulnay himself died. Then followed the most curious part of this whole history, that somehow seems farther away than the struggles of Rome and Carthage — La Tour reappeared and married Madame D'Aulnay!"

Castine does not look out upon the river, but is some distance back from "the point," where Dice's Head light-house sheds its rays upon the intricate channels; and it faces a snug little harbor within the mouth of Bagaduce river. Those who have read Noah Brook's finely illustrated article, *An Old Town with a History*, in The Century for September, 1882, need no account of this harbor, nor of the picturesque water-front of the antique town. But Castine is by no means superannuated. It has large and living interests in ship-building, deep-sea-fisheries and the canning industries, and among its residents are many wealthy men, while more than one distinguished name occurs in its modern annals.

"Faint traces of St. Castin's fort are seen, and on the hill behind the village the English Fort St. George is well preserved. The remains of various American batteries and field-works are found on the peninsula, while the harbor is commanded by a neat little fort recently erected by the United States. Castine is a favorite summer resort, by reason of its seclusion, its heroic memories, its fine boating and fishing facilities, and the salubrity of its sea-breezes."

Its modern name recalls one of the most romantic figures among all the knightly Frenchmen of two centuries ago, who seem so out of place on these wild shores. In 1667 Vincent, Baron de St. Castin, a man of education and high breeding, formely colonel of the Royal Carrignan regiment, came to the Penobscot trading-post from Quebec, married one or more daughters of Modocowando, chief of the warrior-bred Abnakis — whose just hatred of the English dated from the day when, in 1605, Weymouth kidnapped some of their people at Pemaquid, — and became a sort of demigod among all the Indians. During thirty years, with only a few scattered and distant priests for intelligent neighbors, he made Pentagoët his home, building there just such a four-bastioned stockade as I have seen again and again at posts of the Hudson's Bay company in the far northwest.

The English, covetous of its value and fearful of its influence, attacked the trading-post time and again, and here was kindled the spark which lit the wide-spreading flame of King William's war. St. Castin not only defended his own, but sailed with Iberville against the Massachusetts fort at Pemaquid and destroyed it by the aid of his Indians. After the Nova Scotia campaigns of 1706-7 he seems to have returned to his home in the Pyrenees, leaving his son (by the Abnaki princess) to become the *sagamo* of the Penobscot tribes, ruling them in peace and with nobility until 1720, when he was led prisoner to Boston. The next year he went to France, and claimed his father's estates. Though lineal descendants of Vincent St. Castin have been chiefs of the Abnakis ever since. Whittier seems to have taken much poetic license with dates, when, in *Mogg Megone*, he makes Castin a contemporary of the destruction of Norridgewock.

"No matter," cries Prue, her eyes flashing. "What a fine picture we get of the chivalrous old soldier —

> His step is firm, his eye is keen,
> Nor years in broil and battle spent,
> Nor toil, nor wounds, nor pain have bent
> The lordly frame of old Castin."

With the close of Indian warfare settlements sprang up all along the coast and on the rivers; and in 1779 England thought it worth while to seize Castine, and build a fort there (Ft. St. George) against the rebels, the remains of which, on the hill-top above the village, furnish one of the best preserved relics of that period in New England.

Massachusetts at once sent against it a large fleet, carrying 344 cannon, and 2,000 soldiers. They spent several days in bombarding, but finally effected a landing, and would doubtless have reduced the fort, had not seven British frigates suddenly appeared in the river, and attacked the Americans. Never was rout so complete. After one broadside, the American line was broken and a helter-skelter flight ensued on sea and land. Every vessel of the fleet was destroyed.

"I believe Paul Revere was one of the runaway Yankees in that engagement," remarks our member — our malicious member — from Manhattan.

"Yes; and the poet's grandfather, Peleg Wadsworth, was second in command; but Longfellow didn't seem to regard that incident as a good sort of thing to celebrate in his hero of the 'midnight ride.' Old Peleg himself, a little later, was captured and confined in the fort here, whence he and a companion made their escape through an adventure which forms one of the most thrilling traditions of the war. Another participant in the same fight has been sung about, — a British officer who became that Sir John Moore, of Corunna, who, in death,

> —— lay like a warrior taking his rest
> With his martial cloak around him."

Leaving the little harbor, whose green hills have echoed to the cannon of five naval battles, we steered eastward into the river-like Eggemoggin Reach, which separates the archipelago from the mainland by a straight channel a dozen miles in length. The shores are bold and irregular, farms sloping back to the uplands and alternating with rocky and forested promontories. At the head of one of the indentations into the mainland, stands Sedgwick, and nearly opposite, the northern landing on Deer Isle. This, and the adjacent islands, form a township which contains about 3,500 regular inhabitants, all of whom are more or less dependant upon the sea for their living. The recent changes which have come about in the abundance and distribution of deep-sea food-fishes, and the methods of catching them, have been more unfortunate for the dwellers on this line of coast than anywhere else; and had not the people welcomed the "summer boarder," who at this opportune moment began to find out what grand possibilities of pleasure awaited him there, it would have gone hard with the native population. The last blow to their industries was the disappearence of the menhaden, or pogies, which now cannot be caught north of Cape Cod, though a few years ago the annual catch was 100,000,000. On Deer Isle may be seen one local custom more conspicuous than graceful; this is scores of women and girls, their skirts trussed up and stowed away in an enormous pair of oilskin trousers, such as the fishermen wear, and their feet bare or lost in rubber boots, busily digging clams on certain wide mud-flats. In Harper's Magazine for August and September, 1880, appeared two illustrated articles entitled *Fish and Men in the Maine Islands*, which deal with this interesting part of the coast.

The course, after Naskeag point has been passed and the Reach is escaped, winds among green islands, of every size and shape — some rising high and peaked, others low and bare, or mere reefs, or masses of dark forest. There were so many of them that they sometimes completely shut off the view on all sides. Then a vista would open out to sea, and we could feel the steamer swing easily upon the long swell coming in from the Atlantic; or through an opposite gateway our sight might reach across a wide area of placid water and rugged shore northward, to where Blue hill, 1,000 feet high, reared its faithful landmark. "Far before us, on the right, rose the blue summit of Isle au Haut, as the early French navigators named it — a mountain rising from the waves. Before us the peaks of Mount Desert came gradually into view, at first misty and blue, then green and wooded, until as we advanced, still loftier summits showed themselves in grim and stony desolation."

Another and shorter route between Rockland and Mount Desert may be taken by steamers following a more outside course than we pursued, stopping at landings in North Haven, Vinal Haven, to Deer Isle (Green's Landing) where boats can always be engaged to go to Isle au Haut. Isle au Haut can also be reached by a regular steamer from Bar Harbor.

The Blue Hill Steamboat Company also sends boats to and fro among the islands by several devious routes between Rockland, Blue Hill and the many villages. There is no lack of means, therefore, for getting promptly to almost any one of the islands or mainland landings all over this amphibious region.

CHAPTER VII.

MOUNT DESERT.

*Planting strange fruits and sunshines on the shore
I make some coast alluring, some lone isle,
To distant men, who must go there, or die.*—EMERSON.

NOW there began to rise well into view a head, a cluster of mountains, which more and more fixed our attention as we drew near.

An hour later we were close under their "gray turrets," and saluting with three blasts of the whistle the light-house clinging high up the pink precipices of Bass Harbor head, the southernmost point of Mount Desert island. Hearing this friendly blast, a woman runs out of the house and rings the fog-bell with one hand while she waves us a greeting with the other, and then hurries back into her kitchen, as though begrudging time spent in such formalities.

Our course lies south, on the outside of Mount Desert, and we soon turn between the well-populated Cranberry islands, and steer around into Southwest Harbor, formerly the principal settlement on this island, but now eclipsed by Bar Harbor. Here we were at the entrance of Somes' sound, and thought it high time to study our map.

Mount Desert is a hardly detached piece of the Maine coast, standing higher out of water than any other Atlantic promontory, because it holds a group of granite mountains, the tallest of which is not less than 1,500 feet above its surf-smitten base. These mountains stand in long parallel ridges, tending north and south, between which the deep and narrow valleys would be fiords like those which penetrate the coast to the westward, were they not above the reach of the tides. The largest of these valleys, however, does admit the water in a long, river-like channel quite to the heart of the land, giving the island the shape of a pair of well-stuffed saddle-bags, hanging over the head of Somes' sound. Several of the valleys contain ponds, all of which are elongated in narrow basins parallel with the ridges and the sound. The southwestern extremity of the island is a comparatively level plateau, penetrated by the Bass Harbor inlets; but the northern half contains a rugged, irregular region of foothills, smoothed down into a pretty wide area of arable land along the northern shore, where the narrows, which separate the island from the mainland, are crossed by a bridge.

At Bar Harbor, again, enough reasonably level land exists for a large village, or even the city of the future. The southern and eastern shores, however, possess only a narrow rim, and sometimes no space

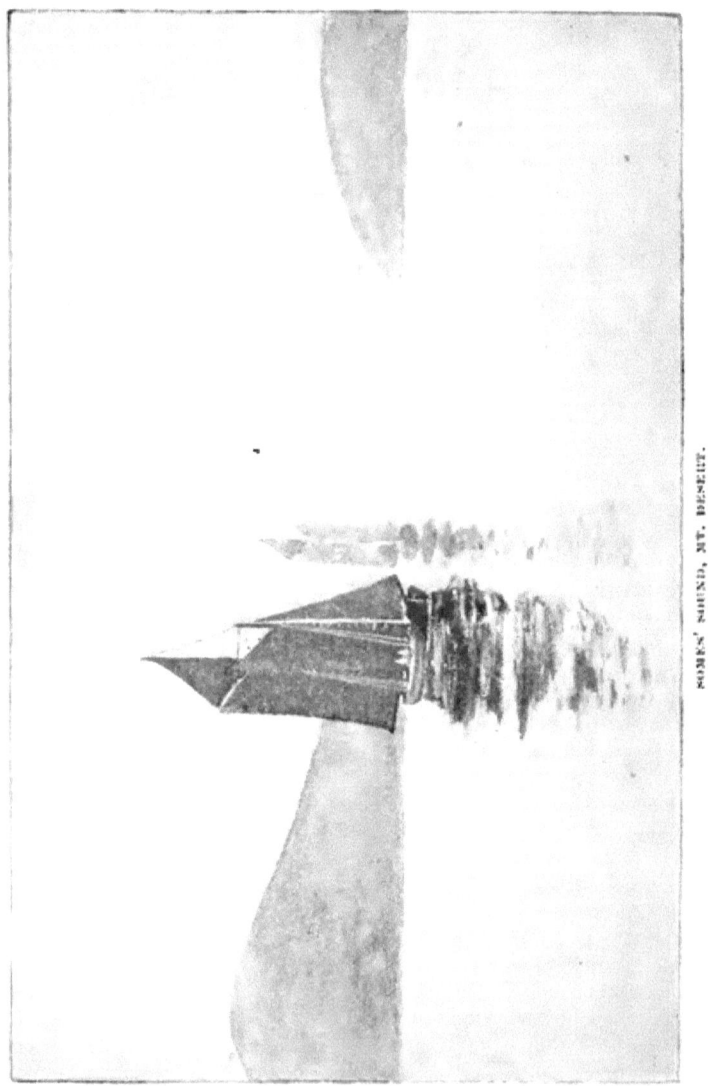

SOMES' SOUND, MT. DESERT.

at all between the abrupt walls of the mountain and the ocean, ever raging at their foundations.

With the *Guide*, written by the skilful pen of Mrs. Clara Barnes Martin, open before us, as we steer out of Southwest Harbor, we scan the passing shores. "The western hills recede," we both hear and see, as Prue reads, "and the remarkable inlet of Somes' sound opens. The Flying mountain juts out across its mouth, but for a short distance there is a view of the steep eastern face of Dog mountain, and further inland the narrows between Robinson's mountain and Brown. Moving farther eastward the other Twin comes out from behind Sargent. Dry mountain separates itself from Green, and Newport's narrow ridge resolves itself into the rounded spurs of its southern face, and so one can count from first to last the 'eight or nine notches in the Isle of Mt. Desert' which Champlain saw.

"This scenery of the shore is impressive. The mountains stand shoulder to shoulder, well braced together, ranks even, trappings rich in color, erect, stern, uncompromising, heroic."

"Big words for little mountains," says Baily, with a shrug in his voice as well as his shoulders, which irritates me, and I fly at him.

"What of it! In poise and outline, as seen from anywhere in this offing, they suggest the finest ranges of the Rockies; and in color are often as magnificent as the Alps. I know they are small, and close at hand; but I tell you truly that you can get profiles of this range from the sea or the islands southward, which shall be as majestic as any of Washington. I have gazed across the heaving rollers of the Pacific at mountains ten times their height and felt no greater satisfaction. Bigness does not necessarily mean beauty, young man, any more than careless contempt is criticism!"

"Go for him!" cries my wife, in great glee; and in the next breath urges Baily to stand to his guns. "Don't let him browbeat you," she entreats. Evidently that wicked young woman wants to see two old friends lose that calm of philosophers, which has been, and remains, their pride,—but she fails. How can any one quarrel or shut their eyes in scowling, when the great green rollers, so sleepy we scarcely feel them out here, wake into leonine strength over there under the pink gates of Otter cove, and with a swing of their whole weight, banners of spray unfurled, hurl themselves upon the brilliant cliffs, slide far up their polished faces, then shrink back baffled. Here, again (we are getting round to the eastern side, now), where the cyclopean masonry of Great Head is so ruined at the top, but so firm and whole at the bottom, see how the breakers never tire of battering, and the shrillest scream of the sea-gull can hardly be heard above the roar and striving of the surf. Next, a little farther on, comes Schooner Head, sending far out upon the wastes the boom of its spouting horn, as the rollers, caught in the hollow, explode through the crevice above like the bursting apart of the cliffs themselves; and, beyond it, trace that wall of iron, where a ship's timbers would crush and collapse in a shoreward gale like a vessel of paper. Ah, the wreckage these rocks have seen,

and the drowning cries they have heard! What tales can be told in
the winter firelight by these old island-men who have fought and
conquered the storms of Maine for so many years!

> For here, when the night roars round, and under
>   The white sea lightens and leaps like fire,
> Acclaimed of storm and applauded in thunder,
>   Sits death on the throne of his crowned desire.
> Yea, hardly the hand of the god might fashion,
>   A seat more strong for his strength to take,
> For the might of his heart, and the pride of his passion
>   To rejoice in the wars they make.

But no wrath of storm and wreak of whirlwind are in the air now.
The sun glints on lace-like lines of spume, trailed across the verdant
waves of Frenchman's bay, and in the sky the few soft clouds hardly
change form or position. We never tire of the shore, each feature of
which is plainly visible. The land fronts the ocean in an abrupt low
wall, or bluff of rock, cracked and excavated into a hundred crannies
half hidden by foliage, where the waves ripple and spout. This bluff
is covered with trees of many kinds, while in some places hanging
vines loop the rocks together with living cables of leaves and flowers.
Now and then we get glimpses of a road, and on the southern shore
saw many cottages; but here by Schooner Head, the tremendous wall of
Newport mountain confronts us, terrible in its sternness, yet lovely in
its warmth of color, above the steely sea,—a wall of bluish-gray granite,
with satiny brown reflections under the noonday sunlight, thinly clothed
with trees that lend a purplish-brown tone, seamed with cracks like
curving strata-lines, and crossed by upright gashes and channels,
where, after rain, the water trickles.

Next is passed the little hassock-shaped islet, the Thrumcap, by
which time Bar Harbor is in sight, and everybody makes ready to go
ashore; some with countenances as rueful as if they expected to be
torn in pieces by the army of hackmen and hotel boys who crowd the
wharf. But for us, at least, the bark of the tooter is worse than his
bite, and handing our baggage checks to a man whose cap bears the
name we want, we are soon rattling up the hill in a half-frantic pro-
cession of buckboards and dog-carts, phaetons, and road-wagons,
which deploy at the top of the street, and go plunging away to the
various hotels as if panic-stricken.

This main front street is set with fantastic shops, several of which
are conducted by leading Boston dealers. The biggest hotels, also,
are down in this democratic, level end of town; and their balconies
are crowded with people in comfortably *negligè* attire, who gaze at us
with welcoming curiosity as we hurry past. One of the biggest of all
these hotels, standing on the front street and looking more like a huge
factory than a hotel, save for its spacious portico and wide-open doors,
is thus spoken of by Charles Dudley Warner: "—a sort of big board-

, hesitating whether to be a hotel or not; a go-as-you-please, If sort of place, which is popular because it has its own and everybody drifts into it first or last. Some say it is an

BAR HARBOR, MT. DESERT, ME.

people do not take to it at first. The big office is room, where new arrivals are scanned and dis-

and the drowning cries they have heard! What tales can be told
the winter firelight by these old island-men who have fought
conquered the storms of Maine for so many years!

> For here, when the night roars round, and under
> The white sea lightens and leaps like fire,
> Acclaimed of storm and applauded in thunder,
> Sits death on the throne of his crowned desire.
> Yea, hardly the hand of the god might fashion,
> A seat more strong for his strength to take,
> For the might of his heart, and the pride of his passion
> To rejoice in the wars they make.

But no wrath of storm and wreak of whirlwind are in the
The sun glints on lace-like lines of spume, trailed across the
waves of Frenchman's bay, and in the sky the few soft clou
change form or position. We never tire of the shore, each fo
which is plainly visible. The land fronts the ocean in an abr
wall, or bluff of rock, cracked and excavated into a hundred
half hidden by foliage, where the waves ripple and spout. Th
is covered with trees of many kinds, while in some places h
vines loop the rocks together with living cables of leaves and t
Now and then we get glimpses of a road, and on the souther
saw many cottages; but here by Schooner Head, the tremendous
Newport mountain confronts us, terrible in its sternness, yet lo
its warmth of color, above the steely sea,—a wall of bluish-gray g
with satiny brown reflections under the noonday sunlight, thinly
with trees that lend a purplish-brown tone, seamed with crack
curving strata-lines, and crossed by upright gashes and chan
where, after rain, the water trickles.

Next is passed the little hassock-shaped islet, the Thrumcap
which time Bar Harbor is in sight, and everybody makes ready to
ashore; some with countenances as rueful as if they expected t
torn in pieces by the army of hackmen and hotel boys who crowe
wharf. But for us, at least, the bark of the tooter is worse th
bite, and handing our baggage checks to a man whose cap be
name we want, we are soon rattling up the hill in a half-fra
cession of buckboards and dog-carts, phaetons, and ro
which deploy at the top of the street, and go plungin
various hotels as if panic-stricken.

This main front street is set with fantastic shops
are conducted by leading Boston dealers. The h
are down in this democratic, level end of town;
are crowded with people in comfortably *negligè* atti
with welcoming curiosity as we hurry past. One of
these hotels, standing on the front street and lookin;
factory than a hotel, save for its spacious portico an
is thus spoken of by Charles Dudley Warner: "—!

ing house, hesitating whether to be a hotel or not; a go-as-you-please, help-yourself sort of place, which is popular because it has its own character, and everybody drifts into it first or last. Some say it is an

BAR HARBOR, M⁺ DESERT, ME.

acquired taste; that people do not take to it at first. The big office is a sort of assembly-room, where new arrivals are scanned and discovered, and it is unblushingly called the 'fish-pond' by the young ladies who daily angle there." We didn't wonder at his "first impression," as we dashed by and got a glimpse of "a bewildering number of slim, pretty girls, nonchalant young fellows in lawn-tennis suits, and indefinite opportunities in the halls and parlors and wide piazzas for promenades and flirtations."

> No hiding-place is this for mournful fate,
> No sorrow here is guest;
> These summer palaces are dedicate
> To pleasure and to rest.
> Here fashion plumes her brilliant, airy wing
> And brightens sea and shore,
> A rainbow-colored, transitory thing,
> Now here, now seen no more.
> Pleased with the brief, exotic revelry,
> Of this ephemeral train,
> In proud delight the city of the sea
> Assumes imperial reign.

The amount of room my clothes took in the two trunks that comprised our family baggage wasn't *much*; you must not expect much change in *my* personal appearance, therefore, throughout this tale. But Prue not only gets along on rather short commons, poor girl, in the matter of dress-appropriations, but is a wonderful manager in making a trunkful go a long way. I sometimes fancy she has a magical power, or juggles with her modest wardrobe in some way, so varied and fresh were the costumes which came out of that same old "Saratoga." Why, she would take a dress she'd worn ever so many times, and make it appear, even to me, new and lovely, through twisting some soft gauzy thing across her bosom, or by some other feminine trick of good taste.

Prue, therefore, held her own very well during these few days in the gay and semi-swell society to which we were introduced at one of the quieter hotels up toward the wooded hills, where some friends were stopping who had arranged for our coming.

But Baily! Look at *him* now, as on the next morning, early, he joins me on the piazza that overlooks the shining tract of Frenchman's bay! His head is crowned by a white hammock hat, his broad chest enveloped in a gray flannel shirt, with its collar loosely confined in a dull red scarf, well displayed by the open jacket; while his legs, encased in knee-breeches and 'cycling stockings, stand firm and straight in a new pair of lawn-tennis shoes. Prue comes to the door, but does not join me. Glancing over my shoulder, I break into a shout of irrepressible mirth. She doesn't recognize our chum, and is hanging back because she thinks I am talking with a stranger! It is a long time before Baily hears the last of that, and he menaces revenge.

Yet he was right in his "get up" and I was right in my ordinary travelling suit, and Prue was sure to be right whatever she wore, for at Bar Harbor every man and woman does pretty much as he pleases in the matter of clothes, and sets before himself the having a good time, "regardless," as the first object of existence. Here again Mr. Warner has caught the sentiment in one of his happy word-sketches. "Except in some of the cottages" at Bar Harbor, he wrote in Harper's Magazine a short time ago, "it might be said that society was on a lark. With all the manners of the world and the freemasonry of fashionable life, it had elected to be unconventional. The young ladies liked to appear in nautical and lawn-tennis toilets, carried so far that one might refer to the 'cut of their jib,' and their minds were not much given to any elaborate dressing for evening. As to the young gentlemen, if there were any dress-coats on the island, they took pains not to display them, but delighted in appearing in the evening promenade, and even in the ball-room, in the nondescript suits that made them so conspicuous in the morning, the favorite being a dress of stripes, with striped jockey cap to match, that did not suggest the penitentiary uniform, because in state-prisons the stripes run round. This *negligé* costume was adhered to even in the ball-room. . . . . . But the principal occupation at Bar Harbor was not dancing. It was out-door exercise, incessant activity in driving, walking, boating,—rowing and sailing,—bowling, tennis, and flirtation. There was always an excursion somewhere, by land or sea. watermelon parties, races in the harbor in which the girls took part. drives in buckboards which they organized,—indeed, the canoe and the buckboard were in constant demand. In all this, there was a pleasing freedom—of course under proper chaperonage. And such delightful chaperons as they were, their business being to promote and not to hinder the intercourse of the sexes.

"This activity, this desire to row and walk and drive, and to become acquainted, was all due to the air. It has a peculiar quality. Even the skeptic has to admit this. It composes his nerves to sleep, it stimulates to unwonted exertion. The fanatics of the place declare that the fogs are not damp as at other resorts on the coast. Fashion can make even a fog dry. But the air is delicious. In this latitude, and by reason of the hills, the atmosphere is pure and elastic and stimulating, and it is softened by the presence of the sea."

We came to know (and hereby testify to) the solemn truth of all that, excepting perhaps the dry fogs, of which we heard much but saw nothing, though it was a good year for fogs.

"What shall we do first?" we ask, when we meet our friends at an early breakfast—no city hours for Mount Desert!

"Better go at once to the top of Green mountain, for it is clear to-day, and you are not sure of it to-morrow. That off your mind, the state of the weather will not give you any anxiety."

This is sound advice and we adopt it. As soon as possible a double-seated buckboard is brought around, and we start.

The road wound along the shore and over the ridges where the finest of the cottages were perched among the rocks above us, or stood in wide lawns down by the shore on the right, and the whole scene was lively and gay. Then we entered the woods and rattled around to the left, under the flank of the mountains, where heights came into view through the trees at unexpected places, until, with the suddenness of a surprise, we were brought out at the end of a pond, stretching away down a narrow woodland valley into a deep horseshoe of mountains. This was Eagle lake, so christened by the painter, Church. On its right were The Twins or Bubbles — bold hills; ahead the craggy peak of Pemetic, and all along the left the steeps of Great hill, White Cap and, towering over all, Green mountain.

> How long the fair expanse, so beauteous still,
> Only the eagle knew;
> When to his eyrie on yon frowning hill
> With eager cry he flew!

Here we alight, in company with a genial lot of sight-seers who have come from the hotels in plebeian barges, or from cottages in patrician phaetons and landaus, and seat ourselves under the awnings of a little steamboat which carries us across the lake to the foot of Green mountain. Baily sniffs at this luxurious way of making the ascent, and I agree with him so far as to say that if there were no other opportunity for ambitious climbing I should prefer to walk; but the railway is a great boon for those whose indolence or infirmity forbid the exertion, and for those whose time is short. There is, indeed, a wagon-road to the summit, built as far back as 1850, but it is no longer kept in repair, and serves only as a bridle-path.

The railroad is like that which later we saw upon Mt. Washington. "There is the same apparatus of cog-wheels and massive brakes, but unlike that road there is no high trestle work. Except for a few feet over a brook, the road bed is made throughout its entire length of timber bolted directly on the solid rock." The distance is about one and a fifth miles, and the average rise, one foot in four and a half. The car hangs very low, and moves so slowly that a nimble person could easily step off or on. Nearly 10,000 persons ascend it annually, and accidents are almost impossible. Twenty-five years ago the summit was an important station for the Coast Survey, which had a building there. When, more recently, Mount Desert began to be haunted by city people and was disclosed to the world of fashion and summer travel, a small hospice was erected, where visitors spent the night; for two days were generally devoted to this excursion in those leisurely and remunerative days. This house was burned in 1884, whereupon a much more pretentious hotel, overlooking Bar Harbor and conspicuous from almost everywhere, was erected in its place.

As we neared the top, and the world widened and widened around us on every side, the light-headed burst into a fusilade of Oh's! and

A LEAF FROM SKETCH BOOK, MT. DESERT.

Ah's! but the more thoughtful grew silent. Our own group sought a certain knob of stone, and buttoning our coats, for the wind was cool and strong, gave up our eyes to seeing and spoke but little at first.

Nowhere else on the eastern coast of America can such an outlook be taken. In front of us the limitless expanse of the gray sea sloped heavenward to a horizon as high as our station — a most curious effect! — and so distant that ships far this side were the merest dots of white. Eastward, this silent and flashing plain, melting from gray to a warmer tone, mingled with a coast almost as low and level as itself:

> Every wave
> Is turned to light and mimics the blue sky,
> As if the ocean were another heaven.

Northward, the whole sky-line was notched with a continuous sierra, mystical and blue in the distance — farthest and bluest, Katahdin. It lay straight north, and was distinct over the crinkled line that elsewhere limited vision, — "some fragment of a wall which anciently bounded the earth in that direction." No mountain in New England is so fancy-spurring as this lone, remote, winter-hoarding monarch of the great north woods. Westward, the Kennebec hills grew higher, as they neared the coast, and then were hidden by the lofty masses of Megunticook at the mouth of the Penobscot. In that filmy paling round the world was enclosed a gray-green area of tree-land, specked with a dozen or so white settlements at the head of sparkling inlets.

In this direction we overlooked a large area of our island; could pitch our sight straight down the brush-clothed flanks of our pedestal into the oblong surface of Eagle lake; could look over the heads of all the mountain-ridges crowded before us, to ocean and islands away toward Pemaquid; or, a little more to the westward, sweep that marvelous mingling of water and land, forest and fishing-ground, upland and salt-meadow, immovable rock and fluent tide, that form the Penobscot archipelago, and fill the scene between the tall dome of Blue Hill and the "titan-fronted blowy steeps" that mark far Isle au Haut.

And so we were brought around to the ocean again, which most often claimed our eyes, and longest held the imagination: —

> I heard or seemed to hear the chiding sea
> Say, Pilgrim, why so late and slow to come?
> Am I not always here, thy summer home?
> Is not my voice thy music, morn and eve?
> My breath thy healthful climate in the heats,
> My touch thy antidote, my bay thy breath?
> Was ever building like my terraces?
> Was ever couch magnificent as mine?
> Lie on the warm rock-ledges, and there learn
> A little hut suffices like a town.

The streets and prettily winding roads which stray among the rocks, groves, and half-hidden houses of the foothills, or curve along the shore, are populous and gay with strollers in the long twilight.

while each hotel soon becomes a perfect beehive of pleasure-seekers, — a honey-comb of sweetness, as Baily once phrased it, refering to the girls, I presume, instead of to the moist sugar he happened to be stirring in the bottom of a tumbler.

Nor were we behindhand in patronage of Vanity Fair, which Prue rightly remarked to be much more *fair* than *vain*. Of "society," and the entertainments of those who own their own houses, modest or magnificent, I have no occasion to speak. They do at Mt. Desert what they are accustomed to do in New Orleans or New York, Baltimore or Boston. What interests me now is the hotel life, open to everybody. It is possible, I concluded, to amuse one's self, and be amused at Bar Harbor and thereabouts more variously and more rationally than at any place I know of, and one who does not enjoy for a season the whirl of genial gayety that eddies round each hotel every evening — well he's something extraordinary. Nor is it necessarily a very expensive treat; you can suit almost any purse capable of pleasure-buying at all. On the other hand, so bountiful in resources is this sea-girt rock that none are keener to praise her than these exceptional ones to whom the painter's brush, or the naturalist's outfit, or the paddle of a birch-canoe, is all sufficient for vacation joy.

As for Prue, she just revelled in innocent glee. One evening I recall particularly. Our friends had introduced to her a batallion of young fellows, and I took good care to keep quite out of sight, and let her disport herself once more in the warmth of admiration and compliment. It didn't do her a bit of harm; and it left me to two or three very charming young misses who were kind enough to be oblivious to the gray hairs — there are not so *very* many! — and whose rippling badinage I enjoyed all the more because Baily had been entrapped by a couple of grandmothers who knew his mother or some of his aunts, and held him like dear old cuttle-fishes.

In the day time we went walking, riding and boating. Earlier in the season picnicing is much in vogue, especially at the time when watermelons are ripe. Of course champagne on ice, and a few other items help out the melons on the cloth spread under the greenwood tree. It is not a fact, however, that these parties are dull and silent affairs, simply because everybody keeps Mumm. One favorite picnicing ground is the shore of Jordan pond; but pitch up a stone almost anywhere and it will fall in a good place to consume watermelons, biscuit and champagne, at the elbow of a pretty girl.

Later, these alfresco feasts give way to pedestrian jaunts — long tramps with a bracing breeze in your face and a hard roadbed under your feet. Our party walked a good deal. We went to all the beaches and climbed all the hills in the neighborhood, getting a new point of view each day for the pretty picture of the clustered town with its many-gabled red roofs and azure bay, with the rugged Porcupines and the knolls of Gouldsborough for a back-ground.

Nowhere in America are lovelier summer-houses than these hillsides hold, or that border the shore north of the landing. Some have been lodged among rocks, gnarled trees and natural vinery, in situations that were inaccessible to goats until roads had been cut. Others occupy the brows of hills commanding a wide prospect, or are tucked away in sheltered nooks where the owner can rest at home from beholding the splendor of the world and so preserve his appetite for nature. To many, the edge of the water seems best, so that the island is almost engirdled with a row of cottages, great and small.

COTTAGE AT BAR HARBOR.

But the word "cottage" here is as expansive as at Newport (Mt. Desert is, in fact, a combination of Newport and Saratoga, remodeled after its own original fashion), and scores of the houses in the outskirts of Bar Harbor, are not only ideals of architecture but very substantial and more costly than the average of city homes, even in wealthy quarters. Nowhere in the Union, I feel sure, can the equal, or similitude of the Bar Harbor heights be found, in combined architectural and natural picturesqueness. Nor is this an ephemeral thing, for every year adds many names to the catalogue of rich and cultivated men who are buying land and building houses here which they mean to occupy permanently.

These facts and many others as to the remarkable growth here were given to us by a gentleman who was one of the earliest to appreciate the excellence of the spot, and one who has not only profited most largely by his early investments, but has wisely guided the hurried improvements since effected. The rise in the value of real estate has been most extraordinary. A lot of forty acres, including a shore-front, was bought seven years ago for $2,500, which has since paid its owner $46,000. Land at Bar Harbor, is now cheap at the rate of $25,000 an acre, and for some a rate of $125,000 has been paid. Desirable cottages have appreciated in proportion; one small one, pointed out to us, having gone from $3,000 to $11,000 between 1882 and 1885. The only fault ever found with Bar Harbor was on the score of bad drainage; and this has now been remedied by a scientific system of sewerage.

The people of the whole island are thriving greatly under this new state of things, and exhibit their bettered circumstances not only in improved farming, but in better houses, better clothes, better schooling and more amusement, so that Mount Desert, from being one of the most forsaken, hardest-working and poorest-living corners of Yankee land, has become one of the most prosperous and easy.

One of our first excursions was along the southern shore, past Schooner Head, where we halted to hear the heavy rollers go booming into the Spouting Horn,

> And see the elastic banners of the dulse
> Rock softly, and the orange starfish creep
> Across the laver.

Then on past Great Head to the cliffs of Otter, and its pretty cove held in the lap of the mountains; and, farther yet, to Northeast Harbor, where there is a large colony of summer houses, and an intellectual circle, represented by two or three university presidents, and a number of literary and professional men.

"To appreciate Great Head," says Samuel Drake, whose winter visit here is a notable contribution to the literature of the locality. "One must stand underneath it. . . . By dint of perseverance I at last stood upon the ledge beneath, that extends out like a platform for some distance toward deep water. It was the right stage of the tide. I looked up at the face of the cliff. It was bearded with icicles like the Genius of Winter. Along the upper edge appeared the interlacing roots of old trees grasping the scanty soil, like monster talons. Stunted birches, bent by storms, skirted its brow and at sea add to its height. From top to bottom the face of the cliff is a mass of hard granite, overhanging its foundations in impending ruin, shivered and splintered as if torn by some tremendous explosion."

This is the route of the "twenty-two mile drive," which from Northeast Harbor goes north along the flanks of the mountains far under some of their cliffs, yet hundreds of feet above Somes' sound, disclosing here and there fine seaward glimpses; and thence descends to the valleys at the head of the sound, where it turns eastward and winds among the hills and past Eagle lake back to Bar Harbor.

In a two day's drive, stopping for the night at Bass Harbor, the whole circuit of the island can be made comfortably, and new roads in all directions are constantly being opened, or old ones repaired, so that the variety of walks and drives available in all directions has become very great; with Mrs. Martin's excellent guide-book in hand no one need get bewildered. This authority cautions travellers not to omit Bass Harbor Head, since it affords a superb view, only surpassed by that from Green mountain.

Southwest Harbor bids fair to rival Bar Harbor in population and

OTTER CLIFF, MT. DESERT.

attractiveness. Its neighborhood abounds in opportunities for walking, driving and sailing. Here is that wonderful natural sea-wall, piled up in a long windrow by the fury of the winter gales, of which so much has been written, — best of all, the poem by Frances L. Mace, with the firm faith of its last stanza : —

> But while the tide shall come and go
> While tempests rage and sunbeams smile,
> Safe guarded by its giant wall
> Shall bloom the Mountain Isle.

Opportunities for sea-fishing are particularly good here, while trout are within reach at several inland ponds. A ferry makes frequent trips to the Cranberry islands, and occasionally, on fair days, a party sails out to the lone reef where Mount Desert light, built in 1830, rears its solitary beacon, — most distant of the light now visible from the top of Green mountain. This light-house occupies a mere summit of granite, towering just out of reach of the waves, and sometimes a boat cannot land there for weeks together.

> All shores about and afar lie lonely,
> But lonelier are these than the heart of grief,
> These loose-linked rivets of rock, whence only
> Looks one low tower from the sheer main reef,
> With a blind wan face in the wild wan morning,
> With a live lit flame on its brows by night,
> That the lost may lose not its word's mute warning,
> And the blind by its grace have sight.

Around Southwest Harbor, too, centres the history of the island. No doubt Mount Desert was sighted, and perhaps examined, by the Viking sailors of Red Eric, for its heights can be seen sixty miles at sea. Hence the island early appears in American history. "It constituted a part of the ancient Acadia, for the possession of which there was a contest more or less sanguinary between England and France which lasted for more than a hundred and thirty years. The French founded their claim on the discovery of this coast by Verazzano in 1524, on the discovery and occupancy of Canada by Cartier in 1535, and on the grant to De Monts in 1603. The English claim was based upon the discovery of Cabot in 1497, upon the occupancy of Newfoundland by Gilbert in 1553, by the subsequent voyage and landings of Gosnold, Pring, and Weymouth and others, by the charter to the Popham colony in 1606, and the occupancy of the soil by that colony in 1607." In 1603, Henry IV. of France granted to Le Sieur de Monts this "Acadia," including all then known of what is now New England and the Maritime Provinces of Canada. In March 1604, DeMonts and Champlain sailed in two vessels for his new possessions, and, after having discoverd the St. John river, made winter quarters on an island at the mouth of the St. Croix (see Chapter X.), sending Champlain on an exploring expedition along the further coast. After various adventures and misadventures Champlain came to an island "very high, and so cleft in places that at sea it appears as if seven or eight mountains were ranged side by side;" and this he named *L'isle des Monts-deserts*. Champlain made no extended stoppage; but a few years later accident sent white people to reside upon the island.

When Henry IV. died, and the Queen-mother reigned in France, Acadia was not forgotten. Her Majesty encouraged Madame de Guercheville to send a Jesuitical colony to be planted among the red heathen, and a well-equipped vessel was despatched under command of M. de la Soussaye, which carried the Jesuits Quantin and Du Thet. They were to stop at Port Royal (near Annapolis, N. B.— see Chapter X.) and take with them Fathers Biard and Masse, after which they were to proceed to Pentagoët. The plan thus far was carried out; but the expedition became enveloped in fogs, and, dreading the rocks ahead, put into a harbor on the coast of Mount Desert, where it was decided to establish their colony, and to give it, in gratitude, the name St. Sauveur.

Both date and place of this incident are uncertain. The former is probably 1613. Some historians suppose their first landing was to have been not far from Bar Harbor — perhaps in the cove near Schooner Head, whence the colonists afterward moved; while others hold that they landed at first where they remained. At any rate the Indians befriended them, guiding them to their own camps; and it seems tolerably certain that the colony was finally settled at Fernald's point, about two miles from Southwest Harbor.

That nothing better than two or three doubtful cellar-excavations remain to mark the traditional site is not strange, when one remembers the slight nature and brief existence of the ill-fated colony. For in 1613, Samuel Argal, one of the boldest (and worst) of the early navigators, who had struck out for himself a short cut to Virginia, and was now attached to the James River colony, came to the coast of Maine on a fishing-voyage. Here he learned from the Indians of the French at St. Sauveur and resolved to dislodge them. "It made no difference to Argal," as the author of *Pen and Pencil at Mt. Desert* has remarked, " that England and France were then at peace." The Jamestown colony, which he represented, regarded all encroachments upon their territory as acts of hostility and assumed the right to keep off all intruders. Argal's approach greatly surprised the French, but having a ship and a barque in the harbor, and a light entrenchment on shore, they did what they could to defend themselves. Argal attacked the place with musketry, and at the second discharge, Du Thet fell mortally wounded, and two young men named Lemoine and Neveau were drowned. The French were easily overpowered and fifteen of the colonists, including Fathers Biard and Quantin, were taken to Virginia. . . . This ends the story of the Jesuit occupancy of Mount Desert island, and whether they were here five years, or only a part of a single year, it matters little now. The ashes of Du Thet repose at

Fernald's point which is the ancient St. Sauveur, and probably other relics of the French mission may be buried beneath the soil, but the description of the harbor, the admirable site for such a settlement, and the boiling springs in the vicinity are the only existing evidence by which we are able to locate the spot.

> Fall softly, blossoms of the century tree!
> Long would we keep our isle's historic fame;
> Teach thy blue waves to whisper, plaintively,
> St. Sauveur's ancient name!

The French, however, still claimed sway, and in 1688 Mount Desert and its neighborhood were granted to a man named Cadillac, who, however, never visited his property. When Acadia was relinquished to England, Massachusetts gave Mount Desert island to Governor Bernard, as a reward for his services. But as he stayed with King George, whom he had served so well before, when the Revolution broke out, the state of Massachusetts confiscated this estate, of some 60,000 acres, but afterward restored half of it to his son, a resident of Bath, who had become a stanch Whig. "Meantime the claim of Cadillac was revived in the person of Mons. Bartholomew Gregoire, and his wife Maria Theresa, who was the great-granddaughter of the original grantee. It was an old and doubtless obsolete claim, but at, and immediately after the close of the Revolutionary war, the government of Massachusetts was especially well disposed toward France and her citizens, and so, in 1787, the Great and General Court first naturalized the petitioners, and then gave them a quit-claim deed of the interest held by Massachusetts in the island, it being one half of it, reserving to actual settlers lots of one hundred acres each. The petitioners settled here, and Theresa Gregoire died at Hull's cove, on the spot now occupied by the large brick mansion house, in 1810. Many of the settlers on the island hold title deeds based upon this grant."

No settler had been safe along this coast, however, until after the French had been driven out, and the Indian wars put at an end; and the first man to make his home on the island was Abraham Somes, jr., who belonged to an old Gloucester (Mass.) family, and came here with his family in a Chebacco boat, which he anchored at the head of the sound that now bears his name, and inhabited during the winter of 1762-3. Thus originated Somesville, in the old staging times an important place, but now devoted to entertaining summer boarders.

Settlers multiplied, fishing, ship-building and other sea-faring industries occupying all the young and sturdy men. Not a Tory could be found in the island when the Revolution began, and no people dared and suffered more for liberty than did these.

Such are hints, here and there, of what we saw and did, or wanted to see or do, at Mount Desert. We walked and we climbed; we rowed and we rode; we danced and we loafed. Bally made diligent enquiry about real estate and bachelor quarters, and picked himself out a place where he proposes next year to begin a long residence. I feel more confidence in this resolution than any I have heard him utter yet, and I am tempted to go in with him, for I have grown strong and refreshed to a most surprising degree already. As for Prue, she has seemed in perfect harmony with the glorious island, and the wan look in her face has given place to that alert air and glowing color which is her natural heritage : —

> For she and the clouds and the breezes were one,
> And the hills and the sea had conspired with the sun,
> To charm and bewilder all men with the grace
> They combined and conferred on her wonderful face.

CHAPTER VIII.

THE PISCATAQUIS VALLEY.

There wild woods grow, and rivers row,
And monie a hill's between—BURNS.

EARLY next morning, as we went on board the ferry steamer,—certainly the handsomest boat, I, for one, ever saw in public service,—which would carry us eight miles across to the mainland (for we were now northward bound), Frenchman's bay lay softly blue and scarcely marred by a ripple. The Porcupine crags, rising sharply out of the shining plain of water, were dark almost to blackness, but the lazy islands along the Gouldsboro' shore gleamed bright in sunshine, where

"The warm, wide hills, are muffled thick with green."

A thousand bare spaces, wet with dew, glistened like burnished mirrors upon the mountains we were so regretfully leaving, and lit up their shaggy sides in barbaric decoration. All too quickly, therefore, the engineer's "slow" bell jarred upon our ears, and with a last fond glance at Newport, and craggy Pemetic, and that observatory-crowned giant which especially is Mount Desert, we gathered up our luggage and made our way ashore at the railway terminus and general steamer-landing, called Mt. Desert Ferry.

The train had several parlor cars which would go straight through to Boston, but we left them to the unfortunates who were homeward bound, for *we* were not going home,—oh, no! We were going to Moosehead lake!

With the exception of the large village of Ellsworth, and Reed's pond, much resorted to by fishing parties in search of land-locked salmon, there is little to entertain the railway passenger between the coast and Bangor. A geologist, however, will be interested in observing the rounded and planed masses of granite exposed by the ravages of fires, in the crannies of which stunted trees can now hardly find nourishment. Prue seemed fascinated by this grim devastation; and Baily told us that it was just like that forlorn Keewaydin region between Lake Superior and Winnipeg. Here, too, are lodes bearing nearly all the precious minerals, and extensive mining for gold, silver, copper, and some other metals has been done.

Before this scenery grows tiresome, we escape it by emerging into the fields and orchards of old Brewer, and look down upon the river, wondering how long it has required for its current to erode so deep a path through the tough rock; then we cross through a covered bridge and roll into the city-like station of city-like Bangor.

Here the Pullman cars, which have just come in from New Brunswick (for this is the outlet of "the Provinces"), are attached to our train which will go on to Portland. But as for us three, we change to a train going the other way, and prepare our minds for a complete contrast to Mt. Desert. All are full of enthusiasm for the change. Even Baily, his countenance round and beaming, breaks into poetry, and, waving his hand impressively, he astonishes us with Wordsworth, most sonorously recited :—

> Oh! what a joy it were, in vigorous health
> To roam at large among unpeopled glens
> And mountainous retirements, only trod
> By devious footsteps; regions consecrate
> To oldest time!

Prue and I said nothing, but, looking solemn alarm at one another, stiffly agreed, for the sake of argument, that it was a joy. Baily's smile gradually faded away, and with some mutterings about "getting even," he marched out of the car. Then you should have heard how we let the seriously-minded farmers and farmers' wives; and the limp little dude beside his unbending dowager of a mother, who might easily have spared a good deal of starch for his benefit; and the boss-lumberman figuring in a worn pocket-book; and the group of factory girls going home to Dover for a vacation; and the brown-eyed little schoolma'm, who was all of a fluster for fear a Boston drummer, across the aisle, was going to try to flirt with her;—you should have heard, I say, how we let all these people know what whole-souled glee sounded like.

"Oh!" cries Prue, "what fun poor Mr. Baily has missed by not staying to hear himself laughed at!"

Meanwhile we had been travelling along the bank of the river, past enormous rafts of logs confined in booms next the shores, over which men in red shirts were skipping like grasshoppers, and now came to Oldtown,—a large, straggling village, where we leave the Maine Central and turn off upon the rails of the Bangor & Piscataquis line.

Here the booms were bigger and the mills more numerous. The falls of the Penobscot furnished the power, to a great extent. "Here," writes Henry D. Thoreau, whose inspiring volume, *The Maine Woods*, we had with us, "is a close jam, a hard rub, at all seasons; and then the once green tree, long since white, I need not say as the driven snow, but as the driven log, becomes lumber merely. . . . Through this steel riddle, more or less coarse, is the arrowy Maine forest, from Katahdin to Chesuncook, and the headwaters of the St. John, relentlessly sifted, till it comes out boards, clapboards, laths and shingles."

Just beyond Oldtown on an island in the river, a large cluster of small houses around a Roman Catholic church is the dwelling-place of the remnant of the Tarratine (Abnaki) Indians,—those who ravaged Pemaquid and were routed at Norridgewock. In the treaty of 1726 they were given possession of the islands in the river, and are paid by the state an annuity of $6,000 to $7,000 in exchange for lands relinquished years ago. Between four and five hundred persons, mostly half-breeds, are now included in their numbers, but the men scatter all over the state, working in the mills and lumber driving, "guiding" hunters and camping-parties through the woods, or hunting and fishing for themselves, while the women at home make baskets or do rough household work in the town. The making of birch canoes is an important industry. Some of the Indians are partly educated and many own considerable property. Thoreau gives an interesting account of what he saw of them, and their characteristics, and their history has been written by their missionary, Vetromile.

At first the Piscataquis railroad runs northwestward, through dense scrub, but in the neighborhood of Lagrange a well-cultivated ridge appears on the right. A view of Katahdin can be had, in clear weather, from South Lagrange, but a far better one is obtained at Milo, a few miles farther on. Mt. Russell appears straight ahead, a round pile, bearing some naked rocks above the rusty woods, and farther away the low dome of Pleasant Pond mountain.

"Why, that's the region, isn't it," Prue asks, "that John Burroughs visited and describes in his 'Taste of Maine Birch?' I remember that he says Pleasant pond was the only strictly silver lake he ever saw,—look, here it is, on this map, just at the western foot of the mountain,—and describes how he counted the bowlders on its bottom in water thirty or forty feet deep."

"And I recall," adds Baily, "that he says of the trout that they were veritable bars of silver until you cut them open, and then they proved the reddest of gold. He thought they were a variety peculiar to that pond. And that was where he found loons that could dodge the bullet from the muzzle-loader every time, but weren't quick enough for his breech-loading rifle."

The next station is Milo, entering which we cross the Piscataquis.

"Strikes me that word, or others very similar, occur elsewhere on the map of the eastern states," some one remarks.

"It does, and naturally enough, since it simply means a big branch, or 'a fork,' as we would say. The Abnaki mind regarded a stream from its mouth up, instead of from the source down, which would seem to indicate that they entered the country along the coast and explored it by ascending the rivers, rather than the reverse."

From Milo, a branch railroad, 19 miles long, goes northward to Brownville and the Bangor and Katahdin Iron Works. Brownville has quarries of peculiarly fine slate, and is the point of departure for the

Schoodic and Seboois lakes, where there is good fishing. An old logging-road runs from Schoodic lake over to the West branch of the Penobscot, passing near the Ebeeme ponds and to Jo Merry lakes, all of which furnish shooting and fishing, amid attractive scenery. That is one route (and a short one) to Mt. Katahdin, by the way of South Twin lake and the West branch.

"Thoreau has much to say about that region," Prue reminds us, turning to page 35 of his *Maine Woods*, and reading to us his experiences in canoeing there thirty years ago.

From Brownville to Katahdin Iron Works the branch railroad runs through a dense forest, with glimpses of Pleasant river on the right. The iron works use the ore of an adjacent mountain to which the Indians had resorted for paint-stuff since time immemorial. The ore is brown hematite, extending from three to twenty feet thick, over many acres, and contains exquisite impressions of leaves, etc. It is manufactured by the charcoal process, especially for making into car-wheels, and the annual product amounts to some 4,000 tons.

Besides the small settlement of people about the furnaces, the Silver Lake House, on the Munolammonungun ("red-paint place") pond, is fast growing into popularity, not only among sportsmen-tourists, but with invalids, who find in the chalybeate springs near by, a tonic additional to the invigorating air and freedom of the woods. A glance at the map shows how many ponds are in the near vicinity, all of which furnish trout-fishing; and in the fall one can obtain excellent partridge shooting, besides having a chance at deer, caribou and the common black bear.

Ten miles up this, the West branch of the Pleasant river, is that exceedingly wild and precipitous "gulf" which comes nearer to a western cañon than any other gorge in this part of Maine. Both Farrar's and Hubbard's *Guides* to Moosehead lake and vicinity (each of which contains a large scale map) give long accounts of it, but it is not yet accessible to the ordinary tourist. The river for several miles has cut its way irregularly into the slate, leaving banks over 100 feet high, which are so vertical and so near together that in one place deer often jump across the chasm. In the bottom is a roaring line of cascades, and above, an arch of dense forest, whence spring the long slopes of high mountains.

June or September are the best months for a camping-trip to this gulf, and the road is under improvement so that ladies may be taken. From that centre the ascent of White Cap (3,700 feet) and several other mountains is feasible; and it is only 15 miles to Moosehead lake. Two miles, by a good path from the foot of the gulf, is Long pond, "the main source of Sebec pond, and the home of the trout and land-locked salmon."

By the time we had discussed these facts we had run on past South Sebec, where stages for Sebec pond and its ancient settlements meet each train; the distance is five miles. There is a steamer on the lake, from whose further borders immense quantities of blueberries are sent to market. The spring fishing for salmon there, is renowned, but during the summer, pickerel and white perch must content the angler.

Then come Foxcroft and Dover,—very pretty towns, in a well-cultivated region. Here, nearly everybody, except the Moosehead tourist, leaves the cars, for this is on the edge of civilization; and the terror of that nervous little schoolma'm, when the Boston drummer also alighted here and politely helped her into the same hotel 'bus with himself, was as meat and drink to our amusement-searching eyes.

A little farther on is Monson Junction, where a narrow-gauge railway runs northward eight miles to the renowned Monson slate quarries, operated by a Lowell (Mass.) company, which proposes to extend the road northward to Greenville and southward to Skowhegan.

"If they do," says Baily, "they'll run it through, what one of the old stage drivers hereabout, used to call, 'a pretty sassy country,' only made, in his opinion, 'to hold the world together.'"

The deep quarries, and the operations of cutting out the slate and splitting it into roof-pieces, are very interesting; and this industry has elevated what was formerly a little cluster of farms, into an energetic and populous community, making Monson a desirable centre for sport and camping. A score or so of ponds are in the near vicinity, most of them accessible by good roads, and several have rude, but comfortable inns on their shores. The local piscatores will give the stranger advice as to the kind of fish and proper season belonging to each body of water; and will cart him and his belongings about, or outfit him for camping, at a very moderate cost. This was the place for stopping over night on the old stage-journey from Bangor; and it was near here that Thoreau and Winthrop saw the moose-horns set on a guidepost at a fork of the road, with the name of each destination painted on their diverging prongs.

Again, I must beg you to remember, that, while I have taken this digression, we are rolling up the Piscataquis, now only an impatient brook. Then we pass Blanchard, and can look off to the left, beyond Mt. Russell, to the more distant hills where spring its fountains. Between Blanchard and Shirley are several high trestles, and a constant outlook far westward across forested ravines pinched between crowding hills. Mt. Russell hangs above us in the rear, and behind him Bald mountain, its smooth face ringed with woods like the crown of one of those friar's, who were the first white men to look upon these hills. Burroughs climbed it from Moxie pond, and found its top one enormous cap of naked granite, seamed, cracked and glacier-plowed,— much such a crest as that of the Mount Desert knobs, I fancy. His description of it is very striking. These hills, richly tinted and changeful, never lose their charm, till nearer and taller the Squaw rears her head, and the gleaming spaces of Moosehead lake, where she watches break suddenly upon our view.

CHAPTER IX.

MOOSEHEAD LAKE.

*Where breezes baffle heat;
Where shaded dells and mossy coverts be.*

SOME of the passengers seated themselves in the hotel coaches waiting at the Lake station and whirled away to Greenville, but the most of us betook ourselves to a neat little hotel a few rods up the road, where dinner awaited us — something we were extremely anxious shouldn't wait any longer.

"I never was so hungry in all my born days!" Prue confided to me, careless of her idioms.

Perhaps the hunger helped our appreciation, but let us give the cook the benefit of the doubt, and simply record our entire satisfaction with that dinner; and then, in better frame both of body and mind, we went out to view the land and the waters thereof.

Only a portion of the lake could be seen, the remainder lying behind points and islands, but this part was promising. Clouds had gathered, but would frequently break, letting the sun strike through and brighten the gray surface of the ruffled water. Straight up the lake, cutting off the view, rose the shapely broad hill on Moose island, — warm, deep, lively blue in color, through which a peppering of dull orange shone. The projecting headlands, and the islets grouped in front of its base, were vivid orange and yellow, where

> Autumn's earliest frost had given
> To the woods below,
> Hues of beauty, such as heaven
> Lendeth to its bow;
> And the soft breeze from the west
> Scarcely broke their dreamy rest.

"What is there in this neighborhood to interest visitors," we ask a comfortable looking lounger on the wharf.

"Oh, slathers o' things! Greenville's got two large hotels and they are full of city folks all summer. No better place now for the lake fishin' than right here, — sometimes they'll bite here when they won't nowhere else. Then there's lots o' ponds and troutin' streams within a few miles, like Gerrish's pond and Eagle stream and the Wilson ponds — calc'late you've heard o' them?"

Baily said he had, often. I, who can not tell a lie, tried to look one, rather than confess ignorance.

"Well, they're three miles off to the east'rd. It's good walkin', or, if you want to take your lady with you, you can go in a carriage to the new hotel on the stream betwixt the two ponds."

"Is the fishing as good there as it used to be?" asked Baily, as if he had been accustomed to spend all his vacations in that vicinity.

"Yes, yes. Sure to get trout, especially in July and August when the fishin's dull on the lake, but you've got to let your bait down to deep water. No jumpin' at make-believe flies for those fellows! It's mighty pretty up there, ma'am, kind o' cosied down in among the mountains as snug as you please; and you'd enjoy goin' up to the upper pond — the carry, you know, and all that — if you aint used to it.

"Greenville's a great place for ladies a-goin' picnicing and fishin' and campin' over night all round this end of the lake; and one of the jolliest ways is to hire a little steamer and go up to McFarland's, or down to some of the islands, or may be across to Squaw brook. I never *did* see folks have such a good time as some of those Boston or New York people do when they go off on a trip o' that kind. Green? Lord love ye! but they don't care — never seem to mind it a bit, just ask foolish questions, and carry on, like a passul o' children out o' school."

"That's about what they are; and I dare say we'd behave as badly as the rest of them," laughs Prue. "But tell me — does any body ever climb that great mountain?"

"Big Squaw? Oh, yes. You go over to Squaw brook in a boat or canoe and then pole up as far as you can, — 'taint far, — and from there a path has been bushed out up to the top. Some fellows call it easy to get up, but I should say it was pretty durned hard work, myself. You certainly do see a heap o' country when you get up there, though — lots o' mountains away up on the Allegash and over in Canada and down Rangely way. Well, good day, ma'am — hope you'll have a pleasant time up to Kineo."

Moosehead lake is the largest of the hundreds of inland seas with which "down east" is provided. It is twice as big as Winnipesaukee, but has not the breadth in appearance (save at one or two points) of even that irregular pond, being elongated north and south, indented by promontories, deluded into prolonged bays or winding coves, and beset with islands, so that in several places it comes near losing its continuity. The length is 38 miles, and the width from one to fifteen. It is 995 feet above the sea, from which it is about 100 miles distant, but its bottom, in some places, is almost at sea-level. The shores, until recently covered with solid forest, are being cleared here and there for farming purposes, since excellent soil exists in several districts. This, however, does not detract from the general interest of the scenery, which can never lose the essential wildness that is its charm, so long as the irreclaimably stony islands, the towering mountains and the rock-infested rivers that make its grand surroundings remain; and when they disappear the lake itself will go with them.

Though innumerable hill-brooks and boggy dells drain thither, and many good-sized ponds overflow into its capacious basin, only one large river — the Moose — contributes its flood. The outlet of the lake is the Kennebec river, which pours out from its western side, at the broadest part, just north of the Squaw mountains, where a most substantial dam has been built for lumbering purposes.

Meanwhile we have started. The steamer is a fine double-decked side-wheeler, which pushes along at a good rate, and we are in every way comfortable and happy. At first there are many birch-covered rocky islands, but these are soon left behind and we get out into the round expanse of Sebamook. Greenville, every house painted white, appears behind us at the head of its bay; and near it, on the eastern shore, are several farms, but elsewhere unbroken woods down to the very edge of the water, with hardly any beach or bare rocks in front. Soon we are out far enough to get sight of the whole mass of Squaw mountain. It is well worth looking at, — a rude, uncivilized, worthy representative of the Maine highlands. Eastward, a more distant group of elevations occupies a large space, and sends spurs down to the shore which is itself ten miles away. There are the Lily Bay mountains, and the lofty groups named White Cap, Baker, Spruce, Saddle-back, Elephant-back, and others that stand amphitheatre-wise around the head of Pleasant river. They make a noble group of rugged peaks, cones and frusta, which were recalled when afterwards we gazed upon the huge upheaval that surrounds old Chocorua. The picture is best between Moose and Sugar island, for after the latter has been passed, though more peaks in number come into view, the "composition" is less admirable. This was one of the most beautiful mountain-pictures we saw anywhere in Maine.

On Deer island is a hotel of good size; and here several gentlemen loaded down with guns and fishing tackle left the steamer, and two of the many canoes lashed outside the guards were let lightly down into the water by the deck-hands, who handled the graceful things "as though they loved them." These gentlemen told us they intended on the next morning to paddle over to Kennebec dam, where the September fishing is particularly good. There is a hotel there, and many persons visit it every year, going by special boat, for it is out of the path of the regular steamers.

Having passed through the narrows between Sugar and Deer islands, we enter the broadest part of the lake, where it is fifteen miles across from Kennebec dam to the head of Spencer bay, the latter locality notorious for its fishing and duck-shooting, and the most remote and solitary part of Moosehead. Into it flows Roach stream, outlet of the large pond of the same name, at the foot of which is Davis's hotel; but the way to get there is by a buck-board road from the tavern on

Lily bay at the mouth of Worth brook, to which the people at Greenville often resort for a day's excursion. Good trout-fishing can be had on Roach; but even better is assured to adventurous sportsmen who follow the logging roads over to the Big Lyfort and other secluded ponds at the head of the West branch of the Pleasant river. These ponds lie right under White Cap, amid savage scenery.

Directly north of the extremity of Spencer bay, two miles, is Spencer pond, to which a canoe can easily be taken. This pond lies at the foot of the dome-shaped hill-top that had been sticking up above islands and capes ever since we started, and, now that Sugar island was passed, came out in full view, with a mate equally big and isolated. Lofty, clean in outline, unencumbered by foot-hills, spurs or neighbors, they hold the eye by their singularity rather than their beauty. But be-

MOUNT KINEO, MOOSEHEAD LAKE.

yond them, like a turquoise wedge laid upon its side above the tree tops, is visible for a moment the monumental Katahdin. In *that* far-away peak it is purely beauty and sentiment which hold our admiring gaze.

Presently the lake contracts, and straight ahead, seen partly over the water and partly beyond the low shores on the right, the crags of Kineo grow darkly into larger and distincter form, till the grand headland stands fully revealed before us, with the green lawns, the white birch-groves, the cottages, warehouses and vast hotel, the steamers and sail-boats, that make the Mt. Kineo House like a bit of Bar Harbor dropped down here in the woods.

It is the next day. A discussion is in progress in the music-room of the hotel. A young man in flannel suit and slouched hat, is speaking with a metropolitan decision: —

"No — I will do anything reasonable, but not that. You may ask me to tramp over to where Rangeley's ripples are throwing kisses back to the moon —"

"Hear! Hear!" shouts a listener.

"— but climb Kineo? No!"

So Prue and I go up the mountain alone, starting soon after luncheon. Formerly, the only way was to row around the peninsula, and then ascend a long path of easy grade. Nimble climbers had a way of scrambling down the south front, just back of the hotel, which made the return (for them) far shorter and dispensed with the boats, but no stiff-jointed or rattle-brained person, nor any woman ever came down that path.

In '86, however, Mr. Dennen built a set of ladder-like stairways up the steepest part of this old line of gymnastic descent, and above that, where the cliff was a little less sheer, fastened a chain, like a hand-rail, by the help of which any ordinarily active and surefooted person can mount to the brink of the rock. Prue made light of the difficulties, and scorning my help scrambled up the rocks, using hands and knees, saplings and chain, all the time bewailing how scared she was, but never stopping nor turning back, so that I paid little attention to her complaints.

A fine panorama southward and westward was spread before us from this first ledge — an excellent chart of our whole steamboat-course the day before; but as soon as we got our breath we turned our backs upon it and trudged up the well-trodden path leading along the margin of the cliff to its much higher extremity at the eastern face. The path was not always an even ascent, however, nor is the summit of the rock as level as it seems to be from below. On the contrary there are two great depressions. The woods were dense, but beautiful, fragrant, and still, and the moss was thick enough everywhere, especially in the hollows, to make a most grateful carpet for our feet. At one spot, half way, we obtained a broader view westward than even the summit afforded, but did not pause, until at last, with a sudden emergence from the cedars, we came to the brink of that great face of the rock looking down upon Kineo bay and the beaches.

It almost took our breath away! Prue sat right down and fairly squealed whenever I moved a step. But after a little, she gingerly advanced and learned to look down the purple walls that fell so sharply away from where we stood. For, though I could have made a running leap which would have dropped me seven hundred and fifty feet into that trembling mirror beneath us, yet the brow of the crag was so rounded off, and treegrown, that it was possible to go quite near the verge, without serious danger; and I know nowhere in the east that such a sense of the grandeur of height can be experienced as here, where the eye can follow the vertical lines of the crag-face, down, down, down, till the heart faints before the awful thought of following the stone you fling out and lose sight of before it strikes.

We wandered about the crest, following various paths through the bushes which would bring us out at new points of view; and at one place I walked out upon the very edge of the precipice, where it really overhangs the beach at the head of the cove; yet this was not so terrifying as the other, for I looked straight down through nothingness to the familiar objects of the shore — though how strangely minified, — and had no curving columns of rock to lead my eyes and measure for me, foot by foot, the awful distance. Prue, however, wouldn't go near the edge, but sat back and wrung her hands, wailed and kept on wailing, until I returned to the

MOOSEHEAD LAKE,
FROM MT. KINEO.

safety of her perch among the rhododendrons. Then we seated ourselves upon the tip-top point and prepared to enjoy the view. Prue, wrapped in my overcoat, lay upon the warm rocks, while I sat in her lee and jotted down the main features of the landscape.

Eastward, the world is comparatively open, and the few mountains are isolated and distinct. Little Kineo, bun-shaped, as seen from here, stands prominent, and beyond it are the high wooded hills towards Lobster lake. Directly east, the most conspicuous objects are the two Spencer mountains, reared out there in the level woods, without a foot-hill. The nearest (Kokadjo) is a three-sided pyramid, even and sharp; the further one (Sabolawan) is more massive and irregular, — in reality a long ridge, seen "end on." To the left of Kokadjo, the northernmost extremity only of Katahdin is visible — a great disappointment to us, who had hoped to see it all. North of it, away over toward the head of the East branch of the Penobscot, half-sunken summits indent the sky with faint notchings.

From the Spencers, southward, there is little to speak of until we get down to the Lily Bay group, over the left of which a pure dome is revealed, which I take to be White Cap. Southward of that are massed the peaked company whose grandeur I have described as we saw it from the lake, and which neither loses nor gains in this new arrangement. A crowd of high hills shut in that end of the lake, the whole southern half of which lies outspread before us as in a chart. Islands so big that we thought them a part of the mainland when we sailed past, now are seen encircled by water. Every bay and cove and inlet, and each little island is plain at a glance.

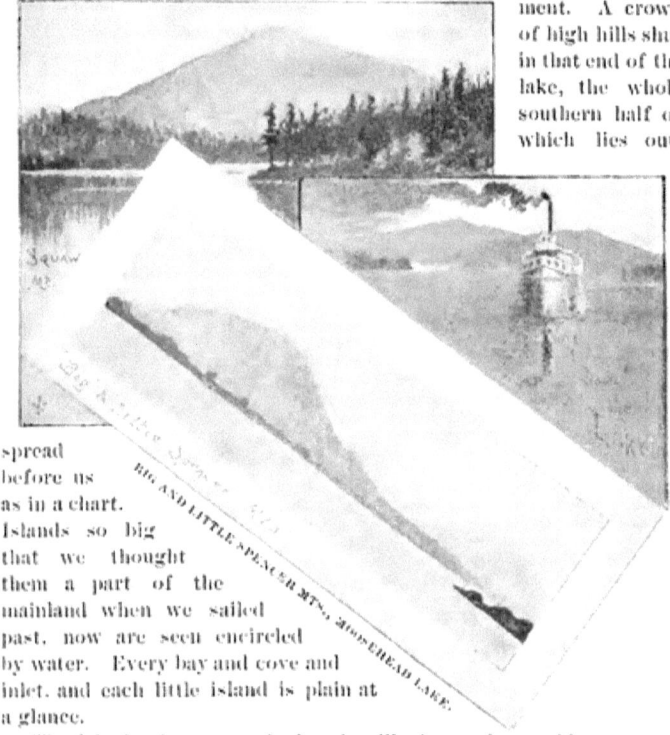

The lake is vitreous and gleaming like ice, and resembles a cameo, whose form has been carved out of the rough epidermis of forest down to some pearly layer underneath. Across it comes the boat from Greenville, like a white bird at the apex of a triangle made by its ever-widening wake; but it is only by long watching that we can see that it moves. Little cats-paws, turning up the blue under side of the wavelets, ruffle the lustrous surface, and by the progress of patches of this deeper color we can trace where some swift zephyr scuds across, or a current is blowing steadily. I am aroused from my revery by my companion's voice, soft, almost sleepy.

"Yes — what is it?"

"Did you say that Mt. Kineo is a mass of pure flint?"

"Yes, or pretty much the same thing. That's what the Indian word means — arrow-head stone. The whole state was supplied with material for sharp stone implements from this place. It's the biggest chunk of hornstone in the world."

"Well, Theo, I was just thinking, you know, that if, some day, that big mountain of iron down at the furnaces, should march up here and pitch into Kineo, how the sparks would fly!"

I decline to laugh, by word or deed, and my wife doesn't seem to demand it, but contentedly nestles into her coat again, and lets her eyes rest in serene delight upon the scene.

Northward, the lake is spread out, keystone-shape, with equal distinctness, and an almost interminable plain of forests, with a few little summits far away as boundary marks. This unbounded forest in every direction forms, indeed, the dominant and memorable feature of the view. As the breadth of the ocean held our gaze on Mount Desert, so here we are held by the expanse of woods. The color is dingy green, and the surface is as uniform and dense as a grainfield. Formerly, the white pines — Sauls of their race — towered up singly or in sparse groves here and there far over the general level, as the standards of an army are lifted above the crowding spears; but these are cut away even from the highest hills and all the remaining trees have the dead level of their mediocrity unbroken. Isolated rocky summits (like our own) sticking up here and there, seemed truly islands. This similitude of the great heaving forest and the sea was intensified moreover by the sound which came up to our ears from all sides — a steady, droning, rustling threnody; a dull suppressed booming, like that of distant surf, yet unlike it; varying with the shifting of the light wind, but never ceasing nor losing its impressiveness. It is the gossip of millions of clashing branches and tens of millions of rustling leaves, and if in a quiet day like this its tones are still powerful, how mighty must be the roar when the storm is hurtling among those pliant tops. It is the harp of the North Woods, vibrating in gentle tones to a zephyr's touch to-day; but capable to-morrow of resounding with what diapason notes!

> A whispered tone of most Æolian sweetness!
> Where many voices seemed accordant blended
> All to a dulcet swell of full completeness,
> Breathing as if by golden harps attended,
> Now lingering slow, now waked to magic fleetness,
> Heaved now in solemn surge, now faintly falling.

Westward, the view is not so satisfactory from here (because of the bushes) as from a point farther back, and after strolling about among the rocks and hoary old trees, and drinking from the spring, which bubbles up at the very top, we slowly return along the woodland path.

Here and there it is dim, the shadows are dense, the thickets would make excellent ambuscades. Prue remembers that she is in the wilderness. She has heard a good many bear-stories of late, and walks on tiptoe, with her eyes open, ears pricked up, and skirts gathered in both hands ready to run *instanter*. Yet she goes ahead—apparently courting the bears, which I try to explain by a reference to that animal's well-known propensity toward hugging, and get snubbed for my pains.

By and by, we come out on the verge of the cliff where the west shines in our faces with sunset smiles. Squaw and the Little Squaw, down at the foot of the lake are black with absolutely unbroken forest; it must have been a large campfire which old Kinneho could see from here. Just across the lake from us is an extension of Kineo called the Blue Ridge, which is one rim, while Squaw is the other, of a vast shallow basin, whose endless forests hide Indian pond, both the outlets to the Kennebec, and a dozen streams; but the background all the way round is filled with the mountains at whose feet lie the Rangely lakes, and along whose farther crests runs the Canadian line.

The sun sinks rapidly. The mountains sway and tremble in the dancing level beams that gush through their passes (for now the sun is half gone), distinguishing each range by some separate color-effect, ineffably soft and rich, while the whole west is veiled in a greenish coppery-mist hardly separable from the glowing sky.

> And the long and level sunbeams
> Shot their spears into the forest,
> Breaking through its shields of shadow,
> Rushed into each secret ambush,
> Searched each thicket, dingle, hollow.

With fast deepening gloom the foreground darkens to greenish-black or dead brown or indigo, and the forested heights far away in the south and east are suddenly dyed in transparent crimson, while the waters between become as a sheet of polished steel.

I am not writing a book about hotels, but here at Moosehead lake the Mt. Kineo House is the whole settlement. Stores, stables, steamers—everything are part and parcel of the property. Nothing could be more fortunate in the way of a site. Right at the side of the huge rock, a few acres of almost level and fertile soil stretch out into the lake, inviting a landing. On this natural location the hotel has been built, but the present building is the enlarged successor of two lesser ones which have been destroyed by fire. "This new hotel," in the succinct statement of its Manager, Mr. O. A. Dennen, "is planned on an ample scale and believed to be second to none in construction, general arrangement and convenience, as well as in its provision for the security and comfort of its guests."

That's just like any popular watering-place, you say. Precisely;

but one might not expect to find such polish in this wild region, and hence I am particular to make the fact plain.

Otherwise, there is a great unlikeness between Moosehead and other watering places. There is no driving for instance. Sailing is another lake-side pleasure little practiced here. Social pleasures take a subordinate place, though the large music-room of the hotel, with its polished floor and airy space, is an ideal place for dancing and by no means left deserted; and though the club house (the very pink and perfection of log cabins) is the prettiest amusement-room the summer tourist of a sun shines upon. Nor does the management trouble itself to entertain the guests by elaborate preparations for their amusement, though it will give sound advice and furnish every material means to carry to success any plan for recreation. The situation, in fact, is much like that of the traveller at the Missouri stage-station, who if he didn't like corned beef could help himself to mustard. Here are the woods and the lake — shooting and fishing. You are welcome to both, or you can take your choice. Nevertheless Cupid is regarded, as well as the Dryads and Naides. A writer in *Harper's Magazine* some years' ago appreciated the case most thoroughly. "Your fishermen," he observes, "may be silent all day while casting his fly, but not so when he has laid his day's sport triumphantly upon the piazza, the envy of unlucky fishermen, and eaten his supper. The walks in the twilight upon the piazzas, the groups of friends clustered here and there, the peals of laughter from the adjoining rooms, the universal stir and movement of the place, the free intercourse of the guides with the sportsman, the admitted privilege of anybody speaking to anybody if he chooses to, the chattering at every available point, make a joyous life whose like can hardly elsewhere be found. It looked dismal at first to interest one's self in this lonely spot of the creation, with mountains and forests as your companions; but each day it is less so. The place grows upon you: the common feeling is, 'It is unlike any place I've been in before.' You eat more and more heartily as the days go on, and grow healthier and jollier; and the great world goes on without you, and you don't care if it does. It is impossible to bring your cares up here into the wilderness. Old men find that they can be young again, and young men have the spice and fun of recreation without dissipation. And so it happens that the people who have the capacity of enjoying themselves in close intercourse with nature come to Moosehead again and again, and those who have to be entertained come but once."

There is no need to go far away for this fishing — some of the best catches on record have been made within hail of the hotel; and Table rock, off Cliff beach, in Kineo bay, always rewards the angler who takes his stand upon it late in the season. Kineo Bay is the favorite terminus of morning walks, and its sandy or pebbly beaches form the most delightful of picnicing grounds or camping places, for visitors often hire tents and camp-outfit and spend their days and nights *al fresco*, taking their meals at the hotel. There you can lie all day in your tent, or float in your birch-bark, teasing the patient echo or studying the lights and shadows on the noble cliff — the purple, violet and black, the silver high-lights where water drips, the hoary tone of lichens and moss, and a thousand changing niceties of color and sunlight.

If you prefer wider excursions, you can paddle or be paddled in the canvas canoes which have pretty well superseded their birchen prototypes (this boat of poetry and romance is not wholly gone, however); or one of the swift steam launches will take you and your canoes together over to a dozen favorite fishing places on the western shore, or clear up to the northern end of the lake if you like, — a trip which will give you a magnificent view of stately Katahdin. Kennebec dam, the western outlet and Churchill stream, with its bead-line of tiny ponds; Brassua lake, Moose river and Brassua stream; the mouths of Tomhegan and Socatean rivers; and Duck cove, on the eastern shore, are the best-known localities.

For beginners, at least, the aid of men familiar with canoes and lake work generally, is necessary both to enjoyment and safety. Probably nowhere in Maine can a better company of these be found than those under patronage of this community. "Most of the guides understand all that can be known about fishing. It is one of the strong points in their profession. They invest but little in novelties. They are not confined to the fly. A stick, a hook, a worm, make their equipment, and you always count on their success. Many a minister, apostolic with his rod if not in his commission, and many a lawyer, have the same tact in catching trout. They know how to do it. They can no more impart the skill to others than you can make the divining rod work with unfitting hands. The birch skiff shoots out from the Kineo pier at 9 A.M., or earlier, often wives and daughters accompanying the fishermen, and go to the famous fishing pools, returning at night with the brilliantly spotted game, which is saved for breakfast the next morning. . . Guides and fishermen rapidly assimilate in appearance as the days go on, till you can hardly tell the bronzed faces, one from the other, and are forced to confess the truth of the saying that dress makes the man — certainly makes the distinction which we too often ascribe to birth and fortune."

Baily did our trio entire credit. Perhaps it was the fact that I, who care nothing for fishing, though I enjoy following anglers in their wanderings, sharing all their preparations and results, was with him; or it may have been the attraction of Prue's bright eyes which quite captured the guide if it didn't the trout; but at any rate Baily got two fishes on his hooks at once, and fought them for forty-two minutes by the watch (it was rather a ticklish place on the western side) before I could get the landing net under their shining bellies and fetch 'em into the canoe.

After he had been at it fifteen minutes or so, skilfully managing the cord that swished through the water as the span of captives darted hither and yon, I asked him how long he intended to keep it up, and was amused by his grim reply.

"I propose," said he, through his teeth, "to fight it out *on this line* if it takes all summer."

We had a fair basketful of good fish already, but these two were worth any half dozen of the others; and having got them we went straight home. Then wasn't it a proud young man who watched them weighed in the centre of an eager circle of envious men and admiring women, and saw them tip the beam at seven pounds! And then Baily put his rod in the scales, and let every body see that it weighed just seven ounces.

"That's good work!" came heartily from a Philadelphian just back from a camping trip up Moose river; "but on single fish I still lead I guess," and he held up one five pounds in weight.

That was champion day for the season, but a few catches every year equal it, though no such giants are ever taken here as nose around the rocky hollows in the Androscoggin lakes.

"Are the trout decreasing here?" we asked.

"Not a bit. More fish were caught this year than ever. The waters are too big and far-reaching to ever feel legitimate fishing injuriously; besides, we have a hatchery here at the house which has turned loose hundreds of thousands of young trout and a heap of salmon, but I'm sorry to say we have never seen any salmon come back. It's a mystery what becomes of them."

But Moosehead lake does not limit the desire of most visitors. The ambition of an explorer enters into a man when he gets on the edge of these great solitudes, and as he looks over the map at the hundreds of connecting water-courses, and then comes to know how capable is a canoe in the hands of his guide, if not in his own, a longing arises to get still farther away into the wilderness, which, if not wholly trackless, at least seems to be so. These woods and waters have been a ranging ground for choppers and sportsmen for a century, but you must look sharply, except at the habitual "carries," to notice any marks of humanity. Maine can repeat Ænone's lament to Ida:—

> They came, they cut away my tallest pines,
> My dark tall pines, that plumed the craggy ledge
> High o'er the blue gorge, and all between
> The snowy peak and snow-white cataract
> Foster'd the callow eaglet, from beneath
> Whose mysterious boughs in the dark morn
> The panther's roar comes muffled.

Yet no one need fear that the forests are tame or the charm of their wildness has departed.

For short trips, near by, there is choice of many secluded and enjoyable places on the winding shores of the lake, or in some of the communicating ponds, I have mentioned, or in the nearer parts of the West branch of the Penobscot, which passes the northern end of the lake at a distance of only two miles, and is reached by the Northeast carry, a steamboat landing at the head of the lake. The voyage down this West Branch to its mouth will well repay one, and many not only go out of the woods that way, but make the trip and return by train to Moosehead from Oldtown. Many men of renown have done it and testified to the great satisfaction it gave them. Thoreau makes it the subject of one of the most entertaining chapters of his *Maine Woods*, and Theodore Winthrop believed that "a breathless dash down the Penobscot" might create in him a more sensitive vitality; and so he and the painter Church came up here to the old Mt. Kineo house, were carried across to the West Branch by the old lumberman's ox-tramway, of which they have left so comical a reminiscence, and were set adrift on that voyage to which we owe that enchanting book, *Life in the Open Air.* "To the lover of scenery," says Hubbard, " the tour down the West Branch offers perhaps more attractions than any other in that part of Maine. There are, to be sure, many carries to make, but the wildness of the river, the picturesqueness of the lakes within access of it, and the grandeur of Mt. Katahdin, which continually discovers some new feature, together form a combination of enjoyments seldom to be found."

A week is long enough for this run if you do not do much fishing or hunting beyond what is permitted by ordinary camping-halts.

The upper Penobscot may also be explored, and many fine fishing and camping places will be found. This part of the river is reached by the Northwest carry to the Seboomook meadows, where many years ago James Russell Lowell met the man whom he admired so much, and whom in his elegant essay *A Moosehead Journal*, he styled "an A. M. and LL. D. in Wood's College,— Axe-Master and Doctor of Logs." The old Canada road runs along the stream, up its middle branch and thence over into Quebec, and it is possible by its help to penetrate the forest and climb some of the great rude mountains of that remote corner of the state. The St. John lies in that direction, also, rising in the almost imperceptible water-shed which divides the rivers of the northern, from those of the southern half of the state. "The country is an archipelago of lakes,— the lake country of New England. Their levels vary but a few feet, and the boatmen, by short portages, or by none at all, pass easily from one to another. They say that at very high water the Penobscot and the Kennebec flow into each other, or at any rate, that you may lie with your face in the one and your toes in the other. Even the Penobscot and St. John have been connected by a canal, so that the lumber of the Allegash, instead of going down the St. John, comes down the Penobscot; and the Indians' tradition, that the Penobscot once ran both ways for his convenience, is, in one sense, partially realized to-day."

The more direct route to the St. John, however, is to go down the West Branch of the Penobscot to the head of Chesuncook, and then up the Umbazookskus and over a carry to Chamberlin lake.

There is good fishing, and a fine chance for sport with the rifle in all that neighborhood, which would make an excellent objective for a limited excursion.

Resuming our eastward route, the canoeist bound for the St. John or East branch of the Penobscot, paddles up the Umbazookskus, where, according to the Indians, moose were always numerous. Meadows now form the hay-fields of the Chesuncook farmers, and moose are less often seen than deer or caribou. Navigation in the upper part of this stream is likely to be obstructed in low water, but a team can always be obtained to haul canoes and luggage over the infamous Mud carry, the unpleasantness of which may be relieved, if the sportsman goes ahead of the baggage wagon, by a shot at ducks on the borders of Mud pond.

This book cannot go into details of the cruise down the succession of lakes which lead to and along the Allegash. From Churchill lake a troublesome series of wadings, carryings and short floatings, through Spider and Munsungan lakes, leads over to the head of the Aroostook, after which that river can be descended to the settlements without much difficulty. This is an old-time trail of lumbermen and fur-traders, but is reputed the least interesting of all the northern Maine water-paths. It is possible from Spider lake, also, to go down the Musquacook, but the excursion has little to recommend it.

Below Churchill lake the Allegash is more river-like, all the way to the St. John. It is only a few miles down that river to the first of the farm-houses, which gradually increase in frequency. Twelve miles below the mouth of the Allegash, the St. Francis, forming a part of the boundary between Maine and New Brunswick, comes in, and may be ascended to a settlement only 20 miles by road from the Intercolonial Railway. Thirty miles farther on is the Madawaska, another tributary from the north, at the mouth of which stands the town of Edmundston. This river may be ascended by canoes to the Temiscuate lake region, in Quebec, which is well settled and only a short distance by stage roads from the St. Lawrence river and the railway on its bank. Or the round trip from Edmundston and back can be made in a week or ten days, under very pleasant conditions.

Edmundston will be the end of his voyage for the average canoeist, as the remainder of the St. John runs through a settled region.

This is the present terminus of the New Brunswick Railway, by which the lower-river towns and seaports of the Province are reached,[*]

---

[*] The routes and resorts through all this region are explained in Ticknor's *Guide to the Maritime Provinces;* and a capital general account of the country and its resources for sporting and holiday pleasure may be found in a little book entitled *Open Season and Resting Retreats*, published a few years ago.

or, one can change at Grand Falls — a fine cataract — to the railroad, and come straight across the state via Woodstock and McAdam Junction to Oldtown or Bangor.

This round trip from Moosehead lake down the St. John and back to the Mt. Kineo house can be made in two weeks (omitting, of course, the side-trips) and will not cost for one man and his guide over $100.

The two or more guide-books to the waterways of this northern wilderness are so circumstantial and complete in their descriptions of each and all routes, and accompanied by so minute maps, that experienced canoeists would find it entirely feasible to go without a guide; but this is inadvisible in any case, and would be wholly wrong on the

KATAHDIN, FROM NORTH BAY (MOOSEHEAD.)

part of a novice. There is no reason why, under proper arrangements, ladies should not form a part of any of these expeditions, but they must be women of the right kind.

The entire camping outfit necessary can be procured at the Mt. Kineo house before starting, and stores can be supplemented at various points, especially on the St. John trip. The guides recommended by the managers of the hotels at Moosehead lake are to be relied upon, and the needful expense and length of the journey can be calculated accurately in advance. Guides of the sort one wants ask from $2.50 to $3.00 a day, and provide a canoe, one small tent and the usual camping outfit for two persons. As to a *good* guide I adopt Mr. Farrar's description: "a guide who wields a strong and skilful paddle, who knows how to handle a setting-pole, who can shoot straight, a good cook, an excellent story teller; one strong, wilful, cheerful, courageous. . . But a cross-grained, lazy slouch, hired because you can get him cheap, is dear at any price."

A few words remain to be said about the ascent of Katahdin. The allurement of this "distinctest mountain," the hub of state and beacon for her remotest sons, is very great. Those who have read the fascinating stories of Thoreau, Jackson, Hamlin and others (not the least of whom is a gifted woman, of unknown name, whose story of how a party of ladies made the ascent, will be found in the volume for 1858 of *Putnam's Magazine*) must long to plume themselves on being among the few who have reached the grizzled summit.

The attack from the West branch of the Penobscot, either by descending it from Moosehead lake or ascending from Mattawamkeag (a railway station on the Maine Central 75 miles east of Bangor), I have already indicated.

CHAPTER X.

BANGOR AND MARITIME PROVINCES.

And then he said, 'How sweet it were,
A fisher or a hunter there,
In sunshine or in shade
To wander with an easy mind,
And build a household fire, and find
A home in every glade!—SCOTT.

BACK in Bangor again, we decide to make a brief halt, for the town is well worth a day's examination. One of the oldest and richest places in Maine, it owes its prosperity to the fact that it stands at the head of ship navigation on the Penobscot, and at the same time is not far below the confluence of the great branches which bring lumber and furs from that large region we have been seeing. It thus becomes the trade-centre of all eastern Maine, and is next in size to Portland.

It is a handsome city, the best residence portions covering two high regions overlooking the business part of the town, which occupies a narrow valley between. In the bottom of that ravine flows the deep Kenduskeag, forming a snug berth for small trading vessels. Many of the best residences are grouped on Thomas's hill, whence a grand landscape is spread out, and Katahdin is said to be visible in clear weather. In this part of the town is situated the Congregational Theological Seminary, which has nearly 700 alumni and a high reputation. The city has upon its roll many honorable names, and counts some famous people among its progressive citizens.

It has been conjectured that this point was the destination of the expedition which inadvertently landed on Mount Desert in 1613. As early as 1629, Jesuit missionaries from Quebec had descended the Penobscot, and the valley was possessed by their countrymen for two centuries, one of the forts being near here. During the Revolutionary period Massachusetts settled here, and in 1791 sent to the government a request for incorporation. Their delegate was the Rev. Seth Noble. The story runs that his instructions were to name the place Sunbury. "Mr. Noble, however, was very fond of the old tune of 'Bangor' (called after an English borough) and perhaps inadvertently had that name given to the new town." During the war of 1812 the Penob scot was held by the British. In 1833 Bangor become a city, and in 1848 was declared a port of entry.

Its men were among the first to respond to the call for troops in the late Rebellion, and this was the home of that 2nd Maine Regiment which was given the finest stand of colors in the army by ladies of New York, Baltimore and San Francisco — colors which they defended and held at Bull Run by the loss of their whole color-guard and nearly the annihilation of the Georgia men attacking them. Parts of many other regiments were recruited here, including a body of Indians.

Bangor is now a considerable railway centre, though the roads are all under control of a single corporation — the Maine Central. This road connects Bangor with Portland and the western part of the state by its main stem down the Kennebec, from which diverge many branches. Eastward the old line of the European and North American road (now the property of the Maine Central company, with auxiliaries southward to Mount Desert and to Bucksport), runs through to St. John, N. B. This trunk-line gives access to the valley of the East branch of the Penobscot; by connection with the New Brunswick Railway reaches the populous parts of eastern Maine, and the salmon-fishing regions of the Aroostook, upper St. John and Mirimichi, as well as the coast-towns and summer resorts upon the St. Croix. It thus constitutes the highway to the Maritime Provinces of Canada.

Now a few words in regard to the tour in the Maritime Provinces — New Brunswick, Nova Scotia, Cape Breton and Prince Edward Island — to which Bangor is the gateway. Should the reader contemplate such a tour (which is well worth the taking), what shall be his course? He is advised to go first to St. John. This is a day's (or a night's) travel; if time is valued the night train (on which are Pullman sleepers) better be taken, for the scenery — almost continual forest — is not of much account.

St. John, with its suburbs, is the largest city in the Maritime Provinces, and is the natural centre of travel. The town is solid and handsome, but quite American, having been rebuilt of brick and granite on Boston models, after the conflagration of 1877. The most interesting part to a stranger is its wharf-front, built to accommodate tides rising some 25 feet, and its cantilever bridge, suspended over those eccentric falls which pitch upstream or down, according as the tide flows in or out of the St. John river. Old Fort Howe, among the officers of whose garrison, at one time, was the great free-trader William Cobbett, and other points of the environs, are full of interest.

From St. John all parts of New Brunswick and the contiguous provinces are accessible by rail or steamboat, and each line of travel presents something different from the others. " The historic and scenic beauties are not concentrated on a few points, but extend throughout the country, affording rare opportunities for journeys whose general course may be replete with interest. The peculiar charms of the Maritime Provinces are their history during the Acadian era and their noble coast scenery, — the former containing some of the most romantic

CANTILEVER BRIDGE, ST. JOHN, N.B.

episodes in the annals of America, and the latter exhibiting a marvellous blending of mountainous capes and picturesque islands with the blue northern sea. And these two traits are intertwined throughout, for there is scarce a promontory that has not ruins or legends of French fortresses, scarce a bay that has not heard the roaring broadsides of British frigates."

Let the first trip be up the St. John river to Fredericton — the capital of the province. The distance is ninety miles by the daily trains or steamboat. This little city is embowered in trees, has handsome government buildings, a cathedral which, "though small, is one

GRAND FALLS, N.B.

of the most perfect pieces of pure English Gothic in America," and it forms a pleasant centre for hunting and fishing trips up various rivers. From Fredericton, the New Brunswick Railway runs northward to Grand Falls and Edmunston, and southward to the main line at Fredericton Junction. All of the remarkable scenery and sporting opportunities mentioned on p. 88, *et. seq.*, are therefore easily accessible from Fredericton.

Returning to St. John let the tourist next turn his face toward Halifax, taking the Intercolonial Railway direct or going by water to Annapolis. We will go by the Annapolis route and return by rail.

The Bay of Fundy opens beyond Cape Spencer, and the course "is laid straight across to the Annapolis basin, which is entered through the remarkable cleft in North mountain called Digby gut. At the head of this basin stands Annapolis Royal, a town of some 6,000 people, on the site of the first French settlement in old Acadia. Discovered by DeMonts in 1604, it was named Port Royal and colonized by Poitrincourt immediately afterward; and from its wharves sailed the expedition of exploration and missionary enterprise of which we have already learned in our visits to the coast and rivers of Maine. Thus the whole harbor glows in imagination with the "historic light of French adventure." A dismantled fortress, built upon the site of previous fortifications, and itself a picturesque relic of British occupation, overlooks the port and an admirable prospect.

The steamboat is now exchanged for the cars of the Windsor and Annapolis Railway (another railroad runs southward along the Fundy coast to the fishing ports of Digby, Weymouth and Yarmouth, opening the Tusket lakes) which extends eastward through the famous farming and fruit-raising valleys of Annapolis and Cornwallis as far as Windsor, passing near the Aylesford and Gasperaux lakes, and skirting the shores of the Basin of Minas, with the Grand Pré of Longfellow's *Evangeline* as one of the stopping places.

The beautiful and pathetically interesting "Land of Evangeline" is easily visited from Wolfville or Windsor, by steamboats on the Minas basin or by this railway and its carriage excursions. Good judges have called the pictures presented to the eye at various points there, the most beautiful in the Maritime Provinces.

"A good road leads eastward three miles from Wolfville to Lower Horton, a scattered hamlet among the hills. By passing down from this point to the meadows just beyond the railway-station of Grand Pré, the traveller reaches the site of the ancient village. Standing on the platform of the station, he sees a large tree at the corner of the field on the left front. Near that point are the faint remains of the foundations of the Acadian church. The tradition of the country-side claims that the aged willow-tree near by, grows on the site of the shop of Basil the Blacksmith, and that cinders have been dug up at its foot. The destruction effected by the British troops was complete, and there are now no relics of the ancient settlement, except the gnarled and knotty trees of the orchards, the lines of willows along the old roads, and the sunken hollows which indicate the sites of former cellars. Near the shore is shown the place where the exiles were put on shipboard."

Between Windsor and Halifax stretches a waste of rocks and scrubby trees.

Halifax needs no description here. Stages or steamboats communicate between it and all the seaports or inland summering places not reached by railroad. The exceedingly wild and tempestuous coast between Halifax and Cape Sable, with its awful rocks, renowned in the death annals of French and British and Yankee seamen, and its many little fishing ports, sending vessels out to the Banks or all along this perilous lee, can easily be reached and examined by the curious.

> The Province craft with ours at morn
>   Are mingled when the vapors shift;
> All day, by breeze and current borne,
>   Across the bay the sailors drift;
> With toil and seine its wealth they win, —
>   The dappled, silvery spoil come in
> Fast as their hands can haul and lift.
>
> New England! New England!
>   Thou lovest well thine ocean main!
> It spreadeth its locks among thy rocks,
>   And long against thy heart hath lain;
> Thy ships upon its bosom ride
> And feel the heaving of its tide;
>   To thee its secret speech is plain.

Or if you prefer to search the still more primitive manners of the northeastern coast, its scanty settlements are attainable by ship, or by going to New Glasgow, on the Intercolonial Railway, and thence by stage to Antigonish, whence connecting stages run to Sherbrooke and its gold-fields, to Capes St. George and remote Canso, and, by a ferriage across the strait of Canso, to the villages on the Bras d'Or, in Cape Breton — a journey vividly described in Charles Dudley Warner's cynical *Baddeck: And That sort of Thing.*

The trip to Cape Breton from Halifax is usually made by one of the frequently going steamers which land you either at Port Hawkesbury, in the scenic Gut of Canso, or at Sydney, the capital of the island, on the northern shore, or one can go by rail to Port Hawkesbury, over the Intercolonial and Eastern Extension Railways. Sydney is in the midst of coal mines, and is connected by railway with the harbor and historic old ruins of the fortress of Louisburg. Baddeck is the picturesque centre of Cape Breton, and in its vicinity profitable hunting for almost every game animal on the American list can be enjoyed. The principal steamers which go to Cape Breton are those of the Quebec and Halifax line, touching at ports in Prince Edward Island and New Brunswick and then ascending the St. Lawrence.

From Sydney, C.B., frequent opportunities occur of crossing to Charlottetown, or Georgetown, on Prince Edward Island. Thence the tourist travels by rail to Summerside, whence he can recross Northumberland strait to Point du Chene, N. B., a terminus of the Intercolonial Railway. This is 18 miles from Moncton, where the main line from Halifax and Truro passes northward toward Gaspé and Quebec.

This is a thinly settled, forested and rocky coast-region; but most of its numerous rivers contain salmon, and some, like the Miramichi, have a world-wide repute in that respect.

"The Miramichi is the gateway to the sportsman's paradise — the forest wilderness of New Brunswick," remarks one writer. Farther on, at the head of the Bay of Chaleur is Restigouche, a port of call for all the coast-wise steamers, a lumber-mart, and a fine centre for shooting excursions, or voyages among those sea-fishing islands in the Gulf of St. Lawrence, which formed the subject of a splendidly illustrated series of articles in *The Century* magazine for 1883-4.

> Who does not long to hear in May,
> The pleasant wash of St. Lawrence bay,
> The fairest ground where fishermen meet?
> There the west wave holds the red sunlight
> Till the bells at home are rung for nine:
> Short, short the watch, and calm the night;
> The fiery northern streamers shine;
> The eastern sky anon is gold,
> And winds from piney forests old,
> Scatter the white mists of the brine.

Restigouche is in the midst of salmon rivers, and Metapediac, still farther on, is another headquarters for this lordly pastime.

Unless our tourist is interested in these special features, or proposes to go through to Quebec and Montreal, he will perhaps not care to take this northerly trip, but will prefer to loiter in the Acadian country between Truro and Moncton, at the head of the Bay of Fundy, and then to go by rail to St. John — a pleasant run through the best farming district of the province.

His homeward trip from that city, if he is wise, will include a visit to St. Andrews, Passamaquoddy bay and the Schoodic lakes.

Two lines of steamers in summer run from St. John to Passamaquoddy bay. Three times a week, one of the large vessels of the International line departs for Eastport, where connection is made with a small steamboat cruising up Passamaquoddy bay and the St. Croix river. If the tourist intends to return to St. John, it is advisable to go out by one route and back by the other; if not, he will get more out of the trip by way of Campobello and Eastport, Me. There is also a railroad (Grand Southern) from St. John to St. Stephen, eighty-two miles, which it is proposed to extend as a coast-line to Penobscot bay. The bay of St. John is interesting both pictorially and traditionally. At Carleton, opposite St. John was built that fur-trading fort of young La Tour the Huguenot, which his wife defended so courageously and where her trust was so shamefully abused.

After the old French rule had begun to wane, this stronghold was left desolate, though many a naval skirmish between French and English took place in the offing; and during the Revolution, when 5,000 loyalists, banished from New England, were brought here in English vessels to become the nucleus of the present capital, the harbor was made a British naval rendezvous.

After leaving St. John, the steamer to Eastport passes well out into the Bay of Fundy, yet not so far away but that in clear weather the amazingly rough and barren shores are distinctly visible. Split rock and Musquash harbor, where two centuries back a naval fight occurred; Dipper harbor, where the frigate *Plumper* was wrecked many years ago; Point Lefreau, bearing a double light-house; and the Wolves, islets of rock with a light 111 feet high, off Beaver harbor, are passed in turn. On the Wolves many a wreck has occurred, and to them might well be applied Swinburne's magnificent poem, *Les Casquettes:*

> Sheer seen and far, in the sea's live heaven,
> A seamen's flight from the wild, sweet land,
> White-plumed with foam, if the wind wake, seven
> Black helms, as of warriors that stir not, stand.
> From the depths that abide and the waves that environ,
> Seven rocks rear heads that the midnight masks;
> And the strokes of the swords of the storm are as iron
> On the steel of the wave-worn Casques.

The steamer now rounds Bliss island, comes within sight of "the rolling hills of Campobello" in the southwest, and traverses the West Isles archipelago, inhabited by fishermen. "Sometimes," notes Mr. Sweetzer, "she meets, in these outer passages, great fleets of fishing-boats, either drifting over schools of fish, or, with their white and red sails stretched, pursuing their prey. If such a meeting occurs during one of the heavy fogs which so often visit this coast, a wonderfully weird effect is caused by the sudden emergence and disappearance of the boats in the dense white clouds."

Soon after passing the White Horse islet, the steamer enters the eastern passage and skirts the shore of Campobello island, now so well known to Boston people as a summer resort.

This island is eight miles long by three miles wide, and belongs to New Brunswick, though it lies right in the harbor of Eastport. It has been occupied for more than a century by the Owens, descendants of a British admiral, to whom it was granted by the crown. He was an eccentric Welshman, and many quaint stories are told of him. His heirs continued to reside upon, and partly cultivate the island. The Owens attempted to gather about them a feudal tenantry, and, had the pre-revolutionary order of things remained, would doubtless have populated the island as an unbroken estate; but the Yankee fishermen, and almost equally independent Bluenoses, thought the time had passed for that sort of thing after *Yankee Doodle* became a national anthem, and they seized land for homesteads on the southern shore, convenient to their labor. The lordly proprietors resisted and literally "fired them out," by frequently burning their houses and schooners; but were finally compelled to let them stay. This settlement is now called Wilson's Beach, and there is another, Welch pool, on the northern shore, to which an hourly ferry-boat runs from Eastport in summer. The island contains nearly 2,000 residents, mainly fishermen and lobster-catchers, who formerly gave much trouble to the authorities by persistent smuggling.

"There was great excitement here in 1866, when many armed Irish patriots came to Eastport, apparently with the design of invading Campobello and twisting the tail of the British lion. The island was nearly deserted by its inhabitants; British frigates and American cutters cruised in the adjacent waters; St. Andrews and St. Stephen were garrisoned by British troops; and General Meade occupied Eastport with a detachment of United States regulars."

This island (like Grand Menan, which lies farther out at sea, and is reached by tri-weekly steamboats in two hours from Eastport) is renowned for the magnificent cliffs with which it confronts the sea, and the deeply-cut, cavernous, romantic coves that indent them; and only less than Grand Menan has it long been the resort of painters, naturalists and persons fond of marine scenes and deep-water fishing.

In 1880, however, when its proprietor decided to go back to England, Campobello was bought by a syndicate of Boston men, who have set up there what bids fair to become a formidable rival to Mt. Desert, and are widely advertising the attractions of their property. The old Owen homestead has been converted into a big hotel, and two other houses, with all the beauty and elegance demanded of the modern seaside hostelry, have been erected, besides many cottages emulating in architecture and refinement of surroundings those at Newport, Nahant or Bar Harbor. Boarders are also taken by the islanders. New landings have been constructed, the old roads repaired, and many new ones cut through to the most worthy points of view or to pleasant residence districts.

Eastport is a town sloping up from its wharves in a pretty way. Or, rather, it *was*, and sometime hence will again be; for in the fall of 1886 a fire swept the town almost out of existence. It is on Moose island, at the head of a harbor, protected from the sea by Campobello; but joined to the mainland by a bridge. Its industries are almost wholly connected with the deep-sea fisheries, and there are here extensive factories for putting up the small herrings which become "sardines" in the market. They are preserved in cotton-seed oil, for the most part, and packed in tin boxes imitating in appearance the imported article. This industry, which amounts to nearly a million dollars a year, has almost supplanted the smoking and pickling of "red" herrings which flourished previous to the rebellion, finding its market in the south, as food for the negroes. Some 370,000 boxes of red herring is the present annual supply of Eastport and its vicinity. The canning of lobsters is another feature of the town's fish-preserving.

Passamaquoddy bay has seen a deal of fighting; and is now guarded by the guns of Fort Sullivan, which was built in 1808, resisted an attack in 1813, but in 1814 was surrendered to a British fleet, whose marines held the town four years.

Five miles above Eastport, on Pleasant point, or Sybaik, stands an Indian village holding a remnant of a once large local tribe, distinguished by its loyalty to the American colonies during the revolution. The story of this band forms a considerable chapter in Vetromile's learned history of the Abnakis. Another remnant of the same band dwells on the Schoodic lakes.

The scenery here is attractive, hills resting the eyes on both shores. On the eastern side of the bay is the forested and rocky region traversed by the Magaguadavic river and lakes, where deer are still numerous and trout-fishing is good. Near its mouth is a remarkable gorge, "through which the waters rush with a roar like Niagara." This furnishes a fine water-power for the cliff-side mills of St. George, a village at the eastern (or northern) entrance to the bay, near which are quarries of a rose-red granite equalling in quality the celebrated "Aberdeen" granite of Scotland. Three miles back, the woods hide Lake Utopia, whence some remarkable pre-historic relics have come to the Canadian museums, and of which still more marvelous legends are related. On a peninsula at the mouth of the St. Croix, stands the provincial seaport and village of St. Andrews.

To the artist and loiterer, St. Andrews is a great comfort. The gratifying assemblage of water and land in its landscapes, whichever way you look; the quaint irregularity of many of its houses; the moss-grown, grass-producing, sleepy appearance of the whole neighborhood; and, most of all, the crumbling old warehouses and rotting, unsafe, delightfully sketchable wharves,— all these are dear to the heart of painter and poet. If it is pathetic, too, this is in a quiet degree, for we feel that the little town, though now under a commercial cloud, is not as one that sorrows without hope; moreover, it is quite likely this impression may give way somewhat as we become better acquainted, and find that the couple of thousand people here are not quite so dead, albeit fully as *reposeful*, as they seem at first sight.

What is the story of this town with its "air of respectability, as if it had seen better days?"

St. Andrews, anticipating the building of an air line railway, the "St. Lawrence & Quebec," in 1852, had prepared elaborate terminal facilities along the margin of her capital harbor, and when these were rendered naught, she had little left to grow upon. St. John already outreached her as a port of entry and commercial centre, and the towns farther up the St. Croix, through their superior milling facilities absorbed the lumber trade. So St. Andrews faded into reminiscences, and became little more than a seashore resort for the people of the province, enjoying in that respect the first place. Several of the most prominent men in Canada are regular residents during the vacation season, when the village is animated by fashionable pleasure-seekers and a host of less fashionable, but quite as jolly, "common folks." Many New England people, also, have formed the habit of visiting it.

Some years ago, a large modern hotel, "The Argyle," was erected in a commanding situation. This has now passed into new hands, has been renovated, and is about to renew the "wide and enviable notoriety" which we are assured it has attained. Its opportunity for pleasant drives; the presence of handsome yachts and the chance for splendid yachting in ample land-locked waters; and the entire and prompt suspension of all annoyance from hay-fever enjoyed by visitors there, are advantages of no light importance in the catalogue St. Andrews offers. "In every respect that can be suggested, the situation of St. Andrews as a summer resort is favorable; and its future popularity would seem to be assured."

Five or six miles up the St. Croix river from St. Andrews is Neutral, or Doucet's island, where De Monts and Champlain built a post for their first winter in the New World (1604-5), and endured extraordinary hardships, according to Les Carbot. "It is meet," he writes, "to tell you how hard the isle of St. Croix is to be found out to them that never were there; for there are so many isles and great bays to go by (from St. John) before one be at it, that I wonder how one might ever pierce so far as to find it. There are three or four mountains imminent above the others, on the sides; but on the north side, from whence the river runneth down, there is but a sharp-pointed one, above two leagues distant." The mountain referred to is the fine peak of Chamcook, which is often ascended for the sake of the view. It is some three miles from St. Andrews by carriage-road, but the base may be reached by the railroad from the latter place. Many small forest-hidden lakes in its neighborhood contain the speckled trout, and the gray spotted trout called *togue*. It was the finding of traces of the French winter-quarters on Doucet's island that proved this river to be the "St. Croix" of the old voyagers, and caused the United States to shrink its claims to additional territory back to this stream. The name is said to be "because it runs in the form of a cross; one branch goes up northeast to the Schoodic lakes that bound the state of Maine and New Brunswick; the other branch runs westward to the Schoodic lakes toward the Passadumkeag river." This is the assertion of the historian of the Abnakis, Father Vetromile, who was missionary to the Indians (Etchimins) of this region; but as the first voyagers were not acquainted with the river to this extent, I fear the good priest is simply emulating the pious zeal which led to its first naming in honor of the Holy Cross, without regard to the geographical accuracy. Another supposition is that the cruciform character of the expansion of Oak bay, 10 miles above St. Andrews, was noticed by De Monts and suggested the appellation. The name of the cape at the northern margin of Oak bay is an opposite case. It is now known as the Devil's head; but was originally Duval's head, from a man of that cognomen who lived there and had no idea of attaining to a satanic immortality like this.

Half a dozen miles farther brings the steamer to St. Stephen, N. B., and Calais, Me., which are only separated from one another by bridges guarded at each end by customs officers. These towns are active and pleasant. The principal industry is lumber-making, the rapids which make the head of navigation furnishing an inexhaustible water-power. The one incident in their history is the peace which reigned, by mutual agreement, between the two localities whose interests were identical during all the British-American war of 1812. "Level-headed men," remarks Mr. Dawson, sententiously, "addicted to the free interchange of commodities, are not carried away by martial ardor."

The New Brunswick Railway runs from St. Stephen to St. John, and northward to Houlton, Woodstock, and Frederickton. From Calais there is a short railway to the Schoodic lakes, and stages to Eastport and Machias, connecting with steamers. From Machias westward, mail-coaches run through the sparse settlements at the heads of the ocean inlets, some seventy-five miles to Ellsworth.

The Schoodic lakes must not be forgotten. They lie along the eastern border of the state, and can be reached at their upper end from Danforth (by wagon) or at Vanceboro on the Maine Central; or at their lower end by the railway from Calais to Princeton. A steamer cruises up Grand river and about the lakes, the most important of which is Grand lake, and there are excellent camping grounds. This is the home of the land-locked salmon, and the fish commissioners of the state, not only, but of the United States, have distributed great quantities of their eggs and artificially hatched young to all parts of the country. The word *Schoodic*, meant lakes surrounded with clearings made by fire; and according to Vetromile the Abnaki name of the St. Croix, *Peskadamink kanty*, has reference to these, and similar feeders. The writings of Hamlin, Scott, Hallock and other authorities on angling give an account of the fishes and fishing here (May is the best season), and should be consulted by any angler about to make his first visit to these or any other of the Maine lakes. Excellent shooting for all classes of game can be had in the neighborhood of these lakes, of course.

The railway northward from St. Stephen runs through a rocky, desolate and monotonous forest to McAdam Junction, where you strike the main line of the New Brunswick Railway. Six miles southward is Vanceboro, whence the daily train of the Maine Central Railroad runs to Bangor by sunset. Or, by going to Eastport you can get a steamer for Portland.

CHAPTER XI.

THE VALLEY OF THE KENNEBEC.

> Come live with me and be my love,
> And we will all the pleasures prove,
> That valleys, groves, and hills and fields,
> Wood or steepy mountains yields.— MARLOWE.

LEAVING Bangor on the morning-express westward bound, no stop is made until Waterville is reached, though "the woods are full" of small stations. About half way, for example, is Newport, whence a branch railway runs north, twenty miles, to Dexter, at the sources of the Kenduskeag, only a few miles by stage from Dover and Foxcroft, and in the midst of hill-farms and trout-brooks. A dozen miles farther we pass Burnham, on the Sebasticook river, whence a branch railroad runs, (thirty-four miles) down through the agricultural towns on the old Waldo patent, (now Waldo county) to the historic seafaring town of Belfast, opposite Castine on Penobscot bay; it was at Belfast that Weymouth set up an Anglican cross in 1605, and wrote that he had discovered "the most beautiful, rich, large, secure, harboring river that the world affordeth."

Waterville is an important and attractive town, bearing the same relation to the upper Kennebec, as Bangor does to its river. Its station is almost within the elm-shaded grounds of Colby University, "which has had in its long history an importance within the Baptist denomination, and a place in the annals of the state, much beyond that indicated by the mere numbers of its students." The traveller sitting on the eastern side of the cars might think himself landed in some princely park, and conceives a most favorable idea of the town which, though a busy trade and manufacturing centre, is one of the most cultivated in Maine.

At Waterville, we had the choice of two routes to Portland. One goes straight down the river through Augusta, Hallowell, Gardiner and Brunswick; the other inland, traversing Oakland, Leeds and Lewiston

The former is the "main line," by which the through trains between Boston and Bar Harbor or St. John go, and very well worth seeing it is. The train leaving the Union station in Portland skirts the shore of Casco bay, traversing the ancient villages Falmouth,

Yarmouth (where the Grand Trunk Railway is crossed) and Freeport, before it reaches Brunswick.

Brunswick, on the site of the colony Pejepscot, founded in 1628 by Plymouth men, is now a lively manufacturing town at the falls of the Androscoggin, where the large river leaps in fine confusion down ledges of rocks, which have now been connected and evened-up by dams, but have lost little of their original picturesqueness. The principal article of manufacture is paper. Here is Bowdoin College, occupying a large and well-shaded campus in the centre of the town, and named in memory of one of its earliest benefactors, James Bowdoin, who was a son of the governor of Massachusetts during 1785-6, and belonged to a cultivated Huguenot family. To him the college owes among other gifts, the foundation of its famous picture gallery, which contains nearly 150 pictures, including two by Raphael and Rubens, many fine copies of the best Italian masters, excellent examples of the Flemish and Dutch schools (including a portrait by Vandyke for which the college has refused $30,000), and several pictures by Hogarth, Copley and other well-known names,— thus New England profited by the edict of Nantes. Bowdoin was opened in 1802, and though its classes were never large they have included some distinguished names, — President Franklin Pierce, Nathaniel Hawthorne, the poet Longfellow, and others. It has built a notable museum of natural history, and is beginning in various ways a new era of prosperity.

From Brunswick, the Maine Central sends a branch eastward to ship-building Bath, at the mouth of the Kennebec, where "through" cars are ferried across to the Knox and Lincoln road, and sent on to Rockland (see page 46). It also owns a branch westward to Crowley's and Lewiston, continuing to all the western part of the state, as far as the Rangeley lakes.

The main line, which our "through" traveller is to follow, strikes straight across from Brunswick to the valley of the Kennebec, which it skirts for nearly fifty miles. "We shall find the river," says a recent book of travels, "full of vessels of all sizes, bearing to every part of the world the solid chunks of comfort from the multitude of ice-houses on the river, in which were stored the past season, more than a million tons of ice. Many of these ice-houses may properly be called *crystal palaces.*"

The stations Bowdoinham and Richmond are favorite summering places, and at the latter the Methodists hold annual camp-meetings.

Gardiner and Hallowell are thriving factory villages, and productive of fine light-colored granite, quarried from the neighboring hills. Next beyond is Augusta, the state capital, which stands at the head of sloop navigation, and was settled before King Philip's war, during which it was laid waste. In 1716 the returning settlers built a stone fort, but failed to defend it during the Indian uprisings of 1724.

Thirty years later (1754) the stronghold Fort Western was built upon the eastern bank of the river, as one of a line of frontier fortifications; and it formed the rendezvous of Benedict Arnold's Quebec expedition of 1775. Under the protection of this fort a strong settlement was made, which continued to thrive after the gaining of our independence. Its central position caused the town to be chosen as the seat of state government; and in 1831, the capitol, a stately structure of white granite, crowning with its solid architecture a noble eminence, was completed. It may be seen from the car windows on the left. On the right, across the river, are the buildings of the hospital for the insane, occupying high ground; and the United States arsenal, filled with munitions of war, lower down. The grounds surrounding both these institutions are carefully ornamented.

The state-house will interest visitors not only by its fine architecture, portraits of men eminent in local history, and a large library, but by the collection of battle flags and relics of Maine troops in the late war. In 1861 this city became a rendezvous for the troops of the state, and many of its regiments saw severe service, but it is said that not a single flag was lost. Five miles southward, at the once popular resort of Togus Springs, is the Eastern Branch of the Soldiers' Home, which now contains about 1700 inmates, and is a charming place to visit. This is only one objective of many charming drives in the neighborhood.

At Augusta the railway crosses the Kennebec on an iron bridge, affording a splendid view up and down the cliff-walled stream, and then runs through the flourishing manufacturing villages Riverside, Vassalboro and Winslow, where it again crosses the Kennebec near its confluence with the Sebasticook.

"The ruins of Fort Halifax are seen on the bluff-point just south of the union of the rivers. This fort was one of a chain erected by Massachusetts to defend the Maine coast from French raids. It was built by Gov. Shirley in 1754, and garrisoned by 130 men, until its abandonment, after the Peace of Paris (1763). Large Indian settlements formerly occupied the intervales in this vicinity, and as early as 1676 envoys of Massachusetts came here to detach the tribe from the King Philip's Confederation, — an unsuccessful attempt."

The next station is Waterville — and so we are back again at our starting point. The main line of the Maine Central Railroad, just sketched, is that followed, as I have already stated, by passengers to Bangor or beyond; and in summer, through cars are run on especially fast and conveniently timed trains, without change, between Boston and Mt. Desert Ferry, so that one can leave Boston in the evening and reach Bar Harbor in season for breakfast; or can go through by day, between breakfast and tea-time in Pullman luxury.

Waterville is the gateway to the upper Kennebec. A railway runs nineteen miles to Skowhegan, picturesquely situated at the falls of the

Kennebec, which furnish the power that drives its many mills. This busy place used to be the starting-point of a regular route to Moosehead lake, but the stages ceased running as soon as the Piscataquis railroad was built. Daily stages and mails still go up the river, however, to The Forks (where Dead river comes in) and on to Canada by a route 156 miles in length.

From Skowhegan to The Forks is forty-six miles, — a day's ride over a good road, — passing near several highly reputed fishing-waters, and exhibiting striking landscapes from the hill tops. Fifteen miles out the road returns to the river, and thenceforth keeps near its banks, which are often precipitous. At Bingham, half way, you penetrate a mountainous and mineral bearing district, full of game. On the opposite side of the river a level plateau is pointed out where Arnold's army encamped, before striking across to the Carrying Place ponds on its march to Dead river.

In Moscow, the next town ahead, lies the pond to which that "author and naturalist of pleasant fame" — John Burroughs — went camping, and procured the material for that little essay in *Signs and Seasons* which keeps for us the flavor of the woods so deliciously well. Burroughs also went to Moxie pond, which lies some five miles northeastward, and is much resorted to by sportsmen. Its outlet is Moxie stream which falls into the Kennebec over a cascade ninety-five feet in height, the beauty of which is much praised. This cascade is three miles from The Forks, and the pond four miles farther, past other minor cascades. Besides the unfailing fishing, deer and caribou haunt the locality.

"Moxie lake lies much lower than Pleasant pond, and its waters, compared with those of the latter are as copper compared with silver. It is very irregular in shape; now narrowing to the dimension of a slow-moving grassy creek, then expanding into a broad deep basin with rocky shores, commanding the noblest mountain scenery. It is rarely that the pond-lily and the speckled trout are found together, — the fish the soul of the purest spring water, the flower the transfigured spirit of the dark mud and slime of sluggish streams and ponds; yet in Moxie they were both found in perfection."

It is three miles from this pond to that Bald mountain, which showed its friar-like head to us from the Piscataquis railway; and other high mountains are within climbing distance.

At The Forks is a settlement of farmers and a well-known hotel, "the centre," says Farrar, "of one of the greatest sporting regions of the state." Up the Kennebec it is fifteen miles to Indian pond, and ten from there to Moosehead lake.

From The Forks a stage runs daily to Parlin pond in the Moose river valley, along the "Canada road." Parlin pond has a commodious hotel and communicates by stream or road with Long pond, Moose river and other streams. Boats and a livery stable are available there, with various quite civilized means of recreation, besides the shooting and fishing which form the chief attractions.

The next stage station is Moose-river village, a considerable settlement; and the end of the route is reached, forty-five miles from The Forks, in Sandy Bay. From there a stage runs thrice a week to St. Joseph de Bauce, in the Chaudiere valley, Canada, from which it is only forty-five miles by rail to Quebec.

At Moose-river village a wide region northward is open to the hunter and explorer, and he can obtain guides and necessary supplies. It is only thirty-five miles down Moose river to Mt. Kineo, — an easy experience in canoeing.

Though the Dead River country is accessible from Skowhegan, by daily stage to North Anson, or by way of The Forks, where it empties into the Kennebec, yet the better way for the person entering from this side is to go to the terminus of the Somerset Railroad at North Anson for a point of departure.

This railroad branches off from the "upper route" of the Maine Central at Oakland, a station six miles west of Waterville, rather strangely described in a recent book as "a growing village sitting gracefully on Cascade falls." Close by Oakland is the pretty lake Messalonskee, which discharges its overflow down a deep gorge in a series of really noteworthy cataracts, hemmed in by slate-crags and densely wooded slopes. At the outlet of the lake stand the large workshops of a tool-making concern. The Somerset Railroad crosses the Kennebec twice, and offers some very pretty scenery in the course of its twenty-five miles.

The midway station is Norridgewock (or *Nauraniswack*) which is only five miles by carriage road from Skowhegan, and is not only one of the loveliest, but one of the most memorable localities in the state.

That the Kennebec was among the first rivers discovered by white men, we have seen; and almost from the first the Indians had explained how it formed a highway to Canada. Down this avenue into heathendom came Roman missionaries of the Cross as early as 1629. The Capuchins had fixed stations on both the Penobscot and the Kennebec at, or soon following that date. In 1646 came the Jesuit father Gabriel Druillette to preach among the Abnakis, whose principal village was at this place. Under one priest or another this mission was intermittently sustained until 1695, when it became a fixture under the care of Sebastian Rale, a learned French Jesuit who had but lately come from labors among the Illinois Indians.

By the papist-burning, French-hating colonists of Massachusetts, this man, whose power began almost at once to be felt, was thought capable of all iniquity. Certainly he stirred up his Indians to resist English encroachment and seek redress for the real and fancied wrongs their nation had suffered at the hands of the Plymouth traders and

British voyagers. He held their allegiance to France, and united them with the powerful bands who had dug up the hatchet all along the coast; but there is every reason to believe that he did this out of a sense of justice, as he saw the facts, and for the glory of the church, and that to the Abnakis he was a kind friend and counsellor. His biography has been sketched by both the learned J. G. Shea, and the Rev. Wm. Ingraham Kip, in their histories of Catholic Missions in the United States; and a "life" of him by the Rev. Dr. Harris will be found in the Mass. Hist. collections, 2d ser. VIII., 250.

A generation had he lived among the Abnakis, and now the whole wilderness was again ablaze with savage warfare. The English knew that the French were secretly fomenting these murderous forays, and furnishing the savages with arms. They believed Pére Rale the agent, and sent an expedition in August of 1724 to attack his fortress, and so strike at the source of the evil. How well that plan succeeded, Whittier has told with nervous power in his startling ballad of *Mogg Megone:* —

> Hark! what sudden sound is heard
> In the wood and in the sky,
> Shriller than the scream of bird, —
> Than the trumpet's clang more high!
> Every wolf-cave of the hills, —
> Forest-arch and mountain gorge,
> Rock and dell and river-verge, —
> With an answering echo thrills —
> Well does the Jesuit know that cry,
> Which summons the Norridgewock to die,
> And tells that the foe of his flock is nigh —
> He listens and hears the rangers come,
> With loud hurrah and jar of drum;
> And hurrying feet (for the chase is hot),
> And the short, sharp sound of the rifle-shot,
> And taunt and menace, — answered well
> By the Indians mocking cry and yell, —
> The bark of dogs, — the squaw's mad scream, —
> The dash of paddles along the stream, —
> The whistle of shot as it cuts the leaves
> Of the maples around the church's eaves, —
> And the gride of hatchets, fiercely thrown,
> On wigwam log, and tree and stone.
>
> . . . .
>
> Fearfully over the Jesuit's face,
> Of a thousand thoughts trace after trace,
> Like swift cloud-shadows, each other chase.
> One instant his fingers grasp his knife,
> For a last vain struggle for cherished life, —
> The next he hurls the blade away,
> And kneels at his altar's foot to pray.
>
> . . . .
>
> Through the chapel's narrow doors,
> And through each window in the walls,
> Round the priest and warrior pours
> The deadly shower of English balls.

> Low on his cross the Jesuit falls;
> While at his side the Norridgewock,
> With failing breath essays to mock
> And menace yet the hated foe, —
> Shakes his scalp-trophies to and fro
> Exultingly before their eyes, —
> Till, cleft and torn by shot and blow,
> Defiant still he dies.

To this long-suffering soldier of the cross, who has been almost apotheosized by his brother Romans, a monument has now been erected on the battle-field where the eastern Indians lost their sway forever; and as the traveller's eye falls upon it from the passing train, he must be a thoughtless man indeed whose imagination is not stirred at the recollections it summons.

North Anson is another door to the fishing and hunting regions of the Maine woods, and particularly to the Dead River district. Dead river (which takes its name from the comparatively still water of its upper part), is the principal drain of a large area between the Androscoggin waters on the south and the St. John's tributaries northward; and it constitutes the most important affluent of the Kennebec below Moosehead lake. It is itself formed by the convergence at the base of Mt. Bigelow of two branches, the northern of which rises in the mountains on the Canadian boundary close to Lake Megantic. From this lake a stream flows into the Chaudiere river, which empties into the St. Lawrence near Quebec; and these two streams early became one of the canoeing routes of trappers, missionaries, and war-parties between Canada and the New England coast, though now they are abandoned almost wholly to the pleasure-traveller. This, indeed, was the route of Benedict Arnold's heroic but disastrous expedition to Quebec, in the cold autumn of 1775, when he attempted to lead 1,000 men in batteaux from Ft. Western, on the Kennebec, to Quebec; and did succeed in taking most of them down the Canadian rivers, until "the little army of gaunt and ragged heroes arose like an apparition from the southern wilderness under the walls of Quebec."

There are now several small hotels, farms and camping-places upon the lower Dead river, or ponds near it. These are reached by stages from North Anson, and invite the camper with no small urgency. He can travel still farther up the river and deeper into the woods, by a stage which goes from North New Portland to Kingfield, and there connects with other stages, or he can paddle up as far as he pleases. But this upper river and its ponds, which form the best part of the district, for the sportsmen, are far better reached by the railroad to Kingfield, via Farmington, of which I shall presently speak.

The ponds alluded to are "too numerous to mention," but may all be found described, together with their approaches, in the excellent *Guide to the Dead River Region*, written and published by A. W. Robinson, which embraces a map. The principal ones are Tim and the

Seven ponds, reached by roads from Eustis. Both of these centres have clearings and cabins upon their shores, where board is furnished by Mr. Kennedy Smith, of Smith's farm, (Franklin county, Me.), who is the traveller's good genius in that region. Guides and boats are available; dozens of minor lakes and connecting streams can be fished and shot upon; ascent of the great unknown Snow mountain is possible; or the boundary hills may be crossed and the canoe launched in Canadian waters. Finally several trails lead over into the Rangeley lakes.

When our fickle minded companion had ascertained these facts, he came to me with the map of Maine in his hand, and called my attention to a place he had marked over on the West branch of the Penobscot, where he proposed next year to build a camp for a fortnight's stay in the woods.

"Now," says he, turning to the westward, "I'm thinking I won't go away over there, but will strike in here on Dead river. You seem to be quite as much in the wild woods, and yet you're not so far away from mail and telegraph; it doesn't take so much time and expense to get there. Yes, sir. I'll build my camp somewhere there by Bigelow; and then from there I'll go to that interesting old St. Andrews for a week, and home by steamer to Portland."

Will he, I wonder?

CHAPTER XII.

KENNEBEC TO THE ANDROSCOGGIN.

And on their way in friendly chat
Now talked of this and then of that.— THE CHAMELEON.

BUT now let us resume our regular course.
From Waterville we had an all-day journey ahead of us, for we were bound to the Rangeley lakes. We had been at the head of the St. Croix and the Machias in the Schoodic lakes; camped on Chesuncook whence "bulges" the Penobscot, and at Moosehead, — reservoir of the Kennebec.

Now we were going to the sources of the Androscoggin river.

Thus far we had been blessed by beautiful weather, but this morning it was raining with long-restrained energy.

"This town's well-named," growled Baily, gazing ruefully at the streams of water coursing down the window-pane.

"No more appropriately than Bangor," quoth cheerful Prue, "which like that tune is all ups and downs."

"Or Bar Harbor," I add, "judging by the empty bottles one sees stacked up at the rear doors of its hotels."

"Or Bath," Prue chimes in, "which sits with its feet in the water; or —"

"Oh go on — go on! You'll be saying next, I suppose, that St. John is 'a voice crying in the wilderness.'"

Well, there is no telling what nonsense might have come next had not the breakfast bell turned our giddy thoughts to a more serious subject. And immediately after breakfast we went to the train.

All day we rode through blinding sheets of rain around the two long sides of a southward-pointing triangle having its apex at Leed's Junction, as the map will show you.

The first half of the journey lay through Oakland, Belgrade, Readfield, Maranacook and Monmouth. We saw misty stretches of ponds, gray and rain-hidden in the bedraggled woods, and crossed many a turbid brook, boiling down its brimfull channel; and we swept by farms and villages which seemed wholly deserted, for your Maine Yankee knows enough to go in when it rains.

All those streams and lakelets are filled with bass and perch and pickerel, and some friends of ours, who spend their summers in this part of the state, assert that in sunshine the scenery has great artistic value. They are esthetic souls, or they wouldn't load down prettiness with such a phrase. We are told that the territorial grant made here was called the "Pond Town Plantation," and that there are forty-four lakes of rare beauty within the limits now comprising Winthrop, Readfield and a portion of Wayne, with commanding sites for summer villas. "Lake Maranacook of itself, as it has been developed by the Maine Central, will surpass any spot in the country for facilities for boat-racing and other out-of-door sports."

At Leed's Junction (this town was the birth place of the soldier-philanthropist, Gen. O. O. Howard), we change to the train from Brunswick headed northward, while our train goes on to Lewiston and Portland by the way of Danville Junction, where it crosses the Grand Trunk leading to the White Mountains.

The region we now vaguely scanned through the obscurity of the rain, seemed to be a sparseley settled farming country with frequent villages devoted to milling by the water power of the rapid Androscoggin, which presently came in view on the left. Livermore Falls is the best remembered of these, and is the town which gave to the political world the Washburnes, statesmen and soldiers — three brothers, — all famous. Farrar's *Guide to the Androscoggin Lakes*, instructed us that here the distant mountains come into view; and we willingly took on trust its statement that "with the sparkling river in the foreground, and the bare-topped mountains in the distance, pretty pictures are formed with every curve of the road." By the middle of the afternoon Farmington was reached.

Farmington is the marketing centre for the Sandy River valley, — a region more populous a century ago than now. Its cultivated homes and maple-shaded streets made it one of the prettiest towns in the state, until two conflagrations, which occured a few weeks after our visit, almost obliterated it. One of the incidents of the first great fire, was the formation of a bucket brigade by some fifty girls from the State Normal School in a heroic endeavor to save the church.

"Case," says Baily, "where something more than Maine strength was necessary."

This school now occupies the old seminary building known as "The Willows," and in the suburb of Little Blue stands the Abbott Family School for boys, founded by Jacob Abbott, the author of the *Rollo* books. From Clear Water pond, five miles distant, and in view of Saddleback mountain, trout weighing fifteen pounds have been taken, according to Farrar.

Farmington is the end of the Maine Central, but a narrow-guage line, called the Sandy River Railroad, continues up the valley as far as Phillips, and we transfer ourselves to its little cars, which have room for double seats only on one side. Prue expresses her delight at this arrangement, and seizes upon one of the single seats, "where she needn't be bothered by any man beside her." We revenge ourselves by going away to the smoker, and a game of whist. The little train jogs out into the rain again and pursues its way over a number of high trestles, spanning gorges whose torrents are galloping noisily down to the swollen river, until it gradually gets nearer the level of the meadows. Grades are climbed again on approaching Strong Village, and, in bright weather, we should have enjoyed some very pretty views across the hills and up and down the fertile valley.

At Strong is the junction with the Franklin and Megantic Railroad, extending fifteen miles northward to Kingfield, on Dead river, whence stages run thirty miles farther, to Eustis, near the confluence of the North and South branches. This is the route by which all sportsmen from Boston, or the West generally, would reach the Dead River streams, ponds and mountains.

Beyond Strong, the Sandy River Railroad works its way around some bluffs, leaps several deep brook-gullies, crosses the river, and enters Phillips, its present terminus.

The day closed with no diminution of storm, and light slowly struggled back to a drenched world the next morning, through a steady downfall of rain. Evidently there was no use of going on to the lakes that day. Prue kept her room all the morning, writing letters, etc. Baily cocked up his heels and devoured a novel, or played billiards. I devoted myself to bringing up my notebook to date and asking questions in regard to the neighborhood, and what lay ahead of us. The trout-fishing is so good in the neighborhood of Phillips, that when the storm slackened a little in the afternoon, Baily unpacked his rubber boots and started out a-fishing, persuading me to go with him, in hope of getting some glimpses of Blue, Saddleback, and the other mountains whose elegant outlines usually make a lovely background to the local landscapes. But the streams were too turbid for angling and the air too thick for sight-seeing; so we returned after a short tramp and resigned ourselves to staying indoors.

This was an easier task here than we had anticipated; for in the hotel we enjoyed, on a small scale, as elegant, comfortable, and city-like accommodations as could be desired.

In the evening we extemporized in the hotel parlor what at home would be called a *musicale*. The air had just chill enough to make a wood-fire grateful, and under the crackle of logs in the fireplace, and their warmth, all the stiffness of strangership quickly dissolved. Prue kindly forbore to exhibit her scientific accomplishments in piano practice, but played a lively little quickstep or something of that kind, that everybody could appreciate. A clever mimic from out west told a capital dialect story of Plains life, standing on his feet and acting the scene out somewhat, yet with a freedom far better than a studied recitation would have permitted; and Baily quite distinguished himself singing a little song to an air out of *Patience*, of which these are specimen stanzas: —

A practical, plain young girl,
Not-afraid-of-the-rain young girl,
  A poetical posey,
  Ruddy and rosy,
A helper-of-self young girl.

At-home-in-her-place young girl;
A never-will-lace young girl;
  A toiler serene,
  In life pure and clean,
A princess-of-peace young girl.

A rightly-ambitious young girl;
Red-lips-most-delicious young girl;
  A morning ariser,
  A dandy despiser,
A progressive American girl.

It was a bright-witted and noble-looking young lady from Washington who played the accompaniment for my friend; she had been spending a part of the vacation with friends in a cottage on Oquossoc lake, as was her annual custom, and now was returning refreshed to her duties in the State Department. I don't wonder the boy forgot all his previous plans and assured her he thought no place equal to the Rangeleys, and meant, next summer, to come here for a long time.

"I shouldn't wonder, Theo," remarked Prue that night, as she blew out the candle and pulled down the window-top, "if he was really smitten."

This was *apropos* of nothing; but I knew whom she meant, and smiled to myself. These women! How little straw they require for a matrimonial brick!

Thus we had utilized our rainy day, defying the gloom; and such an experience is likely to be one of the most unexpected, yet best remembered, incidents of a summer jaunt through New England. Next morning came our sunny reward:—

A night had passed away among the hills,
  And now the first faint tokens of the dawn
Showed in the east; the bright and dewy star,
  Whose mission is to usher in the morn,
Looked through the cool air like a blessed thing
In a far purer world.
. . . .
            I had waked
From a long sleep of many changing dreams,
And now in the fresh forest air I stood
Nerved to another day of wandering.

In Concord coaches we were packed soon after breakfast,—or others were, for we three were lucky and energetic enough to get outside places,—and went rattling up the hard road, toward Rangeley City, "twenty miles away." The Sandy river is a pretty stream, full of attractions for artist and angler as well as mill owner. Madrid, six miles out, is a favorite point for sportsmen, and just above it are some pretty falls. Above the falls the narrow stream tumbles noisily through a great ravine, the brink of which is skirted by the road in crossing breezy Beach hill, whence some admirable views of Blue mountain, and the ranges of Abraham and Saddleback are gained in the north, while southward and westward far-reaching landscapes of great beauty open as the road descends toward the farming district of Greenvale. This town lies at the eastern extremity of the Rangeley lakes, and has a small summer hotel and steamboat landing. Five miles north is Rangeley City — a village of much importance as a supplying point for lumber camps in winter, and a tourist-resort in summer. It possesses a commodious hotel, with a wonderful outlook down the lake toward the sunset, and we reached it in the mood to do ample justice to its table fare. As the terminus of a telephone wire from Phillips, this village represents the forefront of civilization.

A steam yacht, commanded by a lad in a naval cap, awaited us at the wharf, and, after dinner all went aboard in great glee to begin our voyages upon the Rangeley lakes.

CHAPTER XIII.

ON THE RANGELEY LAKES.

Unmolested roved the hunters,
Built the birch canoe for sailing,
Caught the fish in lake and river,
Shot the deer and trapped the beaver.
—THE SONG OF HIAWATHA.

THESE lakes, with their tributaries, are often styled the Androscoggin lakes, because they connectedly drain into that river. The main chain, counting from east to west (down stream), consists of five — Oquóssoc, (or Rangeley proper), Cupsuptic Mooseluemagúntic (or Great lake), Molechunkamunk (or Upper Richardson), Welokennbácook (or Lower Richardson), and Umbágog. Altogether they cover about seventy square miles. Into the first named flows Long pond, often styled the head of the Androscoggin, and several other small ponds and brooks. Into the second, comes Cupsuptic river, enlarging into Cupsuptic lake at its mouth; and into the Rangeley river, which empties Rangeley lake into Mooseluemaguntic, at its point of narrow union with Cupsuptic, is received the strong Kennebago river from the seven ponds and Kennebago lake on the Canadian boundary. The Richardson ponds and several brooks overflow into the next two lakes, which send their overflow through Rapid river to the remoter Umbagog, which receives the strong Cambridge river from the hills south and east of it, and out of which pours the Androscoggin. Into that river, about a mile below its head, comes the Magalloway, which drains Parmachenée lake some twenty-five miles northward (in a straight line), but whose source is on the edge of Canada. The altitude of Umbagog is 1,256 feet above the sea; of the Richardson lakes, 1,456; of Mooseluemaguntic, 1,486; and of Oquossoc, 1,511. No one need be surprised, therefore, at the torrential character of the Rangeley and Rapid rivers.

Except on the northern shore of Oquossoc and the southern shore of Umbagog there are no settlements, and the whole surrounding region is penetrated only by a few trails. These woods are still the abode of large and small game of every kind, and from them rise mountains that tempt the explorer. The fishing in the lakes has long been renowned, for they contain the largest brook trout known in the country, perhaps in the world. This fact, and their accessibility, has caused the lakes to be much resorted to by sportsmen, and upon the shores of each of them club-houses, small hotels, and private cottages, or "camps," have been built. Let me quote a few sentences, just here, from a recent pamphlet written by a Boston man of good authority:—

"Those unacquainted with the resources of this wilderness for fish breeding, would naturally suppose that the enormous drain on these waters would soon deplete them of fish; but such is not the case, owing to the hundreds of ponds surrounding and emptying into the lakes, each furnishing its quota of fish for the larger bodies of water, and to the hatching-houses which have been established for ten years, and from which every year millions of small trout are turned into the lakes, to furnish pleasure and food to the anglers, and keep good the supply. It is a fact, that many sportsmen, who have visited these waters for many years in succession, claim that the trout-fishing is better in the lakes to-day than it was twenty years ago.

"Land-locked salmon, which were introduced to the Androscoggin waters some ten years ago, have also largely increased, and specimens of these fish have been taken weighing over six pounds. The lakes are also well supplied with minnows and chubs, furnishing an abundant and agreeable supply of food for trout and salmon.

"The same praises that are advanced upon the Androscoggin lake region as a game and fish paradise, can also be aptly applied to it as one of the most beautiful summer resorts in the world. The combination in scenery of lakes, ponds, rivers, and mountains, coupled with the pure water and air, and a most agreeable climate, put it far ahead of competition. Persons of consumptive tendency will here obtain a great benefit, and those troubled with hay fever and similar complaints, will find immediate relief.

"The hotels, while not like those at the large mountain and seaside resorts, are neat, comfortable houses, well furnished, with tables supplied with plain, wholesome, and well-cooked food, and are run at an average rate of about $2.00 per day.

"There are three principal routes of entrance to the lake region from Boston: 1st, via Portland, Bethel and Cambridge, to Lake Umbagog; 2d, via Portland, Bryant's Pond and Andover to Lake Welokennabacook; 3d, via Portland, Farmington and Phillips to Oquossoc lake."

To accommodate visitors and to aid the commercial enterprises of the region, steamboats have been placed upon each lake and upon the Magalloway river, and wagon-transfers provided at the carries between them.

The practical side of the picture is represented by the lumbermen, who for nearly a century have floated their rafts and driven their logs down these waters; and by the Union Water Power Company, which controls the whole system, legally by corporative charter, and actu-

A BIG TROUT.

ally by a series of prodigious dams, which reserve the water in these reservoirs more carefully than nature would do, and let it out in the dry season in such proportion as shall sustain the water-power of the Androscoggin river. The object of this solicitude is Lewiston, whose mill-owners are the promoters of this enterprise; but incidentally all the mills along the river are benefitted. Fortunately these works are not of a kind to interfere injuriously with the scenery, which is made by the grandeur of distant prospects, rather than out of something pretty and near at hand.

It was upon the uppermost of the chain of lakes that we were now embarked. The water was smooth and the air deliciously moist and cool, while the sunshine was rapidly cutting long swaths in the mists that still lingered upon the sides of the drenched hills in irregular clouds. About the upper half of this lake, farms overspread the sloping shores, but the forest has only been nibbled away at the edge.

At the foot of the lake, six miles from "the city," near where Oquossoc outlet, or the Rangeley river, goes sliding noisily down its ledges, stands a handsome private cottage and a hotel, the Mountain View House, at which we proposed to spend the night. Baily at once hired a boat and a boy, who paddled him out somewhere near South Bog island, and placed him where he hooked enough trout to establish his reputation on the piazza, and to make us happy at breakfast, next morning. This is where Mr. Page's famous eleven-and-a-half pounder was caught, the skin of which we once saw in the office of a New York angler. Near by is a fish-hatching house, where a million or so brook trout are brought to life every winter and distributed among the various lakes below, as well as put into Oquossoc. Eggs of land-locked salmon and whitefish are also propagated here.

June and September are the prime months for angling in this locality, and during that time the hotels are filled with family parties, who do not care to "rough it" in the remoter camps, and who can here indulge in rowing, driving and hill-climbing more conveniently than elsewhere. The north-shore road from Rangeley City continues two miles further to Indian Rock.

Early next morning we were set across the head of the outlet, and then walked leisurely through the flower-strewn woods behind a buck-board carrying our baggage, until, at the end of a mile, it emerged into the dooryard of the boarding-house at Haine's Landing on Mooseluemaguntic.

We strolled up upon the piazza, where dozens of jointed rods and well-trimmed poles were lying safe and straight on hooks against the wall; and were surprised at the magnificent outlook. This house commands the whole length of the lake, and more; for past its flashing waves and quiet fishing-nooks, its lonely islets of woodbine-painted rock and its gray shores where the herons sit, the vision was carried on to where

> The mountains that infold
> In their wide sweep the colored landscape round,
> Seem groups of giant kings, in purple and in gold,
> That guard the enchanted ground.

But the neat steam yacht which was to transport us down the lake to Upper Dam was ready, and, with the loss of one or two members, the party of passengers speedily put themselves aboard, quite as many sprawling upon the baggage and hanging their feet over the side, as took respectable sittings in the sternsheets. Two or three boats were tied behind and away we went.

Our first destination was Indian Rock, to reach which we headed through the Narrows between this lake and Cupsuptic, northward.

"Well, I shouldn't call these *narrows*," declared Prue. "How can you tell where this lake ends and the other begins?"

"It is rather difficult now," she was answered; "because

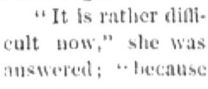

VIEWS FROM RANGELEY LAKES.

the raising of the water by the dam at the foot of the lake has flooded the eastern shore very widely; but originally the connection was through a slender stream."

The steamboat traces this old channel in a most devious course, past many headlands and islands of rock, where bristling fir and feathery birch tuck their toes in common poverty between the bowlders; and sails within stone's throw of Senator Frye's "camp" on top of a mass of well-shaded, solid granite, over-looking the lake, mountains and the mouth of the Kennebago.

Cupsuptic lake, whose small size permits the whole of it to be taken in from one point of view, is the prettiest of this series. It has islands, coves, and good camping-places in the unbroken forest, which sweeps from the water's edge up to the hills around its whole circumference. It is fed by the winding Cupsuptic stream, up which the small lake-steamer can generally ascend as far as the falls (five miles) " through a meadow or swamp, dotted with dead trees. . . . . This was once a favorite feeding-ground for moose, and they are still occasionally met with." At the falls are fishermen's cabins, and a carry a quarter of a mile long to the rapid water above, in which there is canoe navigation eight miles to the beginning of the eight-mile carry across to Parmachenée lake,—a path said to be good, though hilly.

We did not venture into Cupsuptic lake, but turned to the right and entered the mouth of Rangeley river, a flock of herons rising lazily from their feeding on the flooded flats, and trailing off northward with outstretched neck and hanging legs. A young passenger, who was perhaps only thoughtless, and not really abandoned to evil, and who *may* escape a felon's fate, pulled out his gun and was about to fire, when captain, and engineer, and crew, and cook of the steam-yacht, all leaped forward with one impulse, and stopped him, much to our gratification. There is no quicker way to spoil the interest of the wild scenes we have come so far to see than to kill off these birds, and many others, that are not game, yet lend so much charm to the frontier landscape; and it is entirely shocking to all right-minded people, that anybody should want to do so. (The gratifying unanimity of the crew, by the way, was partly due to the fact that one gilt-banded cap covered the steamer's whole *personel*.)

We could get up the Rangeley torrent only as far as the mouth of the Kennebago, a swift current in blue and white that comes rushing down from Kennebago lake and the grand peaks that hold it in their arms. Nevertheless that lake is not reached by an ascent of the river, but by a buckboard road through the woods, seven miles from Rangeley City. There is an inn upon its border, keeping boats and other conveniences for sportsmen, who should go there late in the season after the pestiferous insects have subsided. The same warning applies to all the Dead River country.

At the mouth of the Kennebago, where we made our first stop, is a prominent mass of stone called Indian Rock, and opposite it, on the western banks of the Kennebago and Rangeley rivers, are the headquarters of the Oquossoc Angling Association, occupying a large clearing with several comfortable houses for lodging and board, and a spacious boat-house on the wharf, in which scores of beautiful boats, each bearing the owner's name, are kept and cared for.

We ran in here, but did not stop, except for a few moments, not having an introduction to the privileges of the club. Indian Rock is a postoffice, and is connected by a road with the Mountain View House and Rangeley City, and by trails and canoe routes with the Parmachenee lake and other interior waters. This association has among its members many men of wealth and prominence in all parts of New England, and it has exerted a strong influence for good in aiding its enforcement of the game laws of the state.

Threading our way back again, we headed down the lake, and soon got out far enough to take in the view of the mountainous and wooded surroundings. To the eastward, the fine range of the Bemis borders the shore. Down from their dark bulwark rattles and roars that Bemis brook which stands so high in the estimation of autumnal anglers, and has at its mouth a hotel-camp which forms one of the favorite resting places of the region, and is so well-known that you can buy a ticket from Boston straight thither. Northward, right up Cupsuptic, is planted the isolated cone of West Kennebago, its slopes forming an equal-sided and smooth triangle, meeting in a sharp apex; over its left shoulder peers the more distant East Kennebago, but its outline is not nearly so true and elegant. In the northeast, beyond Oquossoc, are Saddleback, Spotted mountain and other fine elevations, with shapely pinnacles beyond

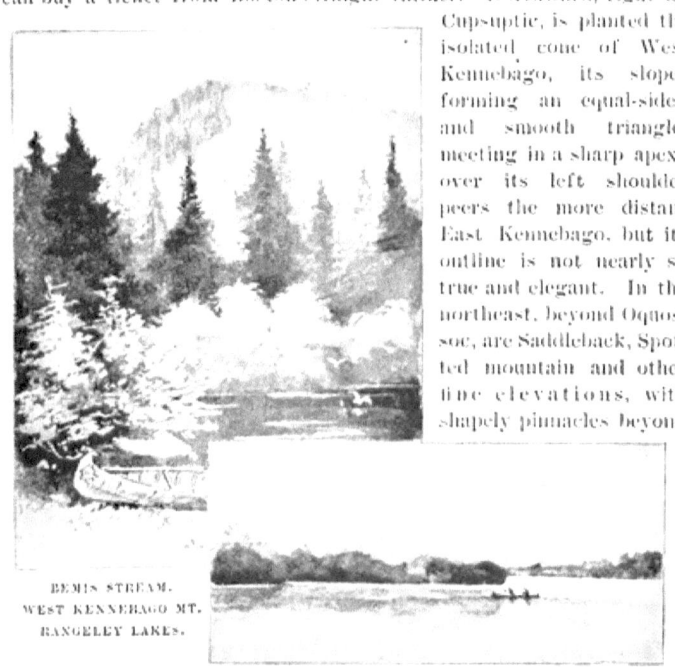

BEMIS STREAM.
WEST KENNEBAGO MT.
RANGELEY LAKES.

them in the far Dead River region. — Bigelow, Abraham and their lofty fellows. Ahead (southward), several blue summits rise into view, prominently Aziscoos, seen just before we reach the landing at Upper Dam.

Nobody awaited us on the little wharf except a French boy, leaning on his yoke of oxen which looked ridiculously powerful in front of the small dirt-cart they had dragged down as a baggage wagon. But this did not mean either solitude or incivility. When we had walked a quarter of a mile along the shore, we came to a low-browed cottage, whose appearance was as inviting as its architecture was nondescript. This is the headquarters of the superintendent of the dams, and has become a hotel by force of circumstances, rather than by intention, now hiding under its spacious roof and

SADDLEBACK MOUNTAIN, RANGELEY LAKES, FROM MOOSELUCMAGUNTIC.

modern additions the "huge log cabin," where Church and Winthrop were offered the freedom of the settlement in a tobacco box. "Its architecture," the latter records, "was of the early American style, and possessed the high art of simplicity. It was solid, not gingerbreadesque. Primeval art has a rude dignity," etc., etc. The old cabin still stands, but is so imbedded in the new that it takes an antiquarian to find it.

Half a dozen ladies and children strolling about in sunshades and comfortably loose gowns were the only persons visible, for all the men were either busy at the repairing of the immense dam and lumber *chutes* (which can raise the height of the lake fifteen feet and are worthy of careful attention), or else were away fishing. But we found our way to quarters without trouble, — what a glorious big stone fireplace that is in the hall! — and neither worried, nor had cause to, about the accommodations. Indeed, I can remember no place where we felt so immediately "at home" and contented as in this little stopping-place at Upper Dam.

By-and-by, as the day declined, canoe-load after canoe-load of anglers and angleresses began to come in, hold up strings of fish to our unstinted admiration, smile through tanned and sunburnt faces their honest satisfaction, and presently reappear in fresh coats and slippers, eager for supper. This meal introduced us to the quaintest little dining room in all Maine — half of the old log house — ceiled to the farthest angle of its steep roof, and so gaily painted in white, red and blue, that one couldn't decide whether he were eating in a Gothic chapel, or in a steamboat cabin.

"It seems to be Friday all summer here," Prue remarks, as we leave the table, after one of those substantial meals at which everybody assembled so promptly.

"Why?"

"Because one gets fish — fish — fish, at every meal."

She refers to stories rather than to provender. Though, in the unhappily short time vouchsafed to most visitors here, no one gets tired of the eating of the ever-present trout, it was the re-catching and re-measuring of them in the conversation of the enthusiastic sportsmen, that had excited my wife's comment. I have sometimes wondered whether there were not more enjoyment in this *postmortem* sport than in the reality; but Baily says he believes that the most fun of *his* year's angling comes in working over his tackle and getting ready, each spring. It is indeed marvelous to one not *fly-bitten* (as Prue scornfully told Baily he was) to see what labor and exposure and privations will be cheerfully undergone here by men, who in town are peevish over getting up before nine o'clock, or at the least irregularity in comfort. Here they are boys again, and not only take their punishment pluckily, but kiss the rod, be it split bamboo, or lance-wood, or what-not.

What a lovely picture was that before us as we sat smoking our cigars on the porch after tea! In the foreground, a cyclopean wall of granite, some massive part of the dam-structure, slanting away at the best angle for composition. Beyond that a broad space of dead water, stuck full of stumps and floating logs, which reaches far to the right, —a tangle of snags—backed by a strip of dense forest stretching across the left half of the scene. This forested point is only a

DEER MOUNTAIN, RANGELEY LAKES.

quarter of a mile away, and is made up of all sorts of trees, whose ruddy tops blaze in the evening light against the background of dappled hillside beyond Molechunkamunk. Only a glimpse of that lake is visible, gleaming white in the heart of the picture, and bounded by a russet-and-indigo slope rounding upward into the ridges of the farther hills, and behind it all the eye is caught and held by the far-distant silhouette of the Grafton mountains—miles and miles away as a bird might fly—washed upon the warm white sky in pale cobalt, even and smooth, with a sharp, clean, attractive outline. It was an evening like that of the burial of Minnisink:—

> Far upward in the mellow light
> Rose the blue hills. One cloud of white
> Around a far uplifted cone,
> In the warm blush of evening shone;
> An image of the silver lakes,
> By which the Indian's soul awakes.

Baily declined to go anywhere except a-fishing during the three days we had allotted to Upper Dam; but Prue and I spent one day in a run to South Arm and back on one of the steamers which the Androscoggin Lakes Transportation Company have put into daily service upon the Richardson lakes. South Arm is the southernmost extremity of the Lower lake (Welokennabacook), and is one of the points of entrance from the outer world. The route thither is by the Grand Trunk railway to Bryant's Pond station. From there, daily stages run northward through the pleasant towns of Milton and Rumford to Andover, where the night must be spent and good inns will be found. Andover is in the broad meadows of Ellis river, and has many good shooting and fishing localities in its neighborhood, and some very pretty mountain scenery. From here it is a ride of twelve miles in a buckboard through utterly uninhabited woods and over high hills, yet upon a decent road, to the A. L. T. Co.'s very comfortable little hotel, the Lakeview Cottage, on the steep shore of the South Arm. Though this entails twice as much staging as the route to the lakes by way of Phillips, the total distance from Portland is much less, and it may be regarded as the direct road to the lower lakes.

"The fishing at South Arm, from the time the ice goes out, up to about the middle of July, is as good as at any other point in the lake region, and trout weighing from a half a pound to five pounds are taken there. . . . Ladies and young people can here indulge in boating with less danger than at any other point on the lakes." So wrote Captain Farrar, in his *Guide;* and he added, as a *viva voce* supplement, that in '85 six trout were caught just opposite the hotel, by one angler, in one excursion, which weighed together thirty-eight pounds. We jarred cruelly upon Baily's sensitive soul, by telling him of this, with due enlargements, when we got home that night; but he retorted by equally large statistics from Upper Dam, where a single fish of seven pounds was caught the same season, and one of over twelve pounds is on record.

South Arm cove is closely shut in by the lofty, rocky, jungle-covered, bear-haunted spurs of the massive mountains southward; and coming out we can see little, except the fine pyramid of Mt. Dustan on the New Hampshire line, which stands squarely ahead, until we get opposite the outlet of the lake, near its centre on the western side, where is the Power Company's middle dam and hotel, toward which our course is shaped.

The names of these dams are given in relation to each other; the lower, or Errol dam, being at the outlet of Umbagog, the middle one here at the outlet of the Richardson lakes, and the upper at the foot of Great lake; several lesser dams obstruct tributary streams.

Middle Dam left behind, we take farewell glimpses of some tall peaks about the Dixville notch, and, there, as we get near to The Narrows, conducting from Welokennabacook, into Molechunkamunk, we catch sight of Aziscoos and Observatory peaks for a few moments, over the near ridges in the northwest. The day is sunny and just breezy enough to roughen the water with little ripples that break the glare. Long patches of deepest Prussian blue lie athwart it, alternating with the sepia tints reflected from the clouds, and touches of color near shore reproducing the bright September tapestry of the hillsides. What a wonderful variety of colors was contained in that tapestry, while every shadow that lurked underneath the crowding leaves was brightest navy blue. There was no white nor black nor gloom anywhere,—all color and sunshine and warmth. Yet Prue wrapped her shawl closely about her, for the air was cool.

As we turn northward into the Narrows, a mob of mountains rises behind us over the lowlands in the south-southwest, in the centre of which, Washington and all his northern companions stand up, filmy and cloud-flecked, but distinct and unmistakable. At this distance inferior heights take their true place, and the shape, the poise, the overtopping height, the color of the Presidents, all testify to their natural supremacy. On the left, towers the nearer and shapely mass of Speckled mountain, at the Grafton notch, and at its left, a little later, the triple-peaked Saddleback, between Andover and Grafton, which stands somewhat this side, and, properly speaking, is a range.

As we emerge into Molechunkamunk lake, the mountains beyond Rangeley come finely into view ahead; the symmetrical cone at the north end of the Observatory range reappears at the left, and is quickly followed by the remaining nameless peaks of that handsome series. On the right, Mettaluk point juts out between the Narrows and Mettaluk brook. The name is that of an Iroquois Indian who lived upon these lakes about forty years ago, and left his name attached to various localities here and elsewhere. Mettaluk brook is frequented especially in July and August, when the fishing in the lake is likely to be dull. Trout of five pounds' weight are said to have been taken from certain pools four or five miles up the creek.

Just beyond, we catch sight of the luxuriously furnished cabins of Camp Whitney, the resort of a coterie of veteran fishermen who never tire of returning.

As the steamer's head turns northward opposite Camp Whitney, slowly there rises over the hills ahead, the rocky, olive-tinted, ponderous poll of Mount Aziscoos, the greatest of all the hills in the lake district and one whose dignity grows upon the beholder the longer he regards it. Passing the row of commodious log houses which entertains the Boston club, we touch at the Upper Dam landing; but as the steamer is to go to the northern extremity of the lake and back, we stay aboard and go with her, passing several fine camps on the shores, and calling at Birch Lodge, "probably the most complete camp in arrangement and equipment of any in the lake country." It stands on the northern shore, between the outlet of the pretty

Richardson ponds, and Beaver brook. Trails lead from there to the summits of both Aziscoos and Observatory peaks, but their ascent is very laborious from this side.

Bidding farewell to our friends at Upper Dam, the next morning, when the sky was overcast with thick clouds fitting our reluctant mood, we took the steamboat for Middle Dam, and there found a buckboard ready to carry us five miles through the silent woods to Sunday Cove on Lake Umbagog. Thinking of its name, that little bay, when we had wearily attained to it, seemed fitly named after the line in old George Herbert's *Sabbath Hymn*, it was " so cool, so calm, so bright;" but, alas! for us sightseers, the " bridal of the earth and sky " was a bank of impenetrable mist.

CHAPTER XIV.

UMBAGOG AND THE MAGALLOWAY.

Rough Coös, whose thick woods shake
Their pine-cones in Umbagog lake.

UMBAGOG! No lake in the country had more excited my curiosity. When I was a boy, a lot of bright fellows in Cambridge used to come up here regularly on natural-history expeditions, and the treasures of ornithology they brought back excited both my imagination and envy. You can find now many a "list" and "paper," in the proceedings of scientific societies near Boston, upon this lake and its environs.

Then its scenery had been so often described to me! The beautiful way in which the sky painted its own hues upon the surface of the water, while the shores, many tinted, now abrupt, now low, forested here, cleared and tenanted there, or walled in with upright crags elsewhere, furnished a glorious frame for the picture. Then the mountains! How on every side they filled the background, towering greater with distance, as do the gigantic figures of ancient history! Eastward, were the rounded masses of the great hills at the head of the Cambridge, with the bald summits of Grafton at the right. Off to the westward, a contrast, in the peaked heights that bristle about Dixville notch. Northward, lone pyramids like Dustan, Aziscoos, and Observatory, dark with unscarred forests and overlooking a hundred lakes. Southward, massively superior to all the rest, Washington and his co-presidents.

All this delight was denied to our eyes; nor was it much consolation to recall that Major Winthrop encountered just such a day here thirty years ago.

"Whiffs of mist," he records, "had met us at the outset. Presently we opened chaos, and chaos shut in upon us. There was no Umbagog to be seen; nothing but a few yards of gray water and a world of gray vapor. Therefore I cannot criticise, nor insult, nor compliment Umbagog. Let us deem it beautiful. The sun tried at the fog, to lift it with the leverage of his early level beams. Failing in this attempt to stir and heave away the mass, he climbed and began to use his beams as wedges, driving them down more perpen-

dicularly. Whenever this industrious craftsman made a split, the fog
gaped and we could see for a moment, indefinitely, an expanse of
water hedged with gloomy forest, and owning for its dominant
height, Aziscoos, or, briefer, Esquihos. . . .

"We enjoyed our damp voyage heartily, on that wide loneliness.
Nor were our shouts and laughter the only sounds. Loons would
sometimes wail to us, as they dived, black dots in the mist. Then we

would wait for their bulbous reappearance and let fly the futile shot
with its muffled report, missing, of course."

Through a similar fog the present writer and his companions
steamed down the whole length of the lake. As the yacht plowed
through the gauzy veil "little islands loomed trembling between sky
and water, like hanging gardens. Gradually the filmy trees defined
themselves, the aërial enchantment lost its potency, and we came up
with common prose islands that had so late been magical and poetic."

Umbagog is a dozen miles long, and perhaps a mile and a half in average width. It lies north and south, sharing its waters between New Hampshire and Maine. Rapid river, the inlet from the upper lakes, enters near its northeastern end; and the outlet is only a short distance below, from the opposite (western) side, where the Androscoggin begins its course. The path of this river is as crooked as its name; and Winthrop thought the queer twist characteristic of colloquial pronunciation in that region appropriate to people who lived near a stream with so scraggy an appellation and tortuous a current.

Our morning's voyage through the "gleaming fields of haze" terminated at the A. L. T. Co.'s excellent Lakeside House, on the lower extremity of the lake in Cambridge, N. H., which is half a mile west of the little settlement of Upton, Me., at the mouth of Cambridge river. The afternoon was spent by Baily and Prue in fishing, each having a guide and a boat, and exerting great rivalry, while I borrowed a gun and went after partridges, getting a fair bag before tea. The fog gradually thinned out and sailed away eastward, in detachments which encamped upon the rugged hilltops, leaving the air clear, the sky

> Of an azure hue,
> Untarnished fair as is the violet
> Or anemone, when the spring strews them
> By some meandering rivulet,

and showing us in new relief the tall mountains northward with which we had become acquainted on the other lakes.

Next morning the steamer took us on its early trip up the lake to the Androscoggin, and down that river to Errol Dam.

The water of this river, raised fifteen feet by the building of the dam many years ago, has invaded the forest on each side and killed a wide belt of trees, the stubs of which now stand in the water, rude cenotaphs of the departed sons of the forest, bereft of bark and branches, bleached and picturesque. Herons, kingfishers and eagles, fitly attitudinize upon these tough old relics, and the water they overlook is as still and smooth as a surface of polished bronze. Says Farrar: "Following the crooked channel of the river, which in the six miles between the lake and the dam makes about thirty distinct turns, you have, as the steamer twists about, views from all points of the compass. From about the middle of July to the first of October the sides of the river are carpeted with water lilies, that present a beautiful sight, and fill the air with their delightful odor. The captain of the steamer is accommodating, and often stops to gather them for the lady passengers, and thus thousands are carried away each year; but the next only sees them more abundant."

A well-known settlement and hotel exists at Errol Dam, connected by an ancient road with Colebrook, N. H., on the Connecticut river, twenty-one miles distant. This road passes through Dixville notch (half way) and forms one of the regular avenues of approach to the lake region, Colebrook being only thirteen miles by a delightful stage-road from North Stratford station on the Grand Trunk Railway.

Dixville notch is "a fine gorge between a crumbling conical crag and a scarped precipice, a pass easily defensible, except at the season when raspberries would distract sentinels." The cleft traversed by the road opens like a Titanic gateway to some region of mysterious desolation. "The pass," to quote Eastman's description, "is much narrower than either of the more famous ones in the White Mountains, and through its whole extent of a mile and quarter, has more the character of a notch. . . . So narrow is the ravine (it can hardly

IN DIXVILLE NOTCH.

be called a pass) that a rough and precarious roadway for a single carriage could only be constructed. . . . No description can impart an adequate conception of the mournful grandeur of the decaying cliffs of mica-slate which overhang the way. They shoot up in most singular and fantastic shapes and vary in height from 400 to 800 feet . . . but are rapidly crumbling away. Some have decayed to half their original height; and the side-walls of the notch are strewn with debris which the ice and storms have pried and gnawed from the decrepit cliffs." So says Eastman. The Rev. William C. Prime pronounces it one of the wildest and most imposing pieces of rock scenery on the Atlantic side of the country; and the drive from Colebrook through the notch to Bethel, the finest he has ever found in America.

It is possible to clamber up to Table rock, 800 feet above the road, and to other pinnacles, whence a view of the whole monument-strewn glen is given, and beyond it, over Umbagog, far down into the heart of the White Mountains, and westward and northward over to Vermont and Canada. Various minor features of interest, trout fishing, and the lovely pastoral region at the western foot of the range, invite a stay of several days in the neighborhood.

Errol Dam is best known, however, as a point of departure for the Magalloway river and Parmachenee lake, a distinction to which it has no better claim, however, than Lakeside. The Magalloway rises in a

WHITE MOUNTAINS FROM UMBAGOG LAKE.

group of ponds and springs among the hills on the boundary of the province of Quebec, in the same highlands that form the nursery of the Connecticut, the Chaudiere and the Cupsuptic. Ten miles southward it "bulges" into Parmachenee lake; and then, augmented by many brooks and pond-outlets, makes its way southward to empty into the Androscoggin two miles below Umbagog. From the time the ice goes out until the middle of October, it is navigated by a steamboat making daily trips from Errol Dam to the Berlin Mills House, sixteen miles up stream, except in low stages of water, when it is compelled to halt at a somewhat lower landing. A short stage-trip then carries the traveller to another reach of steamer navigation; at the end of which he must take to his canoe and his feet in order to reach Parmachenee lake. The distance from Lakeside to Parmachenee, as travelled, is about sixty miles, the major part of which is accomplished by steamboat or stage; two days are required for the through trip, the night being spent at Aziscoos Falls.

We did not undertake the whole journey, but did the first half of it. The enjoyment began when the pilot turned the steamer's prow right into the flooded woods along the Androscoggin, startling the herons and his passengers at the same time, for to our ignorant eyes

AZISCOOS FALLS — MAGALLOWAY RIVER.

no river-mouth could be seen. It opened before us, nevertheless, and presently we were cruising in the Magalloway, a river narrower than the Androscoggin, and hemmed in, not by dead trees, but by walls of living green. "It is not a rude wilderness; all the northern woods have of foliage, verdurous, slender, delicate, tremulous, overhung our shadowy path, dense as the vines that drape a tropic stream. Every giant tree, every one of the pinus oligarchy, had been lumbered away; refined sylvan beauty remained."

We thought the Androscoggin crooked enough, but this proved to be more so,—serpentine is a word that fits it most admirably. Its general width in the lower part is a hundred feet or more, but now and then the stream narrows until the trees bending outward almost touch each other overhead.

"Observe how black and glossy the water is in this deep place," I say to my companions. "It seems never disturbed, except when a trout throws himself, curving above the surface like the flash of a scimitar."

"Never expected to find swordfish up here in the woods!" Baily exclaims in an affectation of pleased surprise.

"Interruptions are impolite, and pointless jests are stupid!" I rejoin, with just severity, whereupon Prue retorts:—

"Oh, come now, that's too hard, Theo! What *could* be more pointed in a joke than a sword?"

I leave this frivolous pair to their own levity. I want to enjoy the river unmolested, and recall how well can be fitted to it Thoreau's masterful description of that other "crooked river," the Souhegan:—

The pines stand up with pride	Whose antiquated graves
By the Souhegan's side,	Its still water laves
And the hemlock and the larch	On the shore.
With their triumphal arch	With an Indian's stealthy tread,
Are waving o'er its march	It goes sleeping in its bed,
To the sea.	Without joy or grief,
No wind stirs its waves,	Or the rustle of a leaf,
But the spirits of the braves	Without a ripple or a billow,
Hov'ring o'er,	Or the sigh of a willow

"On your sail," says the author of Farrar's *Illustrated Guide to the Androscoggin Lakes,* "you will see the brown and bald eagles,—the latter, the typical American bird,—spreading their huge wings in pursuit of some unlucky fish-hawk, who, having worked hard to procure a dinner, is now destined to lose it. The bald-headed eagles in this country are the largest I have ever seen, and they have been shot and measured nine feet from tip to tip of wing. There are many small ponds lying contiguous to the river on both sides and connected with it by short streams, that are often filled with ducks, with blue herons stalking near them. Deer, bear, caribou and moose, are occasionally caught sight of along the river, as frightened by the steamer, they plunge into the leafy cover of the woods. The banks of the stream vary in height from two to eight feet according to the number of gates open at the dam, and a good camping-spot may be found readily.

"About four miles up the the Magalloway you pass some rocks on the left side, then make a sharp turn to the right. Looking back as you make this turn, you obtain the most romantic and picturesque view on the river. About half a mile of the stream can be seen, in some places the trees almost meeting overhead, and the silvery lane of water through this vista of living green presents a picture that you will not soon forget. The country people who go up and

UPPER MAGALLOWAY.

down this beautiful thoroughfare seem generally to care nothing about this scenery; but one day, when coming down the river, as we turned this bend, an old fellow on the boat who caught the view just at the right moment, was for an instant brought to a realizing sense of the beauties of nature, and. looking at me, said, 'I swum now. Mister, if that ain't the purtiest sight I ever saw.'"

Except some stony ledges, like that at Pulpit rock, the foliage and sedge that shut in the river is unbroken for ten miles, at the end of which humanity is recalled by a log cabin at the mouth of Bottle brook. A few moments later the lower landing is reached, among farms, and upon a wagon road along the right bank. Though it is only two miles by land to the Berlin Mills House, the distance is six by water.

This ride of six miles, heading to every point of the compass in

DIAMOND PEAKS.

succession, is a delightful experience. "Mts. Dustan and Aziscoos are dodging around you continually now, first on one side and then on the other, while the peculiarly shaped Diamond peaks, some miles above, occasionally put in an appearance." All of these mountains, with intervening ridges, are lofty and savage heights on the western side of the river, and from the northernmost extension of the White Mountains. Dustan and Aziscoos are beautifully conspicuous from the Richardson lakes and Umbagog, while the Diamond peaks, now first well seen, resemble twin stumps of mountains (exact copies of one another) which have been truncated at a similar level by the plow of the continental glacier, or by some other evenly acting agency. They are reputed to get their name from the Diamond river which flows past them from distant sources in the Coös County forest;

but, perhaps, on the contrary, the river takes its name from them, in reference to their odd angularity.

At Berlin Mills we eat dinner and listen to animated stories of what capital shooting and fishing the vicinity affords, especially at Sturtevant pond. This is the proper point for the ascent of Aziscoos. A buckboard may be driven nearly to its summit, the prospect from which takes in the whole of northern Maine, as far as Katahdin, reaches westward to the heights about Lake Champlain, and southward far into the White Mountains. Nor need any fear of excessive difficulties deter

ON MAGALLOWAY RIVER.

even ladies from availing themselves of this picture and experience, which certainly ought not to be missed.

This is the limit of navigation, because the river above is choked with logs, waiting to be driven out in the spring.

The afternoon was devoted to a ride of half a dozen miles through the woods, with occasional outlooks at mountains, etc., to Fred Flint's house, near Aziscoos falls, and the night we spent there was almost like camping-out in a very comfortable way. The falls are a series of cataracts, boiling over ledge after ledge for a long distance. It is the most dangerous place on the river in running logs, where more than one lumberman has lost his life. At high-water the tumult is very great and makes a picture of grand and perilous force, to which the wild surroundings lend grim emphasis. There is excellent trout-fishing at this place.

From a landing above the falls (which act as a dam, holding back several miles of deep, smooth water), a stern-wheel steamboat runs about fifteen miles up the wriggling stream, which is now six or eight rods in width and strong of current. Camping-places are frequent, ducks and other game always to be had, and the fishing first-rate, especially at the Narrows, where the steamer has a hard pull to get through. Six miles above the Narrows, the Lower Mettaluk pond is reached, which at present forms the head of navigation. The river is to be improved, however, and the boat will then run as high up as the Grass Eddy, but a short distance below the forks of the Magalloway. A trail leads from this point to Lincoln pond, a considerable piece of water two miles eastward. It is said to be well-stocked with trout, disposed to be enticed with bait in May or June, and by a fly after that. Deer, moose, and caribou can often be shot there, in season, and the shore affords good camping ground. It is often reached by a trail from the Upper Mettaluk pond, where there is a cabin for fishermen.

Above the Mettaluk ponds the Magalloway winds for twelve miles through lush meadows beloved of deer and waterfowl. The current is swift through there, and above the meadows, decided rapids are met, where the Little Magalloway comes in from the northwest. This is the end of the canoe-trip, unless the traveller means to take his boat with him, in which case he drags it up the river almost to Parmachenee lake.

The lake is four miles distant by a good path which conducts on through a fine forest to the shore, where a boat will be found or can be signalled for. An island in the lake is occupied by Danforth's "Camp Caribou," a curiously irregular pile of woodland buildings, which has grown year by year from a "camp" to a "hotel." Everything about the place indicates *the sportsman* in both the proprietor and his guests, who come largely from New York City. The walls are adorned with heads of deer, tails of foxes, and other trophies of the chase, while gunning gear and fishing tackle, boats and camp-equipments, old clothes and friendly manners, characterize the settlement. Twenty or more fine boats will be found there, each of which had to be taken through the woods from Rangeley on the shoulders of men. The furniture of the house, like that structure itself, has been made on the spot, for the most part by the ingenious hands of the owner; but all the supplies of every kind must be paddled and carried up the Magalloway, or else "toted" in from Cupsuptic lake along a hilly footpath. The supplies are always abundant, and the equipment comfortable, however, so that ladies form a constant element in the summer colony at this thoroughly out-of-the-way resort.

Parmachenee is celebrated first of all as a fishing and hunting centre. We were told of eighteen trout caught there in one day, lately, none of which measured less than fifteen inches in length, while one reached twenty-three inches. Two gentlemen from New York are reported as taking 2,500 fish, of suitable size for cooking, in eight days, one day's score reaching 900. The scenery about the lake, which is shut in by hills, is utterly wild. Roads and trails or canoe

ON LAKE PARMACHEENEE.

routes diverge to a large number of mountains, ponds, and streams, however; and in the autumn and winter the shooting in that region is incomparable, comprising all varieties of large game. Farrar's guide contains a circumstantial account of the best localities for both forms of sport.

It rained hard during our night at Flint's, and was lowery and cold when we left there on our return in the morning,—ah! what a memorable trout breakfast, we had!—but before we had reached The Berlin Mills House, and reëmbarked upon the lower Magalloway, all the clouds had disappeared, even from the crest of hoary Aziscoos, whose gray poll was almost white with the thinnest possible dusting of hail. Reversing the river pictures, and so finding novelty in them all, we ran quickly down to Errol Dam, and thence into Lake Umbagog. And now what a different scene presented itself, compared with our entrance three days' before! The canopy was unflecked, and the air calm and crystal-clear. The sky-answering water lay utterly still, smooth, and glistening, save where some flocks of ducks and a pair of loons floated upon the burnished surface.

> On its margin the great forest
> Stood reflected in the water,
> Every tree-top had its shadow,
> Motionless beneath the water.

Gliding from the Androscoggin, we swung around to the southward, and there, overtopping all the massive green ridges nearer by, saw the whole Presidential range, peak after peak, towering into the blue sky as if carved from alabaster, for the storm had shed a heavy snow-fall upon them, and the White Mountains were white indeed with the first gifts of winter.

With the speed of thought another slide is shot before memory's lens. Again I am afloat in Hood's canal. Far away over the bronzed backs of my Indian paddlers, beating time to some savage crooning; past the long, gaudy, carven canoe-prow; beyond the shining levels and the clustered spires of Douglas fir upon the shore;—again I see the coruscant pinnacles of the Olympus piercing the blue Pacific sky. The Presidential is five, the Olympic range twelve, thousand feet above the watery foreground; but I avow that this rare picture, seen that early autumn morning from Umbagog, was as lovely in its composition, as brilliant in its color, as impressive in its grandeur and distance, as the other.

So we were glad not only that we had come to Umbagog, and had seen it both in the silvery fog and in the golden sunlight, but that it made for us the *adieu* of the lake region; for we thought if we had begun with *this*, the upper ponds could hardly have sustained the expectation of the first impression. We felt, that in coming down from Rangeley to Umbagog, we had steadily gone from good to better and had the best at the last. And, taking it all in all, we concluded that to him who seeks a vacation in the wilderness, near to nature's heart, the trip across Umbagog, and up the Magalloway to Parmachenee lake will yield more satisfaction with a better economy of time, money, strength and enjoyment, than any other route we know of in New England; but this, of course, omits almost all consideration of the

social element, for which there is nowhere in the Rangeley region such
an opportunity as goes with the out-door life at Moosehead lake.

In summer, there is traffic enough back and forth between the lakes
and Bethel, Me., to support a daily stage each way. The trip takes
about five hours. Climbing the big hill, in the rear of the Lakeside
House, we take our last look at Umbagog and then fix our eyes
upon the mountains in front, chiefly Saddleback and Speckled, between which we are to pass. We note the changes in them, with
never-wearying eyes, until they gradually close about us, and we find
ourselves between shaggy walls of forested and rocky heights where
Cambridge river is a mere brook, and the road crosses and re-
crosses its wrigglings upon bridges of rattling logs. Sometimes there

A GLIMPSE OF SADDLEBACK.

is scarcely room for the wheels to slip between masses of
rock supporting the leafy mountain-sides, and the little stream is an
incessant cascade. Then we find a tiny torrent rushing the other
way which the driver tells us is Bear river, and by-and-by get out
into the sunlight and can look off upon the world once more.

Such is the Grafton notch, and we heard of several curiosities of
scenery in its neighborhood, such as the Screw-auger falls, where
Bear river twists through a spiral channel in a series of sunken cascades; the Jail, a semi-circular abyss worn by some former vagary of
the stream, and the Devil's Horseshoe, — an impression in the rocks
of a cataract-bank, singularly true to the size and shape suggested,

—and finally the profound chasm, or sink-hole into which legend says a wounded moose once plunged. "At the bottom flows a large and noisy stream, which, as if the gloom of the lofty walls which hem it in, and the sombre stillness of the surrounding forest did not sufficiently guard its privacy, plunges beneath a huge mass of superincumbent rock. . . . and disappears from sight."

Grafton notch left behind, the country becomes more open. The old Popple tavern and Newry corners are left in turn, and at the mouth of Bear river the broad intervales of the Androscoggin come in sight, with that crooked river meandering through them. Crossing Bear river we

SCREW-AUGER FALLS, GRAFTON NOTCH.

turn up the main Androscoggin, amazed at the cultivation, serene beauty and warmth of the scene after the cold and almost forbidding sternness of the scenery to which we have long been accustomed; and so roll swiftly into the elm-embowered streets of Bethel.

CHAPTER XV.

BETHEL AND GORHAM.

The mountains, indeed, that they may show their dignity and communicate their favors, require to be approached with great painstaking and peculiar respect.—BARTOL.

HERE, at the entrance to the White Mountains, let us pause for a few moments' study of that region, in general, so that we may proceed more intelligently. "One may travel," remarks the geologist Huntington, "and make extensive tours without map or guide-book, and, at the end of a summer vacation or a year of travel, return to his home and be as profoundly ignorant of the country he has traversed as a man is of astronomy, who has spent his whole life in a mine." Our little party were not of this heedless class; nor do we believe it, gentle reader, of you. Hence the most accurate maps available have been enclosed in this little book for your use.

The White Mountains occupy the whole centre of New Hampshire, between Lake Winnipesaukee and the valley of the Amonoosuc, from the Connecticut on the west to the Androscoggin on the east — an area of over 1,700 square miles. The hills of central Vermont connect them with the Hoosac and Catskill mountains southward, while their extension northward is found in the heights of northern New Hampshire and in the summits along and beyond the Maine lakes, aligning them with the rest of the great Appalachian system fronting the Atlantic coast of North America. Of this system, the culmination of the White Mountains in the Presidential range is the highest expression, except a group of peaks (curiously enough termed The Black) in western North Carolina; but the northern group is loftier in effect and every aspect, save mere measurements, because the more arctic position carries its heads above the reduced timber line, and gives an appearance of alpine altitude denied to the summits of Carolina; while the hard crystalline rocks, and the prevalence of coniferous trees lend sternness and vigor to New Hampshire landscapes, befitting a mountain picture better than the softer foliage and more rounded lines that characterize the still beautiful steeps of Carolina and Virginia.

A glance at the map, or a first acquaintance with the mountains, presents to the eye an almost inextricable jumble; but a little study solves this into two general masses, divided by the valley of the Saco, opening southeastward, and that of the Amonoosuc (whose source is closely adjacent), which opens in the opposite direction. On the north and east are the Mt. Washington or Presidential range (the White Mountains proper), with its outliers, the Pilot, Jackson and Chatham mountains, forming a northerly mass, the general axis of which extends northwest and southeast. South and west of the two rivers mentioned lies the other mass of elevations, represented by the Franconia range, the line of summits extending from Tripyramid to The Twins, Moat mountain, the Sandwich range and the lofty uplift bearing Moosilauke and Kinsman. The general axis of these is nearly north

ENTRANCE TO CARTER NOTCH FROM GORHAM.

and south. The geological survey of the state counts ten distinct groups or ranges; but for my purpose it is enough to indicate these two main masses, which are separated by the Crawford notch.

Though there are hotels and a few small summer settlements in the midst of the peaks, and well-travelled roads penetrate most of the gorges, all the villages are on the outskirts of the mountains, in the valleys of rivers forming the avenues of approach. Railways now skirt the mountains on every side, and cross the middle of them, with branches to Mt. Washington, the Profile House, Bethlehem, Jefferson and Lancaster. Elsewhere, stages run,— the same big, red, four or six-horse coaches identified with all that was exciting and poetic in the mountain tour a generation ago. To every point of importance, and by almost every conceivable route, excursion tickets from Boston to the mountains and return, good for a longer or shorter time according to kind and price, may be bought at the offices of the Boston & Maine Railroad; or, as in our own case, the ticket for a longer journey may be made to include the White Mountain tour.

The most favorable season for a visit to the higher mountains in the opinion of the judicious and experienced editors of both Ticknor's *Guide to the White Mountains* and of Eastman's *Guide*, is July and August, for then the cool air of the highlands affords the most grateful relief to the burning heats of the cities. "The hotels and boarding-houses are then filled with guests, and parties are frequently formed to visit the interesting points in the vicinity of each. Metropolitan society transfers its headquarters and its modified ceremonials to the shadows of the mountains, and the villages are filled with busy and exotic life. On account of the clemency of the temperature, camping-parties can then attack the higher mountains and explore the great ravines. But, for the comparatively few persons who can choose their own time, who have vigorous physical powers, and who love nature with an ardent and undivided love, the months of September and October will be found more favorable for the visit. Then is the season of the harvests, of the magnificent coloring of the autumnal forests, and of clear and bland air. Accommodations are more easily obtained at the hotels; and whereas in August the transient tourist is often obliged to sleep on sofas or floors in overcrowded houses, in the later months he is sure of comfortable quarters and quiet rest. One of the best times to enjoy the scenery is in late September and early October, after the sky has been cleansed by the equinoctial storm and before the higher peaks have been covered with snow."

The clothing provided should be warm and water-proof, in order to meet the emergencies of weather belonging to a mountain climate; and especially stout and comfortable shoes, in order that the walking and climbing may be indulged without stint. Wagon roads and mountain paths in all directions will tempt you, and the danger is rather toward over-doing pedestrianism at first, than toward not being eager enough about it. Almost everywhere good trout fishing may be found.

Of this quiet little village, Bethel, in which we can imagine no greater change to have taken place since his day than the improvement of certain roads and the enlargement of hotels, Starr King remarks, that it is the North Conway of the eastern slope of the mountains. "But its river scenery," he adds, "is much richer than that of the Saco; and it has so many pleasant strips of meadow, like the 'Middle Intervale,' relieved by the broad, winding Androscoggin in front, and by ample hills in the rear, brightly colored to the summit with fertile farms, that, for drives, it is a question if North Conway would not be obliged to yield the palm. . . . . We can see now the wide array of gentle hills swelling so variously that the verdure of the forests, or the mottled bounty of the harvests, drooped from them in almost every curve of grace. Some of these hills were partially lighted through thin veils of cloud; some were draped with the tender gray of a shower, which now and then would yield to flushes of moist and golden sunshine; not far off rose a taller summit in slaty shadow; and between, on the line of the river, the different greens of the intervale would gleam in the scattered streams of light that forced their way, here and there, through the heavy and trailing curtains of the dog-day sky. In the morning or evening light, that horizon must enclose countless pictures which only need selection, and not improvement, for the canvas."

"Now why can't we climb one of those hills?" asks Prue, pointing

A BYE-ROAD AT BETHEL.

to the westward. "I havn't had a good long walk since we left Mount Desert, and they must give a splendid view toward Mount Washington."

The best one to attempt was Mt. Abram, and immediately after luncheon a young man brought around a carriage and drove us swiftly away toward its base. How smooth this road seemed after the wrenching and jolting to which we had grown accustomed in the backwoods! And how doubly pleasant were the farms and orchards and neat houses throughout the valley! Then the way became steep and rocky, as we began to ascend the mountain's flank, and presently the carriage halted in a farmer's dooryard half-way to the top, and a path was pointed out to us by which we must walk the rest of the way, across fields and pastures where cows and sheep were nibbling among ledges of naked rock.

The view was well worth the trouble (which amounted to little, as climbing goes) and lay more or less open to us during all the ascent, since on the western side the mountain is nearly clear of trees, and is a favorite point of pilgrimage from Bethel. In the northwest and north were the high points in the rough region about the Grafton notch, and many of the peaks we had left behind us in the lake country. To the east and southeast, Maine seemed less upheaved; but when we swung round to the southern horizon and crossed again into New Hampshire, all the horizon became ragged with "sierras long."

We remembered this as one of the best views of the White Mountains, though quite different from some more "stunning" ones seen later on. No doubt this high appreciation was partly due to the foreground, since between us and the rough, forested foot-hills, rested the vales of the Androscoggin and Wild rivers, and the green fields and neat villages of Bethel. "Bethel is one of the loveliest and dreamiest of mountain nooks. Its expanses of rich verdure, its little steeple, emerging from groves of elm-trees, its rustic bridge spanning the tireless river, its air of lethargy and indolence captivate eye and mind."

We easily traced the railway around the foot of Mt. Moriah almost to Gorham, and counted loops of the Androscoggin far toward the northwest, where

> —— hills o'er hills lifted their heads of green,
> With pleasant vales scooped out and villages between.

We might have remained contented a long time in that pleasant hotel on The Green in old Bethel. The romantic Wild river remained to be explored, and, besides many shorter drives, that twelve-mile one to the curious Albany basins of which we had heard; but it was Saturday, and we had planned to spend Sunday at Gorham; so the afternoon train bore us westward.

That was a wonderful car-ride! "The brilliant meadows, proud of their arching elms; the full, broad Androscoggin, whose charming islands rise from it on a still day like emeralds from liquid silver; the grand, Scotch-looking hills that guard it; the firm lines of the White Mountain ridge that shoots, now and then, across the north, when the road makes a sudden turn; and at last, beyond Shelburne, the splendid symmetry that bursts upon us when the whole mass of Madison is seen throned over the valley, itself overtopped by the ragged pinnacle of Adams."

The road keeps close to the river, yet just escapes the foothills of Mt. Moriah. In the neighborhood of Shelburne, N. H., the narrow strip of fertile meadow widens out into an elm-shaped vale between the hills, dotted with cottages and two or three hotels, for Shelburne is deservedly one of the favorite stopping-places. Its environs consequently have been well explored, and paths are kept marked to the summits of Mts. Moriah, Ingalls, Winthrop and Baldcap. The latter carries Dream lake, at the height of 2,600 feet, the Giant's falls and other interesting features. The view from Mt. Baldcap (2,952 feet) is described as very remarkable.

The drives along this portion of the Androscoggin valley were long ago conceded to be unsurpassed in all the mountains. Starr King is never weary of extolling them for varied interest in the beauty of the scenery, the historic and traditional associations involved with the prominent points of the landscape, and the scientific attractions connected with some portions of the road.

Gorham (N. H.) is a thriving village on the Androscoggin, at the mouth of the Peabody river, which issues from the deep vale between the White Mountain and Carter ranges. It is twenty miles above Bethel, ninety from Portland, and is noted among tourists as the nearest village to Mt. Washington. Stages for the Glen House (eight miles), leave on the arrival of all important trains; but travellers who hurry on to the Glen, because they suppose there is nothing worth seeing at Gorham, make a great mistake. The hotel, to be sure, does not command encouraging views from its windows; but no point in the mountains offers views to be gained by walks of a mile or two that are more noble and memorable. "For river scenery, in connection with impressive mountain forms, the immediate vicinty of Gorham surpasses all the other districts from which the highest peaks are visible." It is only sixteen miles to the top of Mt. Washington, and Adams and Madison are still nearer. On the south, the Peabody glen opens away into the highlands, flanked on the east by the lofty crests of Mts. Moriah and Carter; and on the northwest are the long serrated lines of the Pilot mountains, the scene of brilliant displays of color towards evening. The rugged hills north of the Androscoggin river tower closely on the north of the village, throwing out their rocky cliffs to the verge of the stream. The roads are admirable in the neighborhood, but those who do not care to tramp about in search of the picturesque can easily get a carriage. Heavy mountain wagons are sent out to the top of Mt. Washington, or on any other desired excursion, whenever a party is made up to fill them. (The same statement might be made of every hotel and large boarding-house in the mountains; nor is the tariff of charges a high one, even to the non-tourist mind. Guides and camp-helpers for rough mountain tramps can always be obtained.)

That first evening we did no more than stroll leisurely up upon the bushy knoll called Soldier's hill, intending to get our bearings and decide upon to-morrow's trip; but the glory of the sunset flames cast upon those hoary giants southward, marking their western angles with strong color, and hiding all the gashes in their eastern slopes under heavy shadow; the alternate glow and paling which made the mountains of the Carter range change their aspect every moment; and the swimming color veiling the upper valley and its softly outlined hills, made us forget our maps and our anxieties for the morrow in the pleasure of to-day. Then, as twilight settles down, we walk arm in arm back through the quiet village streets, watching the stars peep coquettishly over the darkening summits, and go to our beds, glad that once more we are leaning upon the great bosom of the highlands.

"I will lift up mine eyes unto the hills," was the resolution of the sacred psalmist; and, pleased with this doctrine, next morning we hastened to obey it, starting so early as not to scandalize *other* good people who felt in duty bound to go to church.

Steeply from the northern bank of the river, opposite Gorham, spring the battlements of Mt. Hayes, traditionally celebrated for "bears, blueberries and views." Not having lost any bears we were not hunting for them, and it was too late for blueberries; but the "views" remained, for the day was clear and warm. At the end of the street we found a suspended foot-bridge which was slight enough to be decidedly "teetering," yet had no guys or rail within reach of one's hands. Neither the swift water swirling underneath, nor the swinging of the frail structure, disturbed *me;* and probably my sturdy treading in advance (supposing the others would follow as calmly), augmented the shaking, for that bothersome wife of mine at once began to squeal and complain, sidling along with arms outstretched and waving as if she were walking a tight-rope. Baily hurried to her assistance, but was ungratefully commanded to stay where he was, for fear the bridge would break (it was safe enough), which he most gallantly and sensibly declined to do. I unwisely ventured to suggest that had Baily not been there with his solicitude she would not have thought it worth while to say *Oh!* so often. But this was an indiscreet remark, for I was informed that I was a heartless wretch, wouldn't care if she fell off, and — snappishly — that I would "catch it." Hearing this, I gave the bridge a lively shake, whereupon a shriek rent the air, and poor Baily was seized with such a despairing clutch that both of 'em nearly tumbled into the wine-colored whirlpools, seeing which I let the poor things creep on in peace.

All the sunshine that turned the leaves to gold and sent long spear-like rays of gleaming silver through the spruce groves, could not warm Prue's face into a smile as we walked up that sloping road, and I prudently kept out of the way. A little distance beyond the bridge there are the works of an abandoned mine, where the ruins of a stairway offered an easy means of ascent toward a high shoulder of rock which we thought ought to afford a fine look-out. Up these stairs I started, they following; and after getting pretty well out of breath, — evidently the day was too warm for a two-mile tramp to the summit with comfort, — we attained the brow of the crag and received our reward.

Right beneath us the valley held a dark little pond and the flashing eddies of the Androscoggin, with busy Gorham and Gorham Falls. The nearest slope opposite was Pine mountain, densely wooded, and the northernmost ridge of the White Mountain range. Off at the left the many-peaked mass of Mt. Moriah was near at hand, hiding everything beyond, while beside it, toward the right, were The Imp and Carter, their slopes (with Carter's crested ridge in full view) falling away into the Peabody ravine and Pinkham notch, interdigitating (Baily's word — good one, isn't it?) with the long, narrow flanks of the White Mountains.

To be sure of these points we had to consult the map. Now Prue carried this but let me look over it with her, and was as talkative as usual. So I made up my mind that the bridge incident was forgotten, and you may be sure I did nothing to revive it, even by saying I was sorry, (as in fact I was). "Let well enough alone" is nowhere better advice than in a cooling quarrel. On the right, we could see only far enough past our own ledges, up the broad and well-peopled valley of Moose river, to get the profiles of the Randolph and Cherry ranges, themselves standpoints for a magnificent prospect. But these side parts of the picture received little attention; for our eyes were fascinated by the glory of the huge summits lifted into the sky right in front of us,—Madison in all his gigantic breadth, Washington only half-hidden behind him, and a long buttress of Adams sweeping down towards the head of Moose river.

How really mountainous and glacial they looked that morning, the first powdering of snow upon their aged heads! How massive and majestic! The noblest among the mountains that stand around them become insignificant from such a point as this, and we forget them in our homage for these central peaks, sitting like king and queen, high upon their thrones under a royal canopy of purple sky. We bow in admiration before their strength and serenity and grandeur of proportion. The rugged breadth of Washington, especially, was shown to us,— his soldierly erectness and defiance. Though only the slope of the lines and the deep shadows suggest them to our sight, the great gorges that separate him from his peers are easy to realize; and we wonder again at the temerity of men invading the sanctity of that heavenly height, even while we watch sunlit plumes of smoke from the locomotives scaling its crest, and can trace the long line of carriage-road marked athwart its northern slope. Madison is shapely and picturesque, with its deeply-notched top and the mighty buttress bracing it against the weight of Adams; but it has not the majesty and fascinating excellence of Washington.

When noon approached, we began our return. Clambering down over the smooth ledges and steeply inclined thickets, where I helped Prue all I could, we reached the shaky staircase, and I warned my companions who passed ahead of me, to be cautious, as one section of it, at least, down a vertical step of the cliff some twenty feet in height, seemed so loose that a little exertion would push it down.

"Do you think so?" asked Prue, who was standing at its top and looking at it critically; then, "Oh, Theo, I've left my parasol — you'll have to go back and get it. I'm so sorry!"

Her tone was not sincere, nor her look; and suspecting that she had left it "on purpose," I toiled again up those baking rocks and through that confounded brush to get the article, my mood in nowise softened by the echoes of merriment from below. Sliding and crashing back, I regained the stairway only to find the loose section removed, and no way left for me to get down to where those two jokers — I hate practical jokes! — were comfortably reclining on a grassy bank indifferent to my comfort, except by a long detour and bruising scramble over the rocks.

"Thank you, ever so much," were Prue's only words, uttered in the sweetest way, when I handed her the umbrella and brushed the dust from my clothing; but Baily, less sure of his position, felt it necessary to produce the flask in which he kept his stock of apologies in liquid form, so that they would flow more easily than peace-offerings generally do. I accepted the apology, and then we strolled for a mile down through the sunlit woods, with the swift, dark river on one side and the brawny hill on the other, and recrossed to the village by a lower, more solid and extraordinarily picturesque bridge, swung from cliff to cliff above the gorge of the Androscoggin.

> Beautiful river,
> With sunlight a-quiver,
> Rippling and dimpling and sparkling forever!
> Where the cool forests meet,
> Kissing the mountain's feet,
> Then through the valley sweet
> Hastening with footsteps fleet —
> Loitering never!

And Prue, having paid me off, was now all serenity.

We had availed ourselves of only one, and the handiest out of many remunerative excursions in the vicinity of Gorham, where a few minutes' walk only is needed in almost any direction to open pictures to the eye hardly to be surpassed. The loftiest height in New England, for example (counting from where you stand to its summit), is the aspect of Mt. Adams presented from the river-road, about a mile and a half above Gorham; and at the bend of the river, a mile above, is the best view attainable of Moriah, The Imp and Carter.

As for the celebrated drive down the river to the Lead-mine bridge, past Granny Starbird's ledge, it has been called the best in New Hampshire for an artistic mingling of river, meadow and mountain; but a party who drove that Sunday morning to Randolph hill and back, said *nothing* could equal the views they had, so I hesitate to decide.

Nearly all the mountains within sight have paths to their summits, in regard to which a guide-book should be consulted. The Carter range presents the greatest difficulties. Mt. Surprise, one of the lower peaks of Moriah, was a favorite point of pilgrimage with Starr King, and Mt. Hayes, another; indeed, he seems to have been more fond of this eastern side of the mountains than of the other, and is said to have written the greater part of his immortal book at Gorham.

CHAPTER XVI.

THE GLEN.

In lowly dale, fast by a river's side,
With woody hill o'er hill encompassed round.— THOMSON.

"HERE *is* the Glen House?" asked Prue, when we had fixed on a time for going thither.

"In the Glen."

"Ah! So *good* of you! Where is the *Glen*?"

"Between the northern part of the Presidential range and the Carter mountains. If you will look at your map you will find a narrow valley extending north and south and drained by the Peabody river. That is the Peabody glen, or simply The Glen; and the hotel, which is half way up its length, is named after it. At the head of the river the valley narrows into a mere defile, called, in New Hampshire phrase, the Pinkham notch, on the other side of which the Ellis river flows southward through Jackson to the Saco."

"Is it pretty?"

"In my humble opinion it is the best of all the narrow valleys, for while it does not equal in depth and precipitousness the Crawford notch, which is usually thought the climax of White Mountain scenery, and which we are saving to the last on this trip, there is a wider and more varied outlook, more grandeur in the mountains exposed from the higher points of the road, and more picturesqueness of that richer sort which requires some *human* item in its attractions to warm our sympathies as well as to excite a purely mental admiration. Don't you agree with me, Baily?"

"Yes, quite. And I think we shall conclude, after we have seen the whole region, that this eastern side of the mountains is more interesting and delightful as a whole, than its western."

The road from Gorham to the Glen quickly leaves the old highway to Shelburne and Lancaster and plunges into the woods, but is a smooth excellent track all the same. "The ascent is gradual, with no long hills, and the road winds, for the greater part of the way, along the easterly bank of the Peabody river, which, always within hearing, is frequently within sight. Soon after leaving Gorham the burly form of Madison bursts upon the view, apparently barring all further progress, while the Moriah range towers up on the left. The changing mountain-forms furnish a continual study. Washington and Adams come into view before reaching the Glen, and the carriage road is visible from the point where it emerges from the woods almost to the very summit." About two-thirds of the way we halt and make a detour across the river to a point on the road to Jefferson, near a farmhouse nestled against the foot of Madison, whence a view of The

NEAR THE GLEN HOUSE. (PEABODY RIVER).

Imp is obtained, a colossal profile upon a crag of the mountain, directly opposite, to which the face gives its name.

The Glen House is 1,632 feet above the sea and 820 feet above Gorham. The dry, pure, and fragrant air of this locality affords relief and exemption from the annoyances of rose-cold or hay-fever, many of whose victims escape its attacks by sojourning here. The handsome new building occupies a grassy knoll at the foot of Mount

Carter, overlooking the Peabody valley and fronting an amphitheatre formed of the five highest mountains in New England, — Washington, Clay, Jefferson, Adams, and Madison. They are only three or four miles distant, and no hills intervene to cut off the view of their whole vast bulk and altitude. Each is distinct from its neighbors; and all the great gulfs that separate them from one another, and each of the massive buttresses by which the peaks are supported, are in plain view. It is the only point, right at the foot of the mountains, where their unobstructed height and breadth can be gauged; and if in this nearness we lose that tender and idealized beauty which a longer focus gives, we gain an impression of solidity, bulk and majesty.

Moreover, on this side, their lines both of structure and sculpture, are far more strong and noble than on the other, so that, even though we may be quite as near the foot in the upper part of the Amonoosuc valley, the impression of grandeur is far less there. On that (the western) side, the mountain slopes join into a much smoother and more continuous wall-like slope, while here the peaks are separated by profound indentations or "gulfs," between whose "lean and wrinkled precipices" deep shadows lurk while the peaks may be lit up by sunlight, or become marble white under snow. "Mount Madison (5,365 feet) is on the right, left of which is the sharp and symmetrical pyramid of Mount Adams (5,794 feet), then the massive crest of Jefferson (5,714 feet), the low humps of Clay (5,553 feet), and the hotel-crowned peak of Washington (6,293 feet), is on the left, peering over lofty spurs and secondary peaks. The high crags of the Lion's Head are seen on the left, near the opening of Tuckerman's ravine. The deep gorge of the Great Gulf opens into the range towards Mounts Adams and Jefferson, containing the dense forests of the West Branch. This noble view is presented from the piazzas and front rooms of the hotel. On the east, is the high and massive Carter range, which is rarely visited, on account of its tangled thickets; and more to the south are the slopes of Carter Dome and Wild Cat. Below the hotel, on the west, is the pleasant valley of the Peabody river; and above, on the west, is a far-viewing clearing, in one corner of which is a reservoir." (*Sweetzer*).

The Glen House is a headquarters for excursions; Mr. Milliken's stages and mountain wagons are incessantly going and coming; and his claim that his horses and equipments are the best on the Atlantic side of the continent, can no doubt be sustained. Considering the numbers and wealth of the crowds which from May to October patronize them, they ought to be.

Every pleasant morning the spacious piazzas present a scene of active preparation for some outing. "Anglers, with rod and basket betake themselves to the neighboring trout-brooks, artists to the woods or open. Mountain wagons clatter up to the door with an exhilarating spirit and dash. Amid much laughter and cracking of jokes, these strong yet slight-looking vehicles are speedily filled with parties for the summit, the Crystal cascade or Glen Ellis; knots of pedestrians, picturesquely dressed, move off with elastic tread for some long meditated climb among the hills or in the ravines; while the regular stages for Gorham or Glen Station depart amid hurried and hearty leave-takings, the flutter of handkerchiefs and the sharp crack of the driver's whip."

One line of stages runs to Gorham, another makes two trips a day through Jackson (twelve miles) to Glen Station (fifteen and one half miles) on the Portland and Ogdensburg Railroad, connecting with trains to and from Boston and Worcester; and a third leaves morning and afternoon for the top of Mount Washington (eight miles), connecting there with the trains of the Mount Washington Railway down to Fabyan's. In addition, two regular trips in mountain-wagons are made every day to Glen Ellis and the Crystal cascade. Besides this there are various walks to places of interest; to trouting reaches in the gay Peabody river and its tributary brooks; to the Garnet pools,— basins dug by whirling stones in the bed of the river, a mile distant; to Osgood's cascades, one and one fourth miles; and to Thompson's falls and the Emerald pool (the subject of Bierstadt's famous painting), some two and one half miles southward, where an exceedingly good view of Mount Washington and the ravines on its eastern flank can be had. And always and everywhere you can turn your eye from river and lakelet, green meadow or gay woodland, theatrically grouped masses of moss-garnished rocks and smart birches, fragrant brier-thickets, or soldierly firs, to the blanched summits that in sunshine smile so benignly upon the secluded glen, but in storm threaten so terrifically.

The summits of all the surrounding mountains are attainable. Washington has its carriage road along which its conquest is reduced to a commonplace uphill walk. To Madison, a straight path about four and one half miles long, has been cut from the Glen House, by which the summits of Adams and Washington may be reached in five or six hours. About the same time is required for the ascent by the path through Tuckerman's ravine. Carter Dome (4,380 feet), is accessible by a "well-marked, but very steep" path one and one half miles from its beginning in the Carter notch,— that remarkable depression which shows so distinctly from Mount Abram (near Bethel), and from Kiarsarge. Gibson has made a capital picture of it for Drake's *Heart of the White Mountains*, where a thrilling chapter is devoted to a walk through that region. T. W. Higginson in the volume of *Putnam's Magazine* for 1853, gave another graphic account of that district, which is one of the most extraordinary in the state for ruin of rocks, savage forest wildness and a sense of remoteness. Beside the Dome the second Carter peak (almost as high) and Wildcat have paths, and each summit gives very striking views of the Presidential range and a wide horizon elsewhere; but the labor and risk of any excursion on this rough range are very great, and few persons attempt it. The Carter notch, however, is more easily accessible by paths from either the Glen House or Jackson.

Baily and I seriously discussed leaving Madame Prue at the Glen House, where there was a gay crowd of tourists, some staying for weeks, others coming and going, and making some of these longer and rougher tramps, but relinquished the idea, and decided simply to see Glen Ellis and the Crystal Cascade, which we could do all together, and then push on over the summit of Washington.

"This is only a reconnoissance anyhow," I told them, with a sigh of resignation, "and we cannot expect to do more than learn the way. Next year we will settle down at points like this, until we have made thorough explorations of the surrounding country."

"That's just what we *will* do," Baily replied in strong approval. "I mean to come up here early, next summer, and conquer these out-of-the-way cliffs and gorges, if it takes till Christmas."

"How about all your other plans?" I ask.

"They'll have to wait," is his stout reply.

"Even the fishing at Rangeley, when Miss Blank is there?" Prue enquires carelessly.

GLEN ELLIS FALLS.

"Well — I might run up there — it's no great distance, long enough for *that*, you know."

Early in the afternoon a little party of us climbed into one of the big wagons and set off for the cascades,— a trip that is one of perfect entertainment. Whirled along at a rapid trot over a smooth road, the scenery presents some new delight at every stage of advance. For half a mile after leaving the hotel you keep in sight those magnificent lines of Washington's southern crest which are so admirable from the piazza. The changing aspects of the crags of the Lion's Head, and the loftier ridges behind them become very striking as we attain the gentle eminence whence branches of the Peabody and the Ellis diverge in opposite directions from a single pool, and where we begin to descend to the southward. There would be food enough for the eye, even without these crags, in watching the struggles of the little river among its vexing boulders; in noticing the confidential way in which tiny brooks come noisily out of their thicket-shelters, dart across the sunny road and disappear into the wood; or in the lovely contrasts of color which this mixed foliage presents, now that autumn has begun to dye the more tender leaves. At the end of the third mile we come to a somewhat larger stream, swift and clear, where there is a house and country store; and here we get down and follow a path about half a mile into the woods on our right, ascending the stream close to its rocky bed, where at this dry season a dozen rivulets are finding each its own way down among ledges and loose rocks, always on the jump and singing merrily. After a time we come to a shaky bridge laid across the stream upon two long tree trunks, and then climb a steep bit of rocks and spruce-roots to the top of a miniature cliff, and there — right opposite, but coming from one side, at a sharp turn in the course of the creek,— is the Crystal cascade.

Of its kind it is unequalled. Imagine a very steep stairway of rocks perhaps eighty feet high, at the head of an alcove in the forest, the sides of which are tapestried with moss and vines, ferns, and every manner of clinging green thing, the bottom filled with a pure pool, and the whole over-arched with out-bending limbs of trees that seem proud of their charge; and that down this precipitous stairway of natural ledges slides a sheet of diamond-clear water, sporting, pratling and spinning, to splash and glide into the bright pool. I can recall no waterfall in all my travels that is like it, nor can I think of any, great or small, so satisfying in its secluded loveliness. You are not compelled to admiration, nor wonder, nor terror; you simply accept its perfect beauty as what your soul has long been waiting for, and feel that you would never grow weary of it, nor cease to enjoy its music and its lacelike cataracts, any more than a lover expects to to grow tired of the face and voice of his mistress. I have never felt this way elsewhere toward a waterfall but once, and that is on an obscure tributary of the Russian river in California; and now I think that of the two, I like this better.

On this same stream half a mile farther down, reached by another path through the woods at the left of the road, is the Glen Ellis fall, which we next visited, and which is of a quite different order of beauty. Its surroundings are wilder, and you can catch glimpses of the heads and horns of beetling crags, and of slopes of black forest reaching upward thousands of feet. The river, instead of a scattered brook, is now a torrent, plowing its way through closely set rocks and confined in a dark gorge. "Descending by slippery stairs to the pool beneath it, I saw, [it is Samuel Drake who is speaking,] eighty feet above me, the whole stream force its way through a narrow cleft, and stand in one unbroken column, superbly erect, upon the level surface of the pool. The sheet was as white as marble, the pool as green as malachite. As if stunned by the fall, it turns slowly round; then, recovering, precipitates itself down the rocky gorge with greater passion than ever. On its upper edge the curling sheet of the fall was shot with sunlight, and shone with enchanting brilliancy. All below was one white feathery mass, gliding down with the swift and noiseless movement of an avalanche of fresh snow."

This Ellis river comes out of Tuckerman's ravine, an enormous gorge scooped out of the southeastern side of Mount Washington, whose southern wall is formed by the great curving buttress called Boot's spur. The Crystal and Ellis falls are only two out of many less notable cataracts upon its course, which is a headlong rush downward from the "snow-arch" and a circle of snow-banks preserved until late in the season under the shadow of the mighty walls at the head of the ravine.

"Tuckerman's ravine," says Ticknor's *Guide*, "is divided into two sections, the broad vestibule in which are the cascades and Hermit lake, and the inner and higher chasm of the ravine itself. It is the most remarkable piece of scenery of this character in all New England, for though it is neither so deep nor so long as King's ravine, it surpasses it in the steepness and sweep of its cliffs, and in its close relation to the supreme summit. It is, moreover, much easier to traverse, being free from dangerous crevasses, and requiring only a powerful exertion of the thews and sinews. Ladies have frequently traversed the ravine, and encamped in its depths. In view of the possibility of accidents it is not prudent for people to make this excursion alone. . . . The best way into the ravine, for those who wish to see all its glories, is by the Appalachian path, which leaves the Jackson road three miles south of the Glen House, and runs in to the Crystal cascade. . . . It is a hard hour's climb from the snow to the Summit House, the upward route being marked by splashes of white paint on the rocks. The path is kept in repair by the Appalachian Mountain Club, and is a very pleasant forest trail." It is hardly advisable, however, for any but the most vigorous to go on to the summit through Tuckerman's. Better content yourself with the climb to the thick bank of drifted snow, through which the stream cuts a subnivean channel in the spring, leaving an overarching span of ice which lasts until August, and then return to the Glen House by the alternate path.

When we could permit ourselves to stay no longer at the Glen House, we took places in the next morning's stage to the Summit House, and then devoted the afternoon to a drive to Jackson.

The first three miles were over roads with which we were already familiar; beyond the Glen Ellis path-entrance, we trod new ground.

The forest here skirts the road on both sides, and Prue was continually going into ecstacies over some flaming maple, or a birch, dangling golden coins from silver branchlets, intermingled with the shapely spires of evergreens. Out of this universal forest — the great Pinkham woodland from which this defile or "notch" was named — crags and smooth faces of rock would jut in dull blue or black masses, sometimes closely overhead, for we were now in the narrowest part of the pass where the foot of Carter Dome was braced squarely against Washington's extended foot.

"A foot clad in Boots," interjects the punning Baily, referring to the great spur which nearly blockades the valley.

But the woods give us many chances to look out; and at the cottage, halfway (where we stopped to water our horse, and a pretty little girl came out with a tray of apples, pop-corn in tiny bark baskets, and cakes of home-made maple sugar to sell), you look back and get some new and most impressive views of the Presidential summits. This autumn air was wonderfully clear, and the houses upon the summit of Washington were distinctly visible. I think this one of the best views open to the tourist who keeps to the roads, of the Presidential range, and of Washington in particular. The mountains seen from this point are crowded together and appear in profile, where their steepest slopes can take effect. The summits stand high and bold above the trees — higher and bolder than from the Glen House, — recalling to me very vividly the appearance of the Sierra Mojada, in southern Colorado, as you look northward from Walsenburg or Cucharas. The gashes made by trickling water on this well-scarred side — every copse-feathered chasm and cleft — were especially emphatic and sightly, and every jutting crag distinct. But the time of day was right, and the season favorable. Indeed, Starr King thought October the best season for the Glen, since by the middle of that month the summits are often entirely covered with whiteness, as they had not been yet for us, save on that single morning which showed the glorious picture from Lake Umbagog.

A succession of points occured, as we proceeded, where this magnificent picture could be studied behind us at various angles and with differently grand effects; and the traveller who enters the Pinkham notch from the south on a fine day must be filled with enthusiasm, if he has the least capacity for enjoyment of mountain scenery,— and I pity him who has not!

The road down from the Pinkham notch to Jackson, runs along a broadening and always interesting valley, with superb sierras on either hand — heights identified with some of the very earliest tales of exploration. The village itself lies in a lovely nook between the foot-hills of Iron and Tin mountains, with the ragged crests of Mounts Crawford, Resolution, the Giant's Stair, and others in the west, the cone of Kiarsarge in the south, and a crown of lofty peaks northward. All the great heights are far away, however, and the foot-hills near by are mostly cleared, yet dotted with copses and lines of trees that lend a somewhat cultivated appearance to the surroundings, pleasantly relieving the solid woodland that elsewhere overspreads the hills with an unbroken pall. Here are broad meadows, many farms, and a neat little hamlet of hotels of handsome modern architecture and every appearance of comfort, among which, quaint old farmhouses and an elm-shaded meeting-house do not seem out of harmony.

"There is room to breathe here," Prue declared, "and you can see the mountains without being right against them, or half alarmed lest they should slide down upon you some night."

I wonder how she will feel at the Profile House!

CHAPTER XVII.

MOUNT WASHINGTON.

> There, as thou standest,
> The haunts of men below thee, and around
> The mountain summits, thy expanding heart
> Shall feel a kindred with that loftier world
> To which thou art translated, and partake
> The enlargement of thy vision.—BRYANT.

WITH a lurch of the wagon, a rush of four eager horses, and a chorus of "good-byes," we were off for the drive over the carriage-road from the Glen House to the summit of Mount Washington.

With the sunrise a few wreaths of mist, woven among the tree-tops, had risen slowly half-way up the naked shoulders of the range, only to be shorn of their wings and disappear, like the Icarian birds that typified them in the classic fable; and ragged fragments of clouds, hiding from both wind and sunshine, still lurked about the heads of the ravines; but the summits themselves, all five of them, towered sharp and clear into a marvellously blue sky, and had a coppery glow under the fierce sunlight which was reflected from a thousand million mica-points and polished edges in their broken rocks. It is a needless exaggeration to speak of these mountains *glittering* or *sparkling*, as thoughtless writers frequently do. Brilliant color is often present, nevertheless, and makes one of the chief charms of the landscape, especially at dawn and sunset. "More than once," Mr. Oakes remarks, "late in autumn, after the sun had set, and the mountains were becoming dark below. I have seen the whole snowy pyramid of Mt. Washington glowing like a furnace with a bright and intense rose color, fiery and brilliant, but still soft and most beautiful." How glorious are these manifestations of color in the tall, icy and varied peaks of the Rockies, I myself, have heretofore tried to tell in my *Crest of the Continent*.

There was not much to see until we had driven up beyond the line of forests, from which we emerged suddenly, only a few scraggy spruces accompanying us out beyond the crowd of big trees. In the midst of the forest, our road was entered by a new road, lately opened, and connecting by a short cut with the Pinkham Notch road, which effects a long saving both in distance and climbing to travellers from the southward. Wagons are sent to the summit daily on this new cut-off from both Jackson and North Conway, besides private driving parties. We passed many pedestrians, also, going up or coming down.

This carriage-road was begun in 1855, but not finished till 1861. It takes an average grade of only twelve feet in one hundred, and hence winds about a good deal, so that it is twice as long as the old bridle-path whose general direction it follows. The road is well constructed, and whenever the ground falls away steeply beside it, walls have been built, so that it is wholly safe to drive or walk upon, even in foggy weather. A gang of workmen, who live at the half-way house, near the edge of the timber, keep the road in repair, storing up earth and rock-dust for this purpose along the upper part with great care, since anything like soil on the top of the range is about as rare as figs from thistles. The stage-fare from the Glen House is $5 to ascend, or to go up and back, and $3 for the descent alone; but railway excursion tickets include this route. All persons except stage passengers, are required to pay tolls, whether driving or walking. Early in October, when the Summit House closes, the stages are withdrawn, all the bridges (mere culverts over drainage channels) are taken up and stored away, and the road is closed, so far as the responsibility of the company is concerned. This road is visible as a sinuous light line from many of the mountain tops whence Washington is viewed; and it overlooks, in return, a vast area of country in the direction of the Androscoggin, so that to omit it from one's itinerary would be to leave out one of the best prospects open to the tourist; and the *very* best in its reward, compared with labor involved.

Timber-line, on this flank of Mt. Washington, is about 4,000 feet above the sea, and 2,500 above the Glen House, nearly five miles, by the road, distant. It is marked on this range, by "the spectral forest," as King calls it,—a skirmish-line of gnarled and stunted trees, now dead and bleached to the hardness and appearance of antlers. Sweetzer states that this alpine forest-edge was probably killed during the cold season of 1812-16, "through the latter of which years the trees were frozen all the time, 1816 being known as 'the year without a summer.'"

In escaping the forest upon the carriage-road we make a long detour northward, around a subsidiary summit, the end of which (at the fourth milestone) brings us out upon the Ledge (3,900 feet) at the brink of that vast excavation separating Washington from Jefferson, Adams and Madison, called the Great Gulf, (or, at its head, where the railway touches it, the Gulf of Mexico), which at this narrowest point shows all its 2,000 feet of shuddering depth. This chasm balances Tuckerman's on the south side of the spur we are ascending, but is more capacious; whether it is equally interesting is another question. Mr. King thought that looking upward from the bottom (as comparatively few people have done) Tuckerman's was superior, but that seen from the top the Gulf seemed more terrible; and he calls this sight from the Ledge "one of the grandest spectacles which the summit of Mt. Washington affords." Its shadowy trough is carpeted with a dark moquette difficult to realize as a full-grown forest, and the further walls, gashed and broken, soar upward to the ashy dome of Jefferson, behind which stand the spire of Adams and Madison's angular combing. "All around was unutterable desolation. Crevassed with wide splits, encompassed round by lofty mountain walls, the gorge was at once fascinating and forbidding, grand yet terrible. The high, encircling steeps of Clay, Jefferson, Adams and Madison, enclosing it with one mighty sweep, ascended out of its depths and stretched along the sky, which seemed receding before their daring advance. Peering down into the abyss, where the tallest pines were shrubs and their trunks needles, the earth seemed split to its centre, and the feet of these mountains rooted in the midst. To confront such a spectacle unmoved, one should be more, or less, than human."

The view from here is of the Androscoggin and Peabody valleys, in which the Glen House is a mere speck. Gorham is just out of sight behind Pine mountain, which shows beyond and below Madison. Moriah and Carter mountains stop the outlook in their direction, but within this quadrant vision reaches far over the wrinkled tops of Mts. Hayes and Baldcap to the peaks clustered at the Grafton notch.

For some distance the road lies upon the edge of the Great Gulf, then turns sharply to the left and works its way, always upward, across toward the head of Huntington's ravine,—a side cañon from Tuckerman's, and one well worth a visit. The slopes that fall away from the road are here very precipitous, and the sense of height and isolation impresses itself strongly on the beholder. The Carter range is now upon the left,—huge forested knolls and ridges. "A sharp turn around a ledge," writes Mr. Drake, in an account of a walk up this road in May, "and the southeast wall of Tuckerman's ravine rose up, like a wraith, out of the forest. Near at hand was the head of Huntington's, while to the right the cone of Washington loomed grandly more than a thousand feet higher. A little to the left you look down into the gloomy depths of the Pinkham defile, the valley of Ellis river, the Saco valley and North Conway where the familiar figure of Kiarsage is the presiding genius. The blue course of the Ellis, which is nothing but a long cascade, the rich green of the Conway intervales, the blanched peak of Chocorua, the sapphire summits of the Ossipee mountains, were presented in conjunction with the black and humid walls of the ravine, and the iron-gray mass of the great dome. The crag on which I stood leans out over the mountain like a bastion, from which the spectator sees the deeply intrenched valleys, the rivers which wash the feet of the monarch, and the long line of summits which partake his grandeur, while making it more impressive."

Huntington's ravine, to which allusion is made, is a branch of Tuckerman's, near its head, which Prof. J. H. Huntington supposed he had discovered, and which, in 1871, was named after him by a party of "explorers." It was well known long before either of these "discoveries," however, by one, at least, of the Pinkham Notch farmers,—a man named Doloph,—who conducted Prof. Oscar D. Allen, now in the faculty of Yale University, into its almost impenetrable depths and through its whole length.

As the road swings to the right from the head of this ravine, and points more directly up the mountain, splendid landscapes unroll, changing and growing more amazing at every step. Presently, we attain such a height that we can look off eastward to blue heights around Lancaster, seen between the great northern peaks, whose full, fierce majesty is now revealed. All the rents and gashes which frost has hewn and the waters have worn in their ancient forms, can be counted by the eye and explored upon wings of fancy. "The rocks themselves, tormented, formidable, impending, astound by their vivid portrayal of the formless, their suggestions of the agony in which these mountains were brought forth." The seventh mile-post is near the knob where Mr. Chandler died during a storm in August, 1856, and here the view over Mt. Clay, from which the Great Gulf sinks profoundly, reaches the hills of northern Vermont; Lancaster village, embosomed in fine mountains, is framed between Clay and Jefferson; the Pilot range and neighboring peaks are glimpsed in the gaps between Jefferson and Adams, and between Adams and Madison; and to the right of Madison the whole Androscoggin region toward Umbagog is spread before you, whence you swing around past the Grafton peaks to the nearer Moriah, Imp, Carter and Wildcat, and then to Washington's own flanks and the contiguous table-lands of Mt. Pleasant and Boot's spur.

The ride had not seemed nearly as long as the mile-stones measured it, because so exciting; but a chilly breeze was blowing about this "windy cone," and we were all very cold, in spite of the clear sunshine. It was with much satisfaction, therefore, that we came to the stables and station of the stage company, just below the summit, stiffly crawled out of our seats, and, hastening up some flights of wooden steps, presently stood upon the tiptop and very pinnacle of New England.

Fully impressed with this great fact, we yet turned to one another and voiced our common, albeit prosaic, thought — Dinner! The scenery could wait; our mortal frames were another matter.

The top of Mt. Washington, in common with all the rest of the Presidential range, and some other mountains, consists of a micaceous gneiss. This is a greenish-gray, somewhat stratified rock, knit together by innumerable little plates, rosettes and spicules of mica, so that it is exceeding tough and durable. The thin layers, however, let the moisture penetrate it, and the incessant freezing and thawing incident to the weather of this pinnacle, reared out of the temperate zone into an arctic climate, pry the rock to pieces and topple the fragments down. Thus the solid rock-mass forming that rounded summit, which ages ago must have held its peaked head many hundreds of feet higher in the air than now, began at once to crumble at its edges and start that rain of falling blocks which never has ceased, nor ever will, as long as cold and heat ply their elfin tools.

Our pedestal is, therefore, an irregular and ragged heap, like a dump of building-stone thrown down here ready for the Titans to erect their palace, when Olympus should have capitulated; and that must have been long ago, to judge by the weather-stains and lichen-growths on the rocks. These pieces are in size from a band-box to a log-cabin, of all the sharp-edged and slippery shapes imaginable, and set in every position save one comfortable to stand or sit upon. I can think of but one thing in rocks worse to travel over, and that is such a steep slide of small stones, caving under your tread at every step, as Prue and I have more than once toiled for hours upon, in the Rockies.

Of course no vegetation, except the cryptogamous stuff which pastes itself flat down upon the rock, can exist in such a place, while lower down only a scanty herbage finds foothold; and it is to these utterly naked stones, to whose paleness the reflecting particles of mica may lend some additional pallor, that the White Hills are supposed to owe their name. They certainly have a blanched, diluted quality (even when seen so far away as to be dimly blue) which belongs to no other Appalachian range, while close at hand, especially as seen from Fabyan's, they become coldly, mistily gray in tone, under the noonday light, even in the clearest weather.

It was out upon these rocks, with wraps belted tightly about us and hats tied to our heads (for here the winds blow up and the winds blow down without stint or intermission), we carefully adjusted ourselves to see what we should see.

"It strikes me you gentlemen are taking this thing coolly," Prue remarks, referring to lack of emotion rather than bodily temperature.

"Why shouldn't we? Have we endured the trouble of climbing this huge pile to waste ourselves in *Ohs!* and *Ahs!*" I retort. "It is more respectful to this majestic privilege that we take it calmly, as befits those who feel their obligations. The presence of such space and glory as this ought to suppress frivolity. If you had a little of the fear and reverence the simple-hearted natives felt for this noble peak and its invisible divinities, it would do you good."

Prue listens with intent face and anxious eyes, as though she felt my rebuke; but she is an incorrigible fraud, for when I stop, instead of expressing contrition, she asks:—

"Have you a match? Mr. Baily's cigar seems to have gone out."

It hasn't, but he is busy with a map, which he has loaded down with stones at the four corners to keep it from blowing away.

"Gad! this is immense!" he exclaims, looking up from his map.

"If I had a pair of compasses that would stretch a hundred miles or so, I could stick one point among these rocks, and see where to plant the other away beyond Moosehead. Then I could swing it round through the ocean and Massachusetts to the Green mountains, and sweep on through Quebec until I had completed the circle back across the Maine woods."

"Do you mean to say that you could guide with your eye the further point of your compasses, in inscribing such a gigantic circle as that?" Prue queries.

"Touching the highest points along the circumference,— yes."

"Why, that embraces the whole extent of our tour in the east, and as much more toward the west!"

"Yes,— nearly as large an area as the whole of Great Britain."

"Baily is not far wrong. Hear how Eastman sums up the spaciousness of what we are gazing upon, more in amazement, so far as *I* am concerned, at least, than with intelligence, as yet." And I read the following paragraphs:—

"What a stupendous view! A horizon of nearly six hundred miles bounds the prospect! The mountain peaks stand on every side as sentinels over the furrowed valleys of New England.

"If the day is clear, one can see Monadnock loom, as a pale blue film, a hundred miles off on the south-west. Far in the east, Katahdin is driven like a wedge into the sky. Westward, the eye roams almost to the Catskills; northward, into Canada, far beyond the sources of the Connecticut; southward, to the mouth of the Saco. In a clear morning or evening, if there is a silvery gleam on the south-eastern horizon, it tells that the sun is shining on the sea off Portland. Nearer to us on the west, towers the gloomy ridge of Franconia, subsiding towards the Merrimac. That flash now and then through the opaline southern air is from Winnipesaukee, the most exquisite jewel in the necklace of New England. On the near north the twin-domed Stratford mountains tower. Their barren pallor, seen through the uncertain air, counterfeits snow. The cloven Pinkham pass lies directly beneath us, bending around to lovely North Conway. Over this last village we observe the drooping shoulders of Kiarsage, whose northern sides flow from the summit as softly as full folds of drapery fall from a ring. Mt. Crawford attracts attention by his singular knoblike crest; and near him, all the winding Bartlett hills stand up, guarding the shy beauty of the intervales. The long and solid Pleasant mountain draws the eye, set so squarely near the still silver of Lovewell's pond. And farther south the dim, level, leopard-spotted land stretches wide to the horizon haze."

But in the very breadth of the landscape was its defect, as a picture. We were looking *down* upon everything, and this forshortened and flattened each feature. Only the most distant peaks, eighty or one hundred miles away, cut the sky, and thus showed to better advantage than did those in the middle distance. The line of the Green mountains was quite plain, enabling us to count the separate peaks, and see Mansfield and one or two others on Lake Champlain looming behind them. Mr. Eastman puts Katahdin as a visible point in the east. I wish it were so; but the best opinion decides that the turquoise mark set so firmly upon Maine's outermost horizon, as though it were the very last thing in the world, is not that lone sentinel of the east, but Ebeeme mountain, near Millinoket pond, 135 miles distant in an air-line. Whether Mt. Desert, or even Megunticook, is visible is a question.

In the south and west a few sharp and well-marked peaks, like "steel-hooded" Chocorua, and massive Carrigan and Moosilauke, stand boldly out; but in general, the eye is bewildered there by a great wilderness of land-swells, dull indigo or dark olive near at hand, and paling into blue beyond, which after a short time grows oppressive to the sight. We want something more tangible and mobile, and we find it northward, looking over the shoulders of Clay and Jefferson, where roads, villages, rivers, and some human interest occurs. It is terribly lonesome, still, and remote up here. We are glad to get a glimpse of active life down on the earth. Therefore we like to trace rivers,—they are going somewhere,—doing something. "The line of the Connecticut we can follow from its birth near Canada, to the point where it is hidden by the great Franconia wall. Its water is not visible, but often, in the morning, a line of fog lies for miles over the lower lands, counterfeiting the serpentine path of its blue water that bounds two states. Two large curves of the Androscoggin we can see. Broken portions of the Saco lie like lumps of light upon the open valley to the west of Pequawket. The sources of the Merrimac are on the farther slope of a mountain that seems to be not more than the distance of a rifle-shot. Directly under our feet lies the cold Lake of the Clouds, whose water plunges down the wild path of the Amonoosuc."

"How did people come up here before the carriage-road and railway were built,—I mean what were the paths?" is an enquiry by our lady.

"There was a path from the Glen along the general course of the carriage-road, but much shorter, and, of course, steeper," Baily volunteers in reply; "and another from Fabyan's came up the general line now followed by the railway. The steep place where it zigzagged up the spur was called Jacob's Ladder long before any rails were laid there. So much of this path as leads to the summit of Mt. Pleasant, at least. is still preserved."

"Some other routes," I continue, "have been almost or quite lost sight of. The earliest ascents seem to have been made from the Ellis valley. Probably Darby Field came up that way,—he who, in 1642. was the first to reach the peak, in company with two coast Indians,—for the local redskins were too much in terror of the fierce gods reasonably supposed to be enthroned upon these storm-panoplied heights to accompany him. The Gorges party, a few weeks later, certainly ascended through Tuckerman's ravine. But a century and a half elapsed before any real exploration of the range was made, the Indian or other wars making these woods and waters by no means comfortable to pre-revolutionary sojourners. Traditions of diamonds in masses, carbuncles as big as your hat, with silver and gold galore, still kept substance enough to make the mountains alluring, however; and as soon as the Revolution had been accomplished, an expedition was organized by Cutler and Belknap, which reached the summit in July of 1784, by the way of Tuckerman's ravine. They stayed all night,— probably the first experience of that sort. Their quaintly written record still exists in manuscript in the archives of the Massachusetts Historical Society, and it is said, contains the first use of the name *Mt. Washington.*

"After that, I suppose, climbers were common."

"Yes. The Jackson people had paths which came up over the New River cliffs and along the eastern side of Monroe and over Boot's spur. Another ancient route for ascent in this direction was by following up the half-dry ravine of the Mt. Washington river into Oakes' gulf, where it arises, and where legend located a ledge of diamonds. Nobody found the gems, but everybody could catch lots of trout there, and can yet. The 'pastures' on the slope of Monroe along the rim of Oakes' gulf, have always been favorite picking-places for alpine botanists, after one of the earliest of whom (in the United States) the gorge is named. Forty years ago, a proprietor of the Mt. Crawford House constructed a route from his hotel, at the foot of Mt. Crawford, up the Giant's Stairs and then seven miles northward through dense woods upon the Montalban ridge to Boot's spur, and thence pretty straightly up the great cone; but it never became popular, and has almost disappeared. He built it after great discouragement, and Mt. Resolution takes its name in commemoration of his persistence.

"Meanwhile, the farmers who had settled north of the range in the Connecticut and Androscoggin valleys, had marked out routes of ascent over the western flanks of the mountains on their side, not only to Washington, but to the summits of Adams, Jefferson and Madison; and there was even a wagon-route, used in carrying up the lumber for the old buildings. Latterly, several good paths have been blazed by guides to the northern summits, and along their crests to Mt. Washington. This is said to form one of the grandest excursions in all New Hampshire, but it is very arduous, ought not to be attempted without efficient guides, and cannot be done without camping out one or two nights."

"Let's do it next year!" cries the sanguine Baily. "We'll buy some simple camping equipments and take a whole week to it."

"All right. I agree to that. And if we can get two or three donkeys or small mules to 'pack' our luggage, as we used to do in Wyoming, we can have a grand time."

"Then I should think *I* might go," says Prue.

"So you might,— it would be something for a lady to boast of."

"But I haven't spoken yet of the Crawford path, which is the best-known and most often used of any, nowadays. This is about eight miles long, and passes over the four great summits southward, and then down the flank of Mt. Clinton to the Crawford notch. It is called a 'bridle-path,' but a hundred persons walk over it every season for one that rides, and it is more commonly walked *down* than *up*, tourists coming to the summit by rail and then descending in two or three hours of moderate travel. This path is plainly marked and in good condition everywhere above the timber, but within the Mt. Clinton forests is likely to be muddy and rough, since it has been little attended to of late years. Henry Ward Beecher and many other eloquent writers have discoursed of their experiences and delight along this route. One of the most thrilling mountain stories in point, is Drake's account of his wrestle for life with a snow storm on the summits of Franklin and Monroe,— just such a storm as has been the death of those poor fellows whose lives have gone out on the awful summit of this merciless peak. When we go home we must look these stories up and re-read them. They will be ten times as real to us as before."

A few white clouds had been forming in the sky, and dappling the hills with their moving shadows,— one of the strangest spectacles to the person who stands upon a lofty height for the first time; and a feature of the scene in which an old mountaineer never loses his interest and joy. "People in cities," Starr King declares, "who never see the extent and outline of a cloud-shadow, can have no idea of the beauty of a range of hills upon which the lights and shades 'march and countermarch in glorious apparition.' But this is nothing to the excitement, we may almost say the intoxication, of seeing from a mountain-top a huge cloud, miles in breadth, spanning a valley, shedding twilight upon half a dozen villages at once, sweeping along, chased by a broader flood of splendor, to darken for a moment the whole ridge on whose crown you stand, and still flying on before the west wind, to pour its fleet gloom over range after range, till it pauses in the warmer and peaceful spaces near the eastern horizon."

Our eyes had been feasting upon these spectral caprices while we talked, and now and then we had shivered as one of these ethereal mantles had been cast over our own station, intercepting the warmth of the sun. Bryant (whose poetry is not so interesting to the *real* student of Nature as to the recluse who loves to *think* he loves it) must nevertheless have been sometime on a mountain-top, or he never could have drawn the picture in these lines of which we are now reminded:—

> The clouds are at play in the azure space,
> And their shadows at play on the bright green vale,
> And here they stretch to the frolic chase,
> And there they roll on the easy gale.

Suddenly the whole landscape faded out of sight, like a dissolving view, and we found ourselves shrouded in a mass of cold and whirling vapor, which enveloped us in an icy clasp, and wrapped its chilly wreaths about us like numbing arms. The scores of excursionists who had, a little while ago, arrived by the train from the base, and had scattered here and there in a more or less picturesque and entertaining array, vanished as do faces in a dream, though we could hear their voices, sounding unnaturally slight and far away in the thin air. Even the great buildings and the top of the cone itself, only a few rods distant, were completely lost to view; and we realized, as guided by the slope and the noises, we slowly picked our way over the rocks, how perilous it is to be caught in a long-continued and perhaps denser fog,— or worse than all, in a blinding snow storm,— on the freezing wastes of these shelterless uplands. But we were in no danger or serious discomfort, and five minutes later had ensconced ourselves in the warm parlor of the hotel.

As long ago as 1821, a hospice was built upon the summit by Ethan Allen Crawford, but this cabin was swept away in 1826. In 1852, the Summit House was built, and in 1853 the Tip Top House, owned by rival landlords, representing contending claimants to the ownership of the peak. They were low structures, massively built of great stones bolted together and held to their place by cables which passed over their roofs. The latter yet stands unoccupied, and everybody peers curiously into its cave-like interior, where entertainment and romance more fitting the mood of a true mountain climber were formerly met, than the every-day luxury and formality of the large modern hotel can supply, in spite of (or on account of) its magnified comfort. The new Summit House, opened in 1873, is a long, three-story, wooden building, devoid of any architectural pretence, but strongly constructed, and having bedrooms sufficient for 150 guests. There are post and telegraph offices in the building, and the "proper thing" is to write a letter on the hotel paper with its big picture-head, and mail it from the Summit. The railway trains stop on the plank walk in front of the hotel, and a few yards distant is an engine-house. Behind the hotel, on the very highest point, has been erected an observatory, for admittance to which a small fee is charged; and near its base is the editorial sanctum of the bright little daily paper *Among the Clouds*, copies of which are bought by visitors as souvenirs. A few rods distant stands the snug station of the U. S. Weather Service, where two or three observers remain the year round, exposed to those terrific storms of which we occasionally read accounts, and connected with the world for half the year, only by their telegraph and the irregular descents of one member for the station's mail. The station is open to visitors only at certain hours, and the observers are very polite in showing their instruments, etc.; but there is little else to reward curiosity, and nothing to justify the impertinence with which tourists sometimes question these gentlemen and scrutinize their home. The Government's line is the small cable which may be noticed pinned to the ties of the railway track out of reach of the gales; while the ordinary telegraph wire is strung over the mountains on poles,— which Prue thought exemplified the well-known decrease in size of trees with altitude, because toward the summit these poles happen to be very short. This line is taken down on the approach of winter.

Everyone should, if possible, spend a night upon the top of the mountain, to see the setting and rising of the sun, not only, but the wonderful spectacle of the heavens at night, by which many a thoughtful man has been deeply moved, as he gazed into the ebon and star-pricked canopy from this solitary observatory amid the chambers of limitless darkness, vacancy and silence that encompass him. To behold the march of the great peak's shadow, at sunset, upon the slopes of the Carter range, and out upon the plains of Maine like a pointed phalanx; and to see it, undaunted even at the horizon, mount into a mighty pyramid of shadow upon the eastern sky,— such a sight as that, is reward enough for any inconvenience in staying over night, were there no evening or auroral glories to be added into the scale.

Nevertheless, we did *not* stay over night, but made ready to take the afternoon train down to Fabyan's, amusing ourselves meanwhile by looking over an immense stock of knickknacks, photographs, etc., more or less remotely connected with the summit, which are bought as souvenirs by tourists, regardless of cost compared with earthly market rates. Baily explains it by saying that anything but extra high prices would be out of keeping with the supreme elevation of the locality. Prue tells him she supposes that accounts for *his* high spirits, which is a malicious sarcasm, since our comrade has been taciturn and scowling all day. He openly declares that this prodigious, stony-hearted, tempest-nourishing, old king of mountains intimidates and oppresses him, and that he shall be glad to get down. And he goes on to announce, in a vigorous way, his belief,— in which there is no little truth,— that no lofty mountain, and most of all, the loftiest, looks half as beautiful or imposing to the man on top as to the man at its base.

"That may well be," I assent, "all laws of perspective are against the fellow looking down and in favor of the fellow at a distance; but *the man himself* who stands upon the apex of a hard-won height is the bigger for having done so, and that's more to the purpose."

This doctrine Prue reinforces with a bit of the *Lover's Tale:*—

> The joy of life in steepness overcome,
> And victories of ascent, and looking down
> On all that had looked down on us; and joy
> In breathing nearer heaven; and —

"Bosh!" ejaculates Baily, unable to contain himself; then picks up his coat and cane, and strides out of the door, whither we follow.

What a surprise awaits us! The fog has gone and the sun blazes down upon our cone, which is one little island sticking up like an atoll in a boundless Pacific of milky billows. On every side, just below us, stretches a vast expanse of snowy, sunlit, purely-washed fleeces of vapor, heaving and boiling, surging and tossing, bulging upward into rounded volumes or feathery geysers, pressed down by some diving gust, whirling in the dance of an eddy. We stand upon a lone rock in the centre of a shoreless sea. We see the waves rise and sweep, we can feel the dampness, as of spray, flung in our faces, we watch huge rollers dash against the cliffs that bound our islet and sink below that heaving surface. But we hear no sound,—catch no color but the flashing whiteness of snow or silk. It is the top of a mass of clouds, hung a little lower than our peak and overspreading the whole visible earth. The sunshine is brilliant up here, but powerless to penetrate that dense and boiling vapor. Suddenly, there is torn a rent in the veil,—a crack in the cover of the world,—and we get one enchanting glimpse, in blue and green and gold, of the Connecticut valley. Then the gap closes, and again an unsubstantial waste of white, the breadth and absolute level of which is appalling, surrounds us like an ice-pack, and we shudder in the wind that sweeps over it.

"This is sitting on the edge of a damp cloud with a vengeance," mutters Baily, entering a railway car and turning his back on the sight; but Prue and I go forward and seat ourselves on the tender of the locomotive (which goes rear-foremost on the downward trip), fascinated by the wizardly sight and anxious to see every phase of it.

Just as we are ready to start, as if now the exhibition ought to begin, the shining curtains roll up, and under our eyes is spread again the familiar landscape in the west, with the valley of the Amonoosuc directly beneath our feet:—

> Half-drowned in sleepy peace it lay,
> As satiate with the boundless play,
> Of sunshine on its green away.
>   And clear-cut hills of gloomy blue
> To keep it safe rose up behind,
> As with a charmed ring to bind
> The grassy sea, where clouds might find
>   A place to bring their shadows to.

The Mt. Washington inclined railway has been operated so long, and so often described, that surely I need say little about it here. Its inventor was Sylvester Marsh, of Littleton, N. H., and its building began in 1866, but was not completed until 1869. The road has rails to bear the weight of, and guide its cars, laid in a narrow-guage track, like any other road, upon a continuous low trestle-work carrying it evenly over the inequalities of the rocks; nor do the grades seem astonishingly steep, except in Jacob's Ladder and at some other points, where they amount to something over one foot rise in each three feet advance. The total length of the line is two and thirteen-sixteenths miles, and the time of ascent about one and a half hours; but it takes much less time to come down.

JACOB'S LADDER, MOUNT WASHINGTON.

The little locomotives, with their oddly tilted boilers and smokestacks, are able to drag the cars up this hill-track by a mechanism which is complicated enough, when it is remembered that many parts of the ordinary locomotive had to be readapted to meet the novel arrangement, yet is simple in its main principle. This is, the laying down between the rails a third broad rail, which is studded with cleats or cogs, into which there fit the cogs of powerful driving wheels underneath both engine and cars. As these wheels are turned by the locomotive's machinery they at once cling to and advance upon the inclined cog-rail, and step by step (or cog by cog) the machine literally climbs the iron ladder, supported and guided by the outside T-rails upon which the wheels rest. In going down no steam is required, the speed being entirely regulated by the brakes, of which there are several independent sets,—each able to hold the train. There is, in fact, no occasion for fear at all; and persons who come prepared to be panic stricken are almost disappointed, I have sometimes thought, because there is not even a decent *appearance* of danger. It is probable that a quarter of a million passengers have been carried up and down this road since its origin, of whom not a single one has been injured; nor has an accident happened upon the Rigi, in Switzerland, nor at Mt. Desert, where similar railroads, copied from this one, have been constructed.

With entirely easy minds, therefore, and in the midst of a merry party, we ride down to the base, reviewing with entranced eyes, and storing away in our memories, all the landscape westward and northward which we had seen from the top, but now looked at from constantly altering and novel points of view; and we alight at the end of the too-short journey, filled to the very lips with material for joyful reflection hereafter.

There we take our places in open "observation" cars on the branch railway to the base of Mt. Washington, and in half an hour are whirled down the noisy-going Amonoosuc to Fabyan's, where ends this chapter of our tour.

CHAPTER XVIII.

AT FABYAN'S.

A single coal does not burn well. A companionless traveller finds the journey tedious.— BEDAGE PROVERB.

ABYAN'S is the pivot around which all White Mountain touring must revolve. Jackson and the Conways, Mt. Washington, the Glen and Gorham, Jefferson and Lancaster, Bethlehem and the Profile, are about equidistant. It is the Rome of the mountains, toward which all roads lead, and it has been a station on the main avenue of travel through this rugged part of the state as long as the passes have been known.

The mountains stand back at this point, leaving a valley which may be called spacious and level compared with the ordinary openings among these crowded hills, where the main Amonoosuc, coming from the Lake of the Clouds, receives its South branch, draining the rear roofs of the Crawford House. At the junction of these two streams is the Fabyan House, a big, square, dun-colored hotel, of no more architectural presence than a cotton factory; in fact, it does not serve the purpose of a residence to anything like an equal extent with the other great houses we shall visit, but is, for the most part, adopted as a headquarters for excursions — a stopping-place between whiles — a point of going and coming crowds.

Here concentrate all the railways of the White Mountain region, and all travel must filter through this narrow station, after the manner of the sand in an hour-glass. More stir and movement occur at Fabyan's, therefore, than anywhere else, and the great office and bazaar of the hotel are crowded and lively all day long, but especially so at night. The morning trains bring in crowds of people from distant places bound for Mount Washington, or changing cars for some other resort. The expresses whirl away, and one or two of the short accommodation trains, which in summer ply hourly back and forth between Fabyan's and Crawford's, North Conway, the Twin Mountain House, Bethlehem and the Profile House, back up, receive their merry contingents and glide off. Meanwhile, on a side-track, the Mt. Washington train of open cars has been filling with passengers, accumulated from the earlier arrivals, or in waiting over night at the hotel. Here and there, among a motley throng of tourists bubbling over with good nature, careless of how they may look in the eyes of others, eager only to enjoy themselves, or perhaps bent on improvement of mind, will be seen a group whose stylish attire and sedate deportment stamp them as "swells" who have consented to go up the mountain "as a lark, don't you know." These people would feel greatly hurt if anyone were to speak of *their* party as an *excursion*, and still more so, if you were to intimate that *they*, too, had "a good time," for it is a part of their religion not to confess to enjoyment in what is really enjoyable, nor to put themselves in any position likely to stir their hearts with vulgar emotion. This is an artificial mood exceedingly difficult to maintain in the free and bracing air of the mountains, and the few who do sustain it ought to meet with a more respectful consideration, in view of their self-denial, than they usually do.

Often a real excursion, unabashed by that name, sheds its light and its half dollars upon Fabyan's for a few brief moments, or perchance for a whole night, and then rushes off somewhere else. These are the comets in the solar system of summer pleasure, which has its fixed stars, in the "regular boarders"; its planets swinging in defined orbits from perigee in Winnipesaukee to apogee at Umbagog; its meteoric showers of pedestrians and chance visitors; and, beyond all these, cometary bodies of excursionists, who invade the other orbits at all sorts of unexpected angles and seasons, and whirl with amazing swiftness through a path whose returning curve no man can foretell, only to vanish as mysteriously as they came.

Sometimes these excursions are splendid affairs, not "coming," but *arriving*, in Pullman cars, heralded with pomp and ceremony. Sometimes they are military, march by platoons and columns of fours to view the scenery with heads erect and eyes right, while the band plays and the staff appropriates, *ex-officio*, the best point of view. Sometimes they are clerical and benevolent, uniformed in alpaca dusters, and distinguished on the part of the men by shaven upper lips, and on the part of the women by precise curls and gold spectacles. But generally an excursion consists of hundreds of well-to-do farmers and villagers from the rural regions of New England and Canada, or of smart townspeople out for a hard-earned holiday, arranged for them by some Sunday school or social club, and bubbling over with unrestricted Christmas-comes-but-once-a-year gayety which is good to see. Whoever they are, wherever they come from, they tumble out of their cars here, scramble with much struggling of family groups to keep together into the train to the base of the great mountain — that Mecca of all pilgrims — and sit impatiently waiting for the start. The train is pulled out of the side-track and drawn up alongside the station platform, where the amused guests from the hotel are watching the fun; the passenger agents run up and down to see that nobody gets left; tell each other in a loud tone that this is the handsomest party that has gone up this year, and finally the excursion train rolls vociferously away.

At Fabyan's the central group of the Presidential peaks are all in plain view, but the range on this side is so whole and smooth that no aspect is more uninteresting. In other directions the hills are tame, and there is little in the immediate vicinity to reward walking or driving, compared with other centres of pleasure-taking. Half a mile southward the large Mt. Pleasant House is more favorably situated for rambling, and is a favorite stopping-place with many. The White Mountain House, erected as long ago as 1845, stands one mile northward, at the divergence of the road to Bethlehem from that to Cherry mountain and Jefferson. From this hotel, in the old days, a carriage-road extended some distance up the base of Mt. Washington, at the end of which visitors could go upon horseback or walk up a path now abandoned. The views from the tops of the foothills in that neighborhood are very interesting. The Lower falls of the Amonoosuc, of which the old writers were so fond, are only a mile farther down, but have been ruined by sawmills. The Upper falls, two miles above Fabyan's, are still well worth a visit.

Where the Fabyan House now stands there was formerly a long moraine-ridge of gravel, called the Giant's Grave, and identified with the earliest history of the hardy people who took possession of these glens and the valleys, to which the Notch road was the gateway a century ago. Starr King writes at length, and most interestingly, upon these early times and the hardships and privations they had to undergo. The histories, gazetteers and guide-books will enable the reader to learn the adventurous story in detail. The prominent figure of the locality in history is Ethan Allen Crawford, whose monument is seen on the bluff opposite the Fabyan House near the useful " Tourists' Cottage " of the Boston & Maine Railroad.

" Eleazar Rosebrook was one of the earliest of the Pioneers, having removed in 1772 from Grafton, Mass., to Lancaster, N. H., and thence to Colebrook. In 1792, he settled on Nash & Sawyer's location, and built an extensive pile of mills, stables, etc., at the base of the Giant's Grave. Here he died, 25 years later, and was succeeded by his grandson, E. A. Crawford. Ethan Allen Crawford, 'the White-Mountain Giant,' is almost the only resident of the hill-country in whom any interest centres. He was born at Guildhall, Vermont, in 1792, and was carried to the mountains when a child, afterwards inheriting and occupying the house at the Giant's Grave. He was of large stature and powerful frame, and became famous for skill in hunting and woodcraft. His singular adventures with bears, deer, and wildcats are even now remembered and chronicled. He was one of the first and best of the mountain-guides, and made the Crawford-House bridle-path and the first summit-house. In 1803 the first public-house was erected here, and it was burnt in 1819, when occupied by Ethan Allen

Crawford. Two other hotels on this site have since been destroyed by fire, helping to confirm (or perhaps giving rise to) the old tradition that an Indian once stood on the mound at night, waving a torch and crying, 'No pale-face shall take deep root here; this the Great Spirit whispered in my ear.' Some time afterward a new hotel containing 100 rooms was erected on this site, and was kept by Mr. Fabyan until its destruction by fire about 20 years since. The present Fabyan House was erected in 1872-3, and its constructors committed a needless act of vandalism in levelling the mound of the Giant's Grave." (*Ticknor's Guide*.)

Five miles down the once-romantic Amonoosuc all of whose devious windings are, of necessity, followed by the railroad, stands another one of the "great hotels,"—the Twin Mountain House,—none the worse for its seventeen years of age. This hotel is reared upon a terrace, facing east, and in the midst of ornamental grounds. Wooded hills closely engird it behind, so that the only view from the piazzas is over the two Baby Twins or the Sugar Loaf hills, in front, to the lofty summits of the North Twin and Lafayette, with Agassiz and Round Hill at the right, near Bethlehem. By mounting the knoll in front of the house where the flag-staff is planted, the Presidential range and other peaks become visible. It is to its mill-pond, where boating can be enjoyed; to its widely celebrated table; and to the brilliant social play which goes on here in the season, that this hotel owes the favor it has long met with.

The Twin mountains, after which it is named, are two neighboring summits nearly 5,000 feet in height, at the sources of the Merrimac and on the northern edge of the great Pemigewasset wilderness. An observer standing upon the northern summit would overlook, north and east, the whole region embraced between the upper part of the Androscoggin and Lake Champlain, with its green valleys, highways and villages. Westward, the whole Presidential range would be paraded before him; and eastward, the valley of the Connecticut. Southward, there would be nothing visible but an almost boundless stretch of craggy and wooded mountains, limited by the angular crest of the Sandwich range, and unrelieved by any village or clearing, except, possibly, some glimpses of Woodstock. Until recently, however, it would have been a matter of the greatest difficulty for anyone to reach even the base of these forest-guarded mountains; and a pioneer party of the Appalachian Club which marked out a path from the Twin Mountain House, spent four days in the work, although the distance is only six miles.

CHAPTER XIX.

FRANCONIA NOTCH AND THE PROFILE.

Full many a spot
Of hidden beauty have I chanced to espy
Among the mountains; never one like this;
So lonesome and so perfectly secure;
Not melancholy — no, for it is green,
And bright, and fertile, furnished in itself
With the few needful things that life require.— WORDSWORTH.

"WHERE next?"
"Profile House and Franconia notch."
The train left Fabyan's half an hour after breakfast, and was crowded with pleasure seekers, scattering northward. Down the Amonoosuc, now more useful to the saw-mill than lovely to the artist, we hurry past the foothills of Cherry mountain, straight eastward, seven or eight miles, along the wine-colored river, forced thus early in its youth to turn the wheels that grind the very trees upon its banks into boards and shingles. Then we alight at Bethlehem Junction, where two narrow-guage railways diverge,— one to Maplewood and Bethlehem; the other to the Profile House. A large company get out, and the solitary station becomes suddenly noisy with such a crowd as you see in a Boston station toward evening on Saturday, when young ladies predominate. Only here, instead of ravishing bonnets and dainty parasols, are equally ravishing sunhats and glengarries, with substantial umbrellas and haversacks. The rattle of alpenstocks resounds upon the platform, as though half the pretty girls were thumping along on wooden legs. Now in Switzerland, where glaciers are to be climbed and steep inclines of ice and snow to be traversed, the strong, iron-shod alpenstock is of some service; but here the peeled hemlock sticks, with rings of singeing and bows of bonnie blue ribbon, are of no account whatever, practically,— more a nuisance than a help; yet everybody buys and takes one home, as a sign to all men (and more especially to all women) that they have been climbing the White Mountains; everybody, that is, except those who really *do* climb! N. B. We had no alpenstocks, though Prue teased Baily to get one, on the ineffective plea that "its burnt-cream color would match so well with his mustache."

The ride in the cars of the Profile & Franconia Notch Railroad, around the far-reaching flanks of that prodigious pile of rock which forms a monument to Lafayette, is perhaps the most uninteresting dozen miles in all New England. The swampy woods are so thick and tall and tangled, that one might almost as well be in a tunnel. So we unstrapped our books and began to inform ourselves in regard to Mount Lafayette and the wondrous district we were coming to,— an example which, "though I say it as shouldn't say it," it would be profitable for others to follow. Foresight in scenery-hunting, is worth any amount of hindsight.

Lafayette is 5,200 feet in height, and therefore the tallest peak in New England, outside of the Presidential range.

"It is usually regarded as the head and front of the Franconia range, isn't it?" somebody asks.

"Yes, but that term is an indefinite one, applicable properly only to the short line of elevations between the Pemigewasset and its eastern branch; whereas Lafayette is really the dominant summit of a larger wilderness-group, including the Twins, Mount Hale (named after our great preacher and story teller), and the Haystack (recently named Mount Garfield) with their subordinate hills, all of which divide the waters of the Merrimac from those of the Ammonoosuc.

"'Though of similar structure to Washington,' say the books, 'Lafayette shows a marked difference in the sharpness and decision of its lines, and the thin keen profile of its summit ridge, which slopes off sharply into dark gulfs.' President Dwight placed it second only to Washington and Moosilauke in elegance and amplitude, and says: 'It is composed of three lofty conical summits, accompanied by four vast, bold, circular sweeps, formed with a grace to which in objects of this nature I had hitherto been a stranger; and which removed all doubts, in my mind, concerning the practicability of uniting the most exquisite beauty with the most splendid sublimity.' Starr King, I observe, thought it contrasted with Washington as a keen nervous temperment differs from a square-shouldered, burly, billious frame."

"Can it be climbed?"

"Easily. The guide-books describe a bridle path, kept in good repair by toll-receipts, which ascends from the Profile House through a gap in the cliffs that overhang the Franconia notch. and affords many lovely outlooks backward before it emerges upon the brow of the crags and begins to make its way toward the summit of the mountain, which slopes backward from this 'beetling verge' along the narrow ridge already spoken of. I'll read to you a part of Mr. Drake's account: —

"'Although heaped with rocks the way is easy, and is quite level. In one place, where it glides between two prodigious masses of rock dislodged from the cliff, it is so narrow as to admit only a single person at a time.'"

"Then you and I can't go," Prue breaks in.

"Why, pray tell?"

"Because we are not 'single' persons."

"He means only *one* person at a time, you goosey, without regard to any 'previous condition of servitude' in marriage."

"Oh, does he? Well, go on."

Baily grins and I resume:—

"'When I turned to look back down the black ravine, cutting into the south side of the mountain, my eye met nothing but immense rocks stopped in their descent on the very edge of the gulf. It is among these that a way has been found for the path, which was to me a reminiscence of the high defiles of the Isthmus of Darien; to complete the illusion, nothing was now wanting except the tinkling bells of the mules and the song of the muleteer. I climbed upon one of the high rocks, and gazed to my full content upon the granite parapet of Mount Cannon. In a few rods more the path encountered the great ravine opening into the valley of Gale river. Through its wide trough brilliant strips of this valley gleamed out far below. The village of Franconia, and the heights of Lisbon and Bethlehem now appeared on this side.'

"The writer then tells of the little Alpine lakes and the emotions they awakened, and so forth, and so forth. He thinks they look better at a distance than close to their sedgy and brackish shores. Finally he surmounts what he calls 'the first of the great billows which, rolling in to a common centre, appear to have forced the true summit a thousand feet higher;' and then (here I turn a leaf) he continues:—

"'The ascent of the pinnacle now began. It is too much a repetition, though by no means as toilsome, of the Mount Washington climb, to merit particular description. This peak, too, seems disinherited by nature. The last trees encountered are the stunted firs, with distorted little trunks, which it may have required half a century to grow as thick as the wrist. I left the region of alpine trees to enter that of gray rocks, constantly increasing in size toward the summit, where they were confusedly piled in ragged ridges, one upon another, looming large and threateningly in the distance. But as often as I stopped to breathe, I scanned this landscape o'er with all the delight of a wholly new experience. The fascination of being on a mountain-top is yet to be explained. Perhaps after all it is not susceptible of analysis. . . . Had I staked all my hopes upon the distant view, no choice but disappointment was mine to accept. Steeped in the softest, dreamiest azure that ever dull earth borrowed from bright heaven, a hundred peaks lifted their airy turrets on high. These castles of the air — for I will maintain that they were nothing else — loomed with enchanting grace, the nearest, like battlements of turquoise and amethyst, or, receding through infinite gradations to the merest shadows, seemed but the dusky reflection of those less remote. The air was full of illusions; there was bright sunshine, yet only a deluge of semi-opaque golden vapor; there were forms without substance. See those iron-ribbed, deep-crested mountains! I declare it seemed as if a swallow might fly through them with ease! Over the great Twin chain were traced, apparently on the air itself, some humid outlines of surpassing grace which I recognized for the great White Mountains. It was a dream of the great poetic past; of the golden age of Milton and of Dante. The mountains seemed dissolving and floating away before my eyes. Stretched beneath the huge land-billows, the valleys — north, south, or west — reflected the fervid sunshine with softened brilliance, and all those white farms and hamlets spotting them looked like flakes of foam in the hollows of an immense ocean.'

"And then follows," I go on to remark to my companions, "a bit of sentiment which I have often felt like expressing myself."

"Under those circumstances your silence is amazing to us," is Baily's impertinent reply. "Do let us hear it!"

"Very well — listen."

"'Heaven forbid that I should profane such a scene with the dry recital of this view or that! I did not even think of it. A study of one of nature's most capricious moods interested me far more than the study of the topograpy. How should I know that what I saw were mountains, when the earth itself was not clearly distinguishable. Alone, surrounded by all these delusions, I had, indeed, a support for my feet, but none whatever for the bewildered senses.'"

"What season was that?"

"June.— should we go up now, the clear October air would betray all those illusions in clear outlines, and perhaps take away half their beauty."

"Ah!" exclaims Prue, "but think of the peaks, touched with the white of early snow, falling away into that gay drapery of the reddened forests that now must clothe all their slopes and carpet the wild lovely valleys between!"

Then the whistle sounded, we rushed past a bit of blue water which half a dozen passengers told one another, was Echo lake, and came to a standstill among the trees, beside a bustling little cottage-station. The platform was thronged with people, and boys in gilt-edged uniforms were dodging about collecting baggage checks and answering questions, while some men on the other side, whip in hand, were bawling, "This way for carriages to the Flume!"

We gave up our luggage and followed a human current setting through an inclined bridge, or covered way, and in two minutes came out into an open space, boxed in by huge purple cliffs and opening toward the left down a wooded cañon, where stood an old-fashioned, stately, high-pillared, southern-looking building,— the Profile House.

"No situation could be more sequestered or more charming. An oval, grassy plain, not extensive, but bright and smiling, spreads its green between a grisly precipice and a shaggy mountain. And there, if you will believe me, in front of the long white columned hotel, like a Turkish rug on a carpet, was a pretty flower-garden. Like those flowers on the lawn were pretty beauties sauntering up and down in exquisite morning toilets, coquetting with their bright-colored parasols . . . and little children fluttered about the grass like beautiful butterflies, and as unmindful of the terrors that hovered over them so threateningly. Nurses in their stiff grenadier caps and white aprons, lackeys in livery, cadets in uniform, elegant equipages, blooded horses, dainty shapes on horse-back, cavaliers, and last, but not least, the resolute pedestrian, or the gentlemen strollers up and down the shaded avenues, made up a scene as animated as attractive."

Who does not know the Profile House, the Franconia notch, and the Flume, who knows anything at all of the White Mountains? Its story is as old as the history of pleasure-taking in New England. Our great-grandfathers in queues and kneebreeches wooed there the blushing girls in flowered satins and high back-combs who became our great-grandmothers; and their children, with changing clothes, but unchanged hearts, have gone on doing so ever since under the eternally discreet silence of the grand old crags. Other places are imbued with the history of heroism, and shine with the glory of a writer's or a painter's fame; but this glen is illuminated with the perpetual roselight of romance.

By the time we have freshened up and reassembled in the ample, carpeted assembly-room of the hotel, where the clerk's office is merely a convenient piece of furniture, dinner is ready, and we find ourselves seated near one end of the long dining-room, where hundreds can sit at once, and feel themselves almost in a banquet hall; and while we are waited on by the white-capped maidens, whose service in all these mountain houses is such a pleasant change from the Limerick-French men-waiters of city hotels, Prue asks for geographical information.

"We are at the entrance, or within the northern gates of the Franconia notch," she is informed. "This is a narrow gap north and south between the Franconia range on the east and a group of mountains west, of which latter, Kinsman, 4,300 feet high, and Cannon or Profile, 3,800 feet, are the biggest peaks. The waters flow from their western slopes into the Connecticut. Just above us is Echo lake; just below, Profile lake. The former overflows into the Amonoosuc; the latter struggles out through the notch to find its way straight southward into the Merrimac. All along its bank passes a capital turnpike from Plymouth to Franconia and beyond, which has been a stage road for more than fifty years. Franconia is a neat manufacturing village half a dozen miles northward. That stately, dark precipice eastward is Eagle cliff,—a spur of Mount Lafayette; and below it, on the same side, are the frowning battlements of Lincoln and Liberty. The lofty dome and ridge opposite is Mount Cannon, which, at its abrupt southern end "breaks into human expression," the ledges at its beetling summit forming, as we see them from the glen, the Human Profile, or Great Stone Face, or Old Man of the Mountain, which has given to the locality a world-wide celebrity."

"What about the Flume?"

"Half a dozen miles down the notch, and more than 500 feet lower — you can imagine what a torrent the little river is all the way — stands a somewhat smaller hotel, under the same management as this one, called the Flume House, where people stop who care to do more than make a casual visit to the gorge and its wonders.

"Its surroundings are wholly unlike those of the Profile House. There you are outside of the huge upheavals that here hem us in, and you can see the peaks hidden from us behind these imminent crags. 'From the Flume House,' says Starr King, 'the general view is cheerful and soothing. There is no place among the mountains where the fever can be taken more gently and cunningly out of a worried or burdened brain. So soft and delicate are the general features of the outlook over the widening Pemigewasset valley! So rich the gradation of the lights over the miles of gently sloping forest that sweep down towards Campton! So pleasant the openings here and there that show a cluster of farm-houses, and the bright beauty of cultivated meadows enclosed by the deeper green of the wilderness!' In front of the Flume House the long wooded ridge of Liberty has its irregularities so shaped that they form a recumbent figure in which you will please see a resemblance to the Father of his Country, 'dead and turned to clay,' because *that* is Washington lying in State.

"There is an Elephant in this notch, too, quite as good as that owned by the Crawford House; and a little way below is the Pool, — a circular basin reamed out and still being enlarged by the eddying river which pours into it down a white cascade, hidden in the midst of a most secluded and savage mass of rocks and forest. The whirling water is a glossy and lustrous sea-green, and of such marvelous transparency that you see the brilliant pebbles sparkling at the bottom, shifting with the waves of light like bits of glass in a Kaleidoscope. Overtopping trees lean timidly over and peer down into the Pool, which coldly repulses their shadows. Only the colorless hue of the rocks is reflected, —

> 'As if were here denied
> The summer sun, the spring's sweet dew,
> That clothe with many a varied hue
> The bleakest mountain-side.'"

"Don't you think," Baily interrupts, *sotto voce*, "that you'd better hire a hall?"

I look up from my untasted plate, abashed, for all the table are listening, and Prue is dying to laugh.

"Heavens!" I ejaculate. "That isn't *my* eloquence! *I* never *saw* the place! I'm only telling you what I've heard about it!"

Then the laughter came in a burst of gayety at my expense in which I had not only to join to save my reputation, but also to order Bordeaux enough to wash away the memory of my discomforture from the minds of all my tablemates.

That's what I got through playing the prig! and I won't forget it.

Nevertheless, the facts were all true enough, as we proved by a long satisfactory visit of exploration, to which we devoted all the next day, walking slowly down to the Flume House along a park-like road, through groves of birches turned golden by frost. The first object of pilgrimage, of course, was The Flume, just 'round the corner, as it were, a little way up Flume brook, which pitches down from Mount Liberty, and has cut a way for itself through the rocks in the form of a narrow crevice to which the word "flume" very properly applies. It is a wild, pretty little glen, but I do not share in the lavish praise that has been bestowed upon it, or the marvel it has been called. Hamilton Gibson's lovely drawing of it, like almost all the other pictures I have seen, immensely exaggerates, and makes it look like a Rocky Mountain cañon, which it is not, by any means. I could find a dozen crevices in the Virginia mountains far deeper and more interesting. Mr. Sweetzer's straight-forward description fits it best. "The flume," he says, "is a half to a third of a mile from the hotel, and is reached by a good carriage-road which crosses the Pemigewasset river. The road stops near the Flume brook, whose course is ascended by a foot-path leading over clean sheets of granite, broad and slightly tilted, across which the water slips 'in thin, wide, even sheets of crystal colorlessness' for several hundred feet. Farther up, the ledges are more rugged, and the limpid brook lingers in rock-rimmed basins. The Flume is a marvellous fissure in the side of Mount Flume, through which dashes a brilliant little brook. It is about 700 feet long, and is flanked by mural precipices 60–70 feet high. These walls are perpendicular and parallel, and are from ten to twenty feet from each other. A plank walk extends through the gorge, crossing the stream several times. A great boulder for centuries hung between the approaching cliffs in the upper part of the Flume, but was swept away in June, 1883, when a tremendous avalanche, caused by heavy storms on the peaks above, swept through the defile, scouring it out, and increasing its length. The lowlands below were covered with myriads of boulders and acres of rocky *debris*. After the wreck, two pretty waterfalls appeared in the Flume, almost compensating for the loss of the great suspended boulder. The morning is the best time to visit this locality."

The boulder seems to have been the chief object of interest and to have merited this distinction; but in view of its loss it is amusing to read Starr King's rhapsody over "the huge boulder, egg-shaped, that is lodged between the walls just over the bridge where we stand, —as unpleasant to look at, if the nerves are irresolute, as the sword of Damocles, and yet held by a grasp out of which it will not slip for centuries?"

The morning after this great washout, workmen were set digging in the wide mass of debris spread along the outlet of the brook to find it. Before night a boulder had been fished out, set high and dry upon the bank, and fenced in so that it could'nt get away, like the Pilgrim Rock at Plymouth, and, its identity like that historic stone, labeled so that there should be no doubt about it.

"Do you mean to say that you don't believe it?" exclaims Prue, who seems to think I am bound to praise *everything*, irrespective of the way it strikes me.

"This is an age of free thought, my dear," I tell her; "and you can believe it or not without danger of the stake; but it is also an age of skepticism. My honest opinion is, that this fenced-in boulder is a fraud unworthy of the dignity of Franconia notch, than which there is nothing more beautiful in the mountains; and of the people who perpetrate it."

The brook channel supplies a way (not a path) of reaching the tops of the lower Franconia mountains,— Flume, Liberty, and Lincoln, whence the views are grand, and considerably different from that displayed from Lafayette; but the task is an extremely severe one. To Mount Pemigewasset, a spur of Mount Kinsman on the opposite side, a bridle path gives ready access, and ladies often go to the summit. The view is of the same character as that presented from the front-door of the Flume House, but, of course, far wider and more impressive. Starr King makes one of his most delightful paragraphs in telling how the sunset splendor, seen from this high point, must irradiate the eastern heights.

From the Profile House many delightful excursions are open to your choice. You may ramble up Mount Cannon, as did the gay party in *Their Pilgrimage*, and lose your hand where you have already lost your heart; but don't loose your footing! You may go down to Echo lake, and hear the bugle blown and listen to the purple glen's replying; hold your breath while the cannon is fired and count the salvos returned by the water-batteries of Eagle cliff and Bald mountain, and then by the lighter, loftier artillery in the fortresses of Lafayette and the Profile ridge; you may get your insulting yells thrown back in your teeth a dozen times over by the outraged spirits chained to the rocks that tower so menacingly overhead; or, in gentler mood, you persuade your sweet-voiced friend to sing some delicate strain, while you row her to the middle of the blue lakelet, or watch her downcast lashes as she sits in the stern of the little steam-yacht, happy that her voice can be so often repeated by the jealous hills in "the winding wandering music, that returns upon itself." You may drive over to the gay Forest Hills hotel, at Franconia, and hobnob with a crowd that will match your own. You may ride up Lafayette and fish or paddle in Profile lake; and you may — nay *must* — fill your eyes and mind and soul with the Profile itself.

At last then, I have come to this,—the first thing in the Notch; but it is well worth saving until the last in my description.

From the lawns and flower-parterres in front of the hotel, a hard road, overshadowed by the magnificent bronze and purple wall of Eagle cliff, hundreds of feet in almost vertical height, winds down through the birch groves and thickets past a little lake, a quarter of a mile distant. Walk, or, if you please, run, down this road, keeping your eyes off Cannon's ridges upon the west, until you catch glimpses of the shimmering surface of the pond through the dusty white trunks of the trees. Then go slowly, and watch for an opening in the grove upon your right hand.

Suddenly this opening will disclose itself, and there, framed in by the gap, jutting from the very head of the long abruptly ending ridge of Mount Cannon, is the Great Stone Face,—a silhouette of colossal size cut in granite—"a mountain breaking into human expression." And it *is* human expression! Fanciful resemblances to faces and forms of every sort are constantly pointed out upon exposed rocks; but here there can be no more uncertainty than in looking at a portrait-statue. It is, indeed, as if some artist among the Titans, some rude progenitor of the Egyptian sculptors who cut the collossi that look with hollowed eyes from the bluffs of Karnac out across the Nile, had begun to chisel a hero's head from the living rock of the crag; had first completed the face and then ceased his work before isolating the head from the bulk of the mountain. But this is no thick-lipped, round-nostrilled, heavy-lidded Pharaonic face, but an alert, sharp-featured, firm-mouthed and clean-chinned Saxon face of advanced age—a hardy Yankee mountaineer—a type set on high here at the pinnacle of New England of the energetic and irresistible race which was to possess her mountains and plains; and his eyes are fixed steadily toward the west, whither he already sees the star of his empire taking its course. These are the thoughts the face suggests to me. It looks like the portrait of a pioneer,—the presentiment in stone of the spirit of '76; and while for unnumbered centuries it was prophetic, it is now fast becoming a reminiscence, since the lines of that face belong rather to the stern type of a bygone generation than to the more delicately moulded faces of to-day.

Summer houses and seats are arranged by the lake, where you may sit and read the face at your leisure, and dream over its origin and its destiny; or you may take one of the many skiffs, row out upon the mirroring waters and study the head with all its magnificent surroundings; but you will never weary of it, nor lose your sense of its mystery, grandeur, and humanity. It does not simply tickle your sense of wonder—it excites your sympathy; and in sunshine, in shadow, under the varying lights of morning, noon, or night, in clear days and misty days, sharp against the blazing sunset sky or isolated by rising mists, it "speaks a various language" and enforces its personality upon your mind.

Ticknor's *Guide* tells us that it was discovered in 1805, by Francis Whitcomb and Luke Brooks, who were working on the Notch road, and saw it while washing their hands in Profile lake. They exclaimed, "That is Jefferson," he being then President. Hawthorne's tale of *The Great Stone Face*, and a later book called *Christus Judex*, celebrate this marvellous outline. There is a probability that it may not last for many years longer, on account of the rapid decomposition of the granite, which crumbles under the hand, and the geologist Hitchcock, has advised any persons who are anxious to see the Profile for themselves, to hasten to the spot, for fear of disappointment. It is formed of three disconnected ledges of granite, in different vertical lines, their aggregate height being 36-40 feet; and their height above the lake, 1,200 feet. One rock forms the forehead, another the nose and upper lip, and the third the massive chin.

The decay to which it is subject may account for the varying expressions which writers have found in it; differing points of view too, will alter this countenance, while at only a little distance up or down the road, the human resemblance is altogether lost.

One of the oldest descriptions is that of Oakes, who calls it "the greatest object of popular curiosity in the vicinity of the White Mountains," and says: "The expression is severe and somewhat melancholy, and although there is a little feebleness about the mouth, on the whole the face of the 'Old Man of the Mountain' is set, and his countenance fixed firm. He neither blinks at the near flashes of the lightning beneath his nose, nor flinches from the driving snow and sleet of the Franconia winter, which makes the very mercury of the thermometer shrink into the bulb and congeal."

Starr King found in it "an intimation of the human countenance, which is the crown of all beauty, pushed out from the coarse strata of New England thousands of years before Adam. . . . The expression is really noble, with a suggestion partly of fatigue and melancholy. He seems to be waiting for some visitor or message. . . . When, after an August shower, late in the afternoon, the mists that rise from the forests below congregate around it, and, smitten with sunshine, break as they drift against its nervous outline, and hiding the mass of the mountain which it overhangs, isolate it with a thin halo, the countenance, awful but benignant, is as if a mighty angel were sitting among the hills, and enrobing himself in a cloud-vesture of gold and purple." Drake suggests that it was begotten by a thunderbolt, and confesses to a fascination that drew his eyes irresistibly back to it from all other scenery. "The face," he exclaims, "is too majestic, too nobly grand, for any thing of mortal mould. One of the antique gods, may, perhaps, have sat for this archetype of the coming man." An "almost superhuman expression of frozen terror" —a "far-away look"—"an intense and speechless amazement . . . seeming to declare the presence of some unutterable vision, too bright and dazzling for mortal eyes to behold," are the phrases by which this writer tries to convey its effect upon him. "It does everything but speak,— nay, you are ready to swear that it is going to speak! . . . Let the visitor be ever so unimpassioned, surely he must be more than mortal to resist the impression of mingled awe, wonder, and admiration which a first sight of this weird object forces upon him."

Thus I might multiply the record of what men, not easily moved, have thought of this startling accident of rock-crumbling, which so sublimely, so dignifiedly, portrays the human countenance, without a shade of caricature or a tinge of mockery.

CHAPTER XX.

THE CONNECTICUT VALLEY.

The mountains are more grand and inspiring when we stand at the proper distance and look at them, than when we look from them.— STARR KING.

WE NOW turned our faces northward. Returning to Bethlehem Junction we stepped into a second train of narrow-gauge cars and in ten minutes (for it is only a couple of miles) were set down at The Maplewood, in the edge of Bethlehem township, one of the largest and most modern of the New Hampshire summer hotels. In fact, it will soon be a sort of village by itself, for there are so many annexes, cottages, private houses and parks, in the near neighborhood, that the name even now covers much more than a hotel. And what a hotel! Piled up in architecture, like a gentleman's villa rather than a public stopping-place, it is capacious enough to hold 500 guests comfortably, and after that can overflow into annexes which accommodate nearly as many more; and to great size and external beauty it adds many interior luxuries. This is the growth of a few years. "In 1875," records Samuel Drake, "I found a modest hostelry accommodating sixty guests; five years later a mammoth structure . . . had arisen like Aladdin's palace, on the same spot. Instead of our little musical entertainment, our mock trial, our quiet rubber of whist, of an evening, there were readings, lectures, balls, masquerades, theatricals, *musicales*, for every day of the week." Prue went into ecstacies over the pretty Ayrshire and Breton cattle at the stockfarm, and Baily and I agreed that the observatory, on a hill half a mile or so distant, where you saunter along a broad, smooth path, was about the best place in the world to sit and smoke an evening pipe, with the rolling valley at your feet and the grand White Hills to rest your eyes upon. Almost the whole horizon was dotted with familiar peaks, from the Presidential range to the Green mountains, and from Lafayette to where Mt. Starr King and his fellows "struck their javelins up the azure." This observatory-path leads on into the carriage-road up Mt. Agassiz. This mountain (*alias* Round Top) is 2,390 feet high, and has an observatory on its summit whose outlook sweeps the rolling, copse-dotted warm valleys of the Amonoosuc and Connecticut, more beautiful than ever, now

When woods begin to wear the crimson leaf.

That evening, at The Maplewood, the last hop of the season was given. People came over in carriages and by rail from the Profile House, from the Forest Hills hotel at Franconia, from Littleton and Lancaster, Whitefield, Jefferson, and all the houses down the "P. & O." besides the big home-contingent from Bethlehem. We were all in "full fig," and if anywhere in the world a crowd had a better time, or the pearly electric lights shone down upon the happy *dénouements* of more summer flirtations, I have not heard of it.

The next morning, in sunshine sparkling through an almost frosty air which animated our blood and went to our heads like wine, we strode away up the "street" and walked pretty much all over the town of Bethlehem, for neither our spirits were weary, like Rosalind's, nor our legs like Touchstone's. It was with what Baily calls an almost hay-feverish excitement that we went tramping around this summer town, which is so new and shiny that the whole place fairly smells of paint and fresh mortar.

"But this newness which you at first resent . . . is an evident effort to render the place attractive by making it beautiful. Good taste generally prevails. . . . We walk here in a broad, well-built thoroughfare, skirted on both sides with hotels, boarding-houses and modern cottages, in which three or four thousand* sojourners annually take refuge. All this has grown from the 'one small hotel' of a dozen years ago. Shade-trees and grass-plots beautify the wayside. An immense horizon is visible from these houses, and even the hottest summer days are rendered endurable by the light airs produced and set in motion by the oppressive heats of the valley. The sultriest season is, therefore, no bar to out-door exercise for persons of average health, rendering walks, rambles or drives subject only to the will or caprice of the pleasure-seeker. But in the evening all these houses are emptied of their occupants. The whole village is out-of-doors enjoying the coolness or the panorama with all the zest unconstrained gratification always brings. The multitudes of well-dressed promenaders surprise every newcomer, who immediately thinks of Saratoga or Newport and their social characteristics. Bethlehem, he thinks, must be the ideal of those who would carry a city, or at least, suburban life, among the mountains, who do not care a fig for solitude but prefer to find their pleasure still connected with their home life. They are seeing life and pleasure at the same time."

The older writers, therefore, have little to say about Bethlehem as such. The name comes from the religious persuasion of the hardy people who settled there and constituted a Bethlemite church. The sect still exists and has erected a neat church.

---

* The writer is too modest — at least 10,000 people are said to remain more than a week at a time (many during months) within this town, where nearly all other business is subordinate to that of entertaining summer boarders. A census of the boarding-houses alone, on a pleasant Sunday in August, will show nearly 1,500 guests — but you would be lucky to find ten per cent of them at home.

The growth of the Bethlehems (under the skilful management of a few far-sighted men of energy, wealth and good taste) has been due in no small degree to the immunity the locality enjoys from that very distressing catarrhal difficulty called rose-cold or hay-fever, to which so many persons are subject in midsummer on the coast. This is not a peculiar possession, however, for visitors at Gorham, in the Glen, at Jefferson and its vicinity, at the Twin Mountain House, and in many other elevated localities, are equally free from the malady, wherever *Ambrosia artemesiæfolia*, the weed to whose exhalations it is considered due, is not permitted to flourish in the dooryard. In Bethlehem, however, is quartained the headquarters of that society of fugitives called the Hay-Fever Association, which counts upon its rolls so many distinguished names, and makes as merry over its escape from the woes suffered by those who are less fortunate as did the gay guests of Boccacio while Florence was wasting under the plague.

> Why let the strucken deer go weep,
> The hart ungalled play;
> For some must watch, while some must sleep;
> Thus runs the world away.

As to the views? Oh, haven't I written *enough* about this magnificent spectacle of the mountains,—flushed with sunrise; dyed with departing day; sapphire-like at noon; opalescent under the mist when we watch

> The soft white vapor streak the crowned towers
> Built to the sun;

enveloped in gale-torn masses of black storm-clouds, "thunder and splendor of lightning" hid in their folds; gleaming under snow and ice like the polished helmets of an army of Titans advancing in battle array? Up the rapid Amonoosuc see the Presidents — count their names again: — Madison, Adams, Jefferson, Washington. Then turn to the massive summits out of which the Twins stand prominent; to Lafayette, lifting his worn and battered crest high over the dark forests and foothills; and to a horizon-full of noble peaks closing in the west and north. One does not get all this at once, but day after day, as he explores this road or path, that eminence or forest opening, he finds some new picture which he thinks better than the last.

From Bethlehem, it is only a comfortable morning's walk across to Littleton, or you can take one of the frequent stages which run back and forth. Some expensive and beautiful villas are built along this very notable road, whose windows survey magnificent scenery. At Littleton are plenty of good hotels and less conspicuous boarding-houses. This village is a historical place, and now a centre of busy manufacturing. It can be reached in half an hour from Bethlehem Junction by the way of Wing Road. From Wing Road the railroad runs northeast through wild hills to Whitefield Junction, whence the Whitefield & Jefferson Railroad runs down to Jefferson.

Our plan of driving through Randolph and Jefferson while we were at Gorham, was interfered with and postponed, the result of which finally was that we did see one of the most inviting regions of the whole state; but Prue had a friend spending the summer at Jefferson Hill, who used to write capital letters, one of which I am permitted to quote for your benefit,— omitting the private ejaculations!

JEFFERSON HILL, N. H., July, 1886.
MY DEAR PRUE:—

.... I am sitting on the piazza of one of the hotels on the slope of Mt. Starr King. The afternoon air is soft and balmy — just the essence of enjoyment,— while the atmosphere is so clear that our vision in every direction is unobstructed, even by the haze which comes in the dog-days. We seem here to be in a vast amphitheatre.

At our feet lie the Jefferson meadows, forming a richly carpeted floor, with its varied colorings of crimson and green, while roundabout us on every side are mountains, kings rugged and gray and old, their huge sides scarred and seamed in the "battle of the years" with Father Time, yet, with the green midsummer drapery thrown carelessly over them, softening the sharp angles and hard faces, and giving them for a short time, at least, the beauty and freshness of youth.

In front of us, twelve miles in a straight line, "as the bird flies," is the grand "Presidential" range,— Mt. Washington, *as always*, in regal splendor " stands the monarch of the hills in the centre of his court." Far away to the right, their graceful forms outlined against the sky, rise the lesser, but more beautiful peaks of the Franconia range, from Mt. Lafayette to Mt. Kinsman, terminating at Moosilauke, which guards the southwestern horizon like a grim sentinel. At our left, rising in great dignity, is Starr King mountain — so aptly named — along the foot of which runs to the eastward a road known as the Mt. Adams road. This is a most popular drive from Jefferson, as it gives all along its length an almost unobstructed view of the whole Presidential range. Another fine road leads to Lancaster, seven miles westward, which is quite a resort for the boarders at Jefferson Hill.

Coming over this road one evening towards Jefferson, I saw a sight of such wondrous beauty that words seem powerless to describe it. Back of us the western sky was, of course, radiant, while in front of us the eastern sky was even more wondrously beautiful. Great roseate clouds overhung Mt. Washington, and, moving back and forth with a gentle swaying motion, seemed to sift a glow over the whole range of mountains, and to imbue each one with distinctive color of its own; and these colors seemed to vie with the perfect and gorgeous hues of the rainbow. Jefferson meadows also caught the grand reflection and soon the grass was tinged with purple and carmine, gold and blue, while along the entire length of the Franconia range on the south, great amber and blue clouds shone resplendent. We felt, as we stood and gazed, with senses enthralled, as if we were the inhabitants of another sphere of marvellous beauty and brightness, so completely were the "heavens above and the earth beneath" filled with the glory of it.

> Stand well ye mountain monarchs, through all time,
> Work of a master hand divine;
> Thou wert created mighty to endure,
> As God's own promises, eternal, sacred, sure.
>
> ALICE J.

At Scotts a railroad diverges westward on its way through Lunenburg and the Concords (in Vermont) to St. Johnsbury and Lake Champlain; but the main line continues from Whitefield, northward, to Lancaster, the county seat of Coös county, on the Connecticut (in reality on Israel's river near its mouth), the largest village within easy distance of the White Mountains, and one of the most attractive.

It was a party of Lancastrians who, in 1820, applied the names they now bear to the peaks of the Presidential range; but this proves more for their patriotism than for either their "culture" or good taste, when it is remembered how many more appropriate ones might have been given, and how many sonorous Indian names were already attached. About Lancaster cluster traditions of early struggles against Indians, wild beasts and every kind of hardship; and, later, of revolutionary campaigning.

The views from the village itself are extensive and gratifying, and several eminences are within walking distance. One drive is to Dalton mountain, three or four miles from Dalton or Whitefield villages, the summit of which is reached by a path half a mile long. On Kimball hill, near Whitefield, is the Howland observatory, (ten miles from Lancaster) whence a view opens worth considerably more than the twenty-five cents it costs, not to speak of the telescope "thrown in." The peculiar possession of Lancaster, however, is the Lunenburg Heights, on the Vermont side of the Connecticut, which afford a fine prospect toward the crowded and supreme mountains southward; of the Pilot range and Androscoggin country; and of the Percy peaks, with other isolated but shapely hills in the more open country northward. Starr King declared himself unable to conceive of any combination of natural scenery more pleasing, more refreshing or soul-inspiring than the mingled harmony of the rich and varied landscape which greets the eye from Lunenburg Heights.

From Lancaster, the railroad runs northward to a junction with the Grand Trunk, at Groveton. From Groveton it is only a few miles down through the picturesque, view-famous river-villages and lumber-sawing communities of Milan and Berlin Falls, to Gorham, and this somewhat roundabout way is one of the regular avenues of passage between the eastern and western sides of the mountain country. Or, from Groveton you can go northward a dozen miles to Stratford, and then, by the daily stage via Colebrook, reach the Dixville notch and cross through it to Umbagog lake and Magalloway river, as explained in chapter XIII.

CHAPTER XXI.

Through the Crawford Notch.

Shaggy and wild
With mossy trees and pinnacles of flint,
And many a hanging crag.—BRYANT.

WE WERE in the morning express southward bound. We had caught our last glimpse of the far blue Pilots and of the black cone of Cherry mountain. Lafayette had disappeared on our right, the North Twin was sinking behind the ragged heaps of rock through which the upper Amonoosuc fights its way. Now Deception and the rude Rosebrook ledges hem us in, and then the whistle arouses such echoes as even Fabyan's historic old tin horn could never have evoked. Fabyan's has been passed, and we go spinning on across the valley, lovingly looking up to where we can see the black dot of an engine, with its white feather of smoke, climbing that vast pyramid of lapis lazuli they call Mount Washington. We halt in the rear of the Mount Pleasant House, and are reinforced by a troop of homegoing merry-makers, laden with trophies, flirtations and freckles. Before they have got fairly settled in their seats we emerge from a deep cutting and the brakeman calls "Crawford's!" which is "short" for The Crawford House.

Elbowing our way through the crowd at the station, we look about us, up and down a small elongated vale or glen, closely girt by high wooded hills. On rising ground at the right (northward) stands the big white hotel, its lawn sloping down to the station and to a tiny lake, in the middle of which a fountain-pipe is sending up a strong jet, blown to one side like a geyser. Out of the lower end of this lakelet trickles a thread of water which makes its escape a hundred rods below, through a black crevice in the rocks where protruding ledges of the opposite hills all but join. That stream is the head of the Saco, and that narrow portal is the Gate of the Notch. The mountain behind us is Tom,—that in front Clinton; and the little avenue cut through the trees yonder is the beginning of the Crawford bridle-path to Mount Washington. "We are now in the midst of a little plateau, about two thousand feet above the sea. It is the highest point of the valley, and the water flows from it in both directions, the spring near the house discharging its contents down through the notch into the Saco, and that at the stables emptying itself into a tributary of the Amonoosuc, and reaching the sea through the Connecticut."

A GRAY DAY IN CRAWFORD NOTCH.

Though well-known to the Indians, used by them in war raids, and heard of by the whites in the days of the old French-and-Indian troubles, it was not until 1771 that this pass (which is *the* Notch *par excellence*) of the White Mountains, may be said to have been made known to people generally. In that year, Thomas Nash, a hunter, saw, from the top of Cherry mountain this deep cleft in the mountains, and, by way of exploration, passed down the Saco river through its gorge, going on to Portsmouth, where he told Governor Wentworth of his happy discovery. "Wishing to test the value of the pass as a route of commerce, Wentworth requested him to bring a horse through it from Lancaster, offering as a reward in case of success the tract now called Nash and Sawyer's Location, extending from the Gate of the Notch to a point beyond the Fabyan House, and including 2,184 acres. Nash associated with himself a fellow-pioneer by the name of Sawyer, by whose aid he lowered the unfortunate horse over the cliffs and drove him through the rocky river until they emerged at Conway. A road was soon built here 'with the neat proceeds of a confiscated estate,' and a direct route was formed between the coast and the upper Coös country, which had previously been accessible only by a long detour around the south side of the mountains. The first article of merchandise carried through from Lancaster was a barrel of tobacco; and the first freight up from the coast was a barrel of whiskey, most of which was consumed on the way, 'through the politeness of those who helped to manage the affair.'"

The grant soon passed out of the hands of the improvident owners, and other settlers built cabins along the route. Among these were the Rosebrooks, Willeys, and Crawfords. They were such people as are drawn in the *Leatherstocking Tales*, and Abel Crawford might have stood for Leatherstocking himself. He was six feet four in height, and a wonder in strength, even among the big frontiersmen of those athletic days. His two elder sons, Erastus and Ethan Allen, were even taller than their father; Ethan, in fact, measured fully seven feet, and was of prodigious strength. The home of the Crawfords' (built, I think, about 1793) was twelve miles below the Gate of the Notch, and half way between stood Willey's house. Captain Rosebrook's family at the Giant's Grave (Fabyan's), and the farmers at North Conway, were their nearest neighbors.

This pass seemed so important to commerce that in 1803 the state built "the tenth turnpike," in place of the old and badly engineered road, which remains in the existing road. So large a number of market wagons and emigrant's teams passed along this road that a good chance for a public house was presented, and the Willeys built a substantial domicile, which immediately became known as the Notch Tavern, or the Willey House. It was closed for a time, but in 1825 was reopened, and in 1826 became the scene of that fatal June slide which is so renowned in the history of the locality. Later, the Crawfords, who then had the Mount Crawford Tavern, five miles below Willey's, built a second and more pretentious house, just above the Gate of the Notch, which became well-known not only to teamsters and stage-travellers, but had a large custom in summer from the hunting and fishing fraternity, naturalists, artists, and pleasure-seekers, who were the forerunners of that current of summer travel which now sets so strongly through the Notch, and invades every beautiful recess of the old hills. It was at the height of its prosperity about 1840, when Thomas G. Crawford, the third son of Abel, was manager; and it remained as an appendage to the new hotel long after the beginnings of the present structure were opened to the public; but has now been entirely torn away. It is these movings and the ubiquitous character of the Crawfords' actions and influence in the mountains, which have caused their names to be so confusedly applied to various localities; but now there is only one "Crawford's,"—the big hotel half a mile above the Notch-gate. "Hither" says an old guide-book, "every one comes to talk over his plans, and to make arrangements for various excursions." That is true yet, and the guide books inform us that

A LONELY BIT OF MEADOW — CRAWFORD NOTCH.

from the Crawford House "excursions can be made on the same day to the summit of Mount Washington, and return; through the famous White Mountain notch to North Conway and return; to the Glen House, via the summit of Mount Washington, Pinkham notch, Glen Station and the White Mountain notch; to the Profile House, Old Man of the Mountains and the Flume, and return; to Bethlehem, Littleton, and Jefferson, and return. Hurried tourists can visit the Willey House and Mount Willard the same day, or can ascend Mount Washington and return in season to ascend Mount Willard, and get the charming effect of the shadows in the Notch at sunset, a sight of a lifetime, and one which no one should miss."

The view from Mount Willard is down the notch, and possesses singular beauty. Bayard Taylor asserted that as a simple picture of a mountain pass, seen from above, it could not be surpassed in Switzerland. "Under our feet," he writes, "yawned the tremendous gulf of the notch, roofed with belts of cloud, which floated across from summit to summit nearly at our level; so that we stood, as in the organ-loft of some grand cathedral, looking down into its dim nave. At the farther end, over the fading lines of some nameless mountains, stood Chocorua purple with distance, terminating the majestic vista. It was a picture which the eye could take in at one glance; no landscape could be simpler or more sublime. The noise of a cataract on our right high up on Mt. Willey, filled the air with a far, sweet, fluctuating murmur, but all around us the woods were still, the harebells bloomed, and the sunshine lay warm on the granite." The top is about 2,570 feet above the sea, and the road after winding its way up by an easy grade affording many pleasant outlooks, leads out to the brink of a great cliff, whence the whole gorge of the Saco, and the sweep of its steep walls, are under your eye, while many a mountain peak may be recognized, from Jefferson in the northeast, to where, "about south-southwest the weird white crown of Chocorua peers over the dark ridge of Bear mountain." As the distance from the hotel is not too great, many persons find it pleasanter to walk to the top of Mt. Willard, although mountain-wagons are sent twice a day, or oftener, from the Crawford House. The best time to go is toward evening.

The guide-book's further caution, however, is no longer needed, namely: "You should be careful as soon as you arrive, to book your name at this place for a horse to Mount Washington, if you intend to make the ascent within a few days, as often all the ponies are engaged for a day or two beforehand." That was some twenty-five years ago. The price of a horse for the ride up and back, with guides to accompany the party, was only $4.00 to each person. A few still make the ascent each year, and a great many walk down the path. The danger and excitement of it are as great as ever, and severe casualties have occurred upon it, above timber line, within the past two years.

It is through the open grove called Idlewild, along the eastern side of the Glen, where seats have been made overlooking the little lake, the station and the lawn-tennis courts, that we enter upon this path and follow it half a mile or less upward to Gibb's falls, which proves to be an exceptionally rough series of cascades, recalling most forcibly to my mind the way in which the great Rio Grande leaps down from its sources in the Sierra San Juan toward Cunningham gulch. I forget the name of this stream,—perhaps it has none. I care not where it rises nor whither it flows. Nothing about it is of the least consequence except a few rods of snow-white foam and water that come pell-mell, dodging around and under the bulky rocks barricading the deep and sombre chasm; sliding in curves of crystal over floors of granite whose rough lines (where emerald moss clings) seem to writhe under the transparent and wavering currents; resting for a moment in some shaded, sandy basin at the head of the path, only to be deluded at last down a sluice-way into a cataract, where, in a clean leap of fifty feet or more (if there be plenty of water) the stream

THROUGH THE NOTCH.

loses all form of water and becomes merely twisted skeins and ravelings of fleece,— white, blue and green.

"What do you flatter yourself a reader can make out of such a description as that?" asks Prue in somewhat scornful criticism, after she has glanced over my note-book.

"Little that is very definite, my dear. Yet the words are quite as orderly as that struggle of rocks against torrent in the steep forests here at the base of Mount Clinton, which they call Gibb's falls! Now the idylic little stream on the other side of the valley is very different, —let us walk over there."

Returning to the hotel, we light our cigars and join the line of elegant strollers who drift down past the bowling-alley, across the bridge spanning the railway-cut and out upon a plank-walk that leads towards the thicket of young oaks sloping slowly up toward Mount Tom. A broad path leads into this sapling grove and we loiter along it, pausing here and there to catch the notes of a thrush that is beginning to salute the evening from his secluded retreat. After a few minutes we come to a stream-bed, among whose bowlders and gravel clear brown water is gently finding its way in a dozen friendly streamlets, which part but come together again, only to separate and rejoin in a new place, as a bevy of persons might leisurely pass among the trees of an open wood without disturbing their sociability.

Above the pool, is a sloping apron or incline of granite whose ledge-edges have been worn smooth and somewhat overgrown with moss, down which two currents, divided by a jutting diamond of rock above, unite in a merry slide. This is one of the very best standpoints to see the cataract and the clear pool at its foot; and, now that the water is low, we can walk out on the smooth slanting rock and pick our way along the stream-bed; or we may cross to the other bank, where a rude path, getting foothold on roots of trees, and rocks, and earth, helps us to mount to the higher parts of the cascade, as well as by remaining on this side.

There is a turn ahead hiding the upper part of the stream, but we can see a narrow bridge thrown across the little ravine, upon which stands a group of ladies, whose bright dresses look very gay against the sunlit foliage. Climbing up there, we find ourselves overlooking a very pretty and quiet little double waterfall, whose veil of misty white hangs down a vine-clad trough in the granite, and whose musical crashing is not loud enough to o'ermaster, nor be inharmonious with, the golden-mouthed thrush whose evening hymn still floats up to us out of the depths of the woods.

Such is Beecher's cascade, concerning which Henry Ward Beecher, and Starr King, and I know not how many other poets and preachers, have written such rhapsodies of word-expression as I can never emulate. Nor do I wonder,—for truly the place is pretty and inspiring; and you may ramble along the path to higher, and perhaps even more delicious bits of sylvan water scenery, where this wanton little heiress of the hill-snows flings its bubble-pearls by handfuls into the lap of the stolid rocks, and lifts its bright lips to the sunbeam's kiss just before coquettishly darting away down some cascade.

This waterfall is maidenly and coy, pretty and to be sung to. The other is virile and lusty; and the splendor of its charge down the mountain, is magnificent.

Next morning, the weather being beautiful, we decided to take a long walk down the Notch road, and hence declined the courteous invitations given us by two or three groups of amiable people to join them in a wagon-party, in the same direction. Immediately after breakfast, therefore, we trudged away, as blithe as larks. It is noticeable with what an increase of elasticity and solidity of nerve we step out now, compared with our powers of walking and enjoying a walk when we first left home. None of us had been ill, much less feeble, yet had more nervousness, or less vigor, than belonged to proper health. This proper health had now been recovered, and it was with the self-reliance of athletes and the glowing enjoyment of childhood that we set off upon our walk along the railroad track, ready to breast a slope, or leap a torrent, or tramp for many miles if necessary.

The railway alluded to, is the Portland and Ogdensburg,— Prue enquired whether "P. & O." did not stand for Peaks and Ocean,— which runs from Portland to Fabyan's. Leaving the Union Station in Portland it skirts, in Maine, the shores of Sebago lake, passes around the foot of Mount Pleasant, traverses the Fryeburg part of the Saco valley, so renowned for the great battles of Lovewell's war (see Chapter III.), exposing lovely landscapes toward the west all the way, and enters the mountains at North Conway, where it is joined by the Boston & Maine's tracks. For a long time that remained the terminus, and the dashing six-horse coaches which once carried passengers so gayly up this old turnpike to Bemis, Crawford's, and Fabyan's, are all well remembered, and much regretted by old travellers. But by-and-by, money and skill found itself able to hew a long niche-like shelf along the precipitous western side of the dark defile, and, in 1875-6, the impertinent locomotive had passed through its own Gate of the Notch (since the old portal was too narrow), and was flaunting its smoke in the very face of Mount Washington. Pushing northward, the railroad followed down the Amonoosuc to Fabyan's, where it connected with the Boston & Lowell. This accomplished, it had become possible to pass by rail from Boston, Portsmouth or Portland, directly through the heart of the mountains to northern Vermont, Montreal, and Quebec. The hurried traveller between the towns of Lake Champlain or Lower Canada and the New England seaports can therefore see the main features of the White Mountains, without any interruption of his journey, by coming this way,— and that is a great boon.

By the time I had expounded these facts (as I greatly enjoyed doing, for the preacher-blood of my exegetical ancestors runs strong in my veins) we had come to the Gate of the Notch.

The little plateau-valley where the Crawford House stands was once the bed of a lake, held in its oval basin by a barricade of rock at the lower end, extending from that naked bluff, well named Elephant Head, at the foot of Mount Jackson, across to the protruding base of Mount Willard. Over this, a magnificent waterfall then poured with copious volume and an unbroken fall, wearing a deep pit at the outer foot of the natural dam. But as the years went on this waterfall cut a deeper and deeper trough for itself, undermining the frost-cracked rocks on either side, and causing huge fragments to fall from their crags into the gorge below, until at last the cataract had cut a narrow gap in the dam down to the level of the bottom of the lake, which was thus wholly drained away except the little Saco pond still sparkling like a sapphire in the dark setting of the shaggy hills.

Into this gorge, only twenty-six feet in width, cut by the primitive glacier-fed river, and now occupied, half by a slender torrent and half by the turnpike, we follow the latter along the left wall, leaving the railway track to pursue a higher level on the right-hand side.

But it is not until we get twenty rods or so below the portal along the descending road cut into the eastern wall of the Notch, that we begin to perceive how really picturesque the scene is. There the rude, lofty, buttressed wall on the right (as we look back, or upward, toward the Gate) is seen in perspective, and across the tree-filled gorge at our feet, whose depth it is difficult to determine, where the corners of great rocks are dimly discerned through the curtaining foliage and the steady roar of white water sounds in deep diapason above the rustling of the wind,— across this chaotic and resounding chasm rise the bald terraces of a cliff where the foundations of Willard are bared to our eyes in marbled and banded granite, here rough and protuberant, giving mosses, ferns, and blossoming plants a foothold, there smooth, polished, and adorned only with the purple and crimson stains of water. The lowermost part is really separated by a deep gash from the main cliff, but we cannot detect this, and the whole front appears to be one solid escarpment, richly covered with weather-stains and the gay decoration of autumn leaves.

We should have missed the best of this, had we ridden, for the trees along the roadside obscure the view; but we crept through them to where a kind of balcony of jutting rock hung over the bank (you can easily find the place) whence we had a clear view of the chasm, of the jumble of fallen rocks below the Gate, the gray slides thrown down by the railway makers, the gaudy wall above, and the dark crest of the Mount Willey range overtopping the whole picture, which was almost as upright before us as if set upon some gigantic easel.

We could see nothing of the steeps upon our own side, on account of the overhanging trees and crags, until we had wandered a quarter of a mile or so farther down through the grove, along a winding road which now and then disclosed a noble peak in advance. There we came to a great knoll of bare granite that promised an outlook, and a moment's scrambling took us to its top.

The knoll keeps its promise, as we turn our eyes backward toward the Gate, which we can no longer look straight through, as before. At the head of the cañon looms the superb façade of Willard, black and stern as iron, and so steep and smooth that only here and there can a little close-clinging brush keep a foothold upon its face. The rounded summit is almost equally bare and rocky, its scant shrubbery looking like the sparse tufts of wool on an old African's half-bald pate, and I wonder it wasn't called Niggerhead.

At the right, on the eastern side of the gorge and over the Gate, towers the dome of Mount Jackson,— a "beetling cliff," in truth, even bolder (from our point of view) than its *vis-à-vis*, yet much less imposing, because its face is a slope of trees instead of the ledges and slides breaking Mount Willard's front into picturesque groupings of rocks. Down the Notch the lofty cone of Mount Willey dominates the landscape, and presently we come to a place on the road, where the trees on each side framed into a panel of golden leaves just these two peaks, Willey and Jackson — one before and the other behind us — producing a very striking tableau.

When we had gazed our fill at this sight, we walked on down the road, which was by no means deserted or silent, toward the two cascades that descend from the dark shoulders of Mount Webster like a white stole down the black gown of a priest. There seems to be uncertainty as to which should be called the Silver cascade and which the Flume, but we choose to believe that to the first or upper one, the latter name belongs. There is also much difference of opinion among the many writers who have described them in glowing terms, as to which is the prettier, and we debated it, not only with those whom we found climbing about them to get new points for admiration, but even in our own trio. I liked the Silver cascade the better, while Prue and Baily gave preference to the Flume. The beauty of both must depend upon the amount of water coming down.

The Flume is so called from the square-sided and deep channel the swift water has cut for itself in the soft granite at the point where the road bridges the stream, and the word is a very appropriate one. The torrent comes first into view from an invisible crevice in the forest, near the crest of the great hill, and almost at once divides into two parts, parted by a dense company of spruces crowded upon an island-crag; nor, as you stand upon the bridge in the road, can you see where these parts reunite again. But presently a broad single stream, sheeted with spray, comes leaping toward you, then, falling short, gathers into the funnel of the Flume beneath your feet and goes plunging down to the invisible Saco through an arch of interlaced boughs, fallen logs, and rocks, into which the sun strikes, this autumn day, as if through a cathedral window.

The Silver cascade has the most volume, is more torrential, and so steep that it is almost an unbroken fall for some hundreds of feet. "As you stand on the piazza of the hotel, you see this same stream far up the mountain, full a mile distant, leaping over the rocks and flashing in the sunlight like a silvered pinnacle of some mountain shrine. But as you stand on the bridge, or at the very base of the fall, which you can reach with care, the water seems pouring over the edge of the precipice. Just after a heavy rain the huge rock, which just below the summit usually divides the current, is almost entirely concealed by the spray. Like the most of mountain falls, it rather glides over the surface of the ledge than leaps in a clear, unbroken sheet from the summit to the base. At first the water is diffused over a broad surface, and in times of a drought is divided into several small streams. Before it reaches the base, however, all the water is compressed into a very narrow channel. Then, hurrying along over a comparatively level bed, it again, as it reaches the bridge, plunges down a distance of some twenty feet, and, driving through the flume, disappears among the bushes on the opposite side of the road. There is, perhaps, no place on this side of the mountains which so enchains one by its loveliness as the Silver cascade. You may spend hours around it, and yet long to return to its solitary beauty. The very height of the mountains, rising almost perpendicularly on each side of you, causes you to feel the impressiveness and power of the rushing torrent."

Continuing our walk under the base of Mount Webster, we got more and more out of the Notch proper into what is termed the Crawford glen, where the forested heights of Willey, Field, and Cevalon were reared almost to the zenith on the west, and Webster's unclimbable scarp hung over us against the east. Mount Webster is the southernmost of the Presidential range. It is 4,000 feet in height, and from it the White Mountains, proper, run in a pretty straight northeasterly direction to Mount Washington, increasing regularly in height. The summits of both Webster and Jackson, its next-of-kin, are attainable, but it is an exceedingly difficult undertaking, and the reward in scenery is slight. The great feature of Mount Webster (formerly called Notch mountain), is its west side, "where it slopes to the Saco valley in a steep wall, free from foliage and striped with brilliant colorings by the slides which have laid bare the bed rock."

The Mount Willey range, which runs from Mount Willey to Mount Tom, rewards the climber much better. Its principal peak, named after the Willey family who were overwhelmed by the great avalanche from its side in 1826, is 4,330 feet high, and therefore overlooks all the neighborhood; but the view is no more satisfactory than that to be attained from several other peaks much more easily accessible.

There are, however, some fine cataracts, Ripley's and the Arethusa especially, upon the southern flanks of this range. The latter is on Bemis brook, about two miles north of Bemis station, or six and one half miles from the Crawford House, and offer to an adventurous person a capital excursion.

The falls are 176 feet high, and are surrounded by old trees, and rugged groups of water-worn bowlders. The best point of view is about 100 feet below the falls, where their long white line is seen through the foliage.

We had now come within sight of the old Willey House, and not caring to visit it, turned back and were walking homewards when we met a mountain-wagon half full of the casual acquaintances that one makes as he journeys leisurely from inn to inn, where the same faces are encountered again and again, and where the free-and-easy sociability of a walk to some summit or a scramble together in some wild ravine, may introduce a life-friendship.

"Get in with us!" cried these people gayly. "You don't want to walk all the way back again. We're going down to Bartlett to get dinner, and then come back on the express There's lots of room — come on!"

I was willing, and I saw Baily casting longing looks at the back seat, where sat a very pretty brunette,— she was from Michigan, and had all that debonair archness and freedom which is so refreshing to the eastern eye, when, as in this case, it animates perfect decorum and style; but Prue hesitated, not because she didn't want to go, nor because there was any reason under the sun why she shouldn't, but simply out of that meaningless contrariness, or self-denial, characteristic of her incomprehensible sex, always is so ready to give away the rose and keep the thorns.

Ignoring her hesitation, I coolly lifted her up beside the jolly matron of the party, and climbed in behind with the brunette (who welcomed me with just the least bit of well-bred surprise), leaving Baily, mad as a hornet, to find a seat by the driver, throwing me a look of deadly enmity over his shoulder, while my wife's eyes gleamed like that legendary carbuncle hidden in these same old hills. I began to believe the bad spirits reputed to inhabit this dark gorge had entered into the whole party.

Rounding the mighty scarp of Mount Webster, we came into a somewhat broader park, where a rear rank of mountains, west of the lower half of the Presidential range, burst suddenly into view — noble and picturesque summits, bearing names given long ago by the learned Dr. Bemis — Giant's Stairs, with its terraced ledges atop; Resolution, where Davis resolved anew to continue the making of his almost forgotten path to Mount Washington along the high Montalban ridge, upon which these summits stand like sentinel boxes upon a Chinese wall; Crawford, wearing a jaunty *toque* of granite and the name of the hero who dwelt at its base (the old Mount Crawford tavern still stands there); and two or three others. Opposite, and in advance, towered spruce-clothed peaks on the edge of the great Pemigewasset wilderness, along whose base the railway was supported three or four hundred feet above our turnpike.

In the midst of this triangular park, just at the foot of Mount Webster, the Mount Washington river—straight as a birch sapling—came down to join the Saco,—crooked as a whiplash; and here (it was only a few minutes after starting) I discovered that I felt great anxiety to talk with the driver, and asked Baily if he would be good enough to exchange seats with me.

"Why, of course, old fellow, if you really insist upon it; but I am exceedingly comfortable here."

"Ah, that's just it!" I answered, for I wasn't going to confess my real motive; "you're far *too* comfortable; so I propose to root you out, and make you earn your passage by entertaining Miss Michigan with an account of your adventures."

"Oh, I'm sure he couldn't be more entertaining than you have been!" and she said it so heartily that for an instant I was deceived.

But the change was made; and then,— well, you know how it is on a summer day when all at once the clouds vanish and the radiant sun lights up and warms everything? That was the effect of this simple manœuvre. I don't discuss the philosophy of it, or attempt to palliate my part in the mischief,— I simply state the facts.

Next, we rattled over Nancy's bridge, recalling its pathetic romance,— no story brings the pioneers closer, and makes them seem more akin to us than the sad fate of this faithful heart; passed Sawyer's rock, the rum-scented legend of which is of an wholly opposite stripe; and in due time reached Upper Bartlett, which Starr King concisely described as in his day "only a long, winding lane among steep hills, cool with thick, dark, green verdure."

"Upper Bartlett," we read, "is a station on the P. & O. railroad, near which a small hamlet has arisen. It is in the centre of a picturesque amphitheatre of mountains, having Carrigain, the Nancy range, Tremont, and Haystack on the west; Hart's and Willoughby ledges, Mts. Parker, Crawford, Resolution, Langdon, and Pickering on the north; Kiarsarge and Moat on the east; and Table and Bear mountains on the south. Numerous excursions may be made from this point over the adjacent peaks; and there is rich trouting in Albany brook and other tributaries of the Saco. . . . . Mt. Carrigain is seen to the best advantage here, and Champney made his celebrated painting of it from near the old mill. The formidable and frowning peaks which surround the hamlet are finely contrasted with the rich and narrow intervales of the Saco."

Many of the adjacent mountains are ascendable, and the views from the summits of Langdon and Tremont, in particular, have been pronounced "of a high degree of grandeur." Carrigain is more remote, jungle-girt and difficult of access, but is higher than any other (4,678 feet) and divided from Mt. Lowell (3,850 feet) by the Carrigain notch, whose walls are remarkably precipitous. It has often been surmounted, however, even by ladies.

"Mt. Carrigain stands almost exactly in the centre of the vast group of the White and Franconia mountains, and .... is a marked feature in the landscape from almost every point of view. Conversely, the view from Carrigain must embrace the whole mountain mass, and must sweep around over all the principal summits. .... Ranges and notches, huge mountains and broad valleys, never seen from the points commonly visited in this region, are spread all around. From its central position

THE MOUNTAINS, FROM UPPER BARTLETT.

a better idea of the arrangement of the White and Franconia mountains is had than from any other point, perhaps, in the whole group." Close to Carrigain on the other side is the almost unexplored mass of Mt. Hancock, almost as lofty.

Upper Bartlett has long been an important outlet and milling point for the lumbering operations in the Pemigewasset basin; and within the past year a railway has been pushed into the wilderness as far as the Albany intervales. A new and entertaining side-trip is thus opened to tourists, in regard to which I shall have more to say presently.

When the north-bound express came along, we boarded it, on our return to Crawford's.

That ride by railroad through the Notch is, to most travellers, the crowning and best-remembered experience of their White Mountain journeyings.

Almost as soon as the train leaves North Conway it affords a momentary view of Mt. Washington, at the left, and then plunges into the pine woods growing around the base of Mt. Bartlett,—a lesser twin with Kiarsarge. The first stop is at the Intervale House, beyond which beautiful meadows are skirted, and glimpses caught of Double-head mountain, on the right, over the church spire in Lower Bartlett. Then the East branch of the Saco is crossed, the Carter peaks display themselves and Glen Station is reached, where stages are in waiting for Jackson and the Glen House, by way of Pinkham notch (see Chapter XV). The bridge over the romantic Ellis river, just beyond the station, gives a capital sight of Carter notch, while Kiarsarge towers finely in the rear across the Bartlett hills, Moat range lies southward beyond the meadows, and Iron mountain prominently ahead.

PEAK OF MOAT MOUNTAIN, NORTH CONWAY.

The Saco is next crossed, and a little later passengers on the right-hand side of the cars (which is the better henceforth) catch an inspiring view of Mt. Resolution and the Giant's Stairs, up the Rocky Branch valley. The Saco is now upon the right, with old fashioned farm-houses and orchards in the narrow meadows enclosed by its bendings, partitioned by frowning headlands. Carrigain and many lesser peaks crowd the scene ahead, and show how close we are getting to the very heart of the hills. Then the train draws under the Willoughby ledges of Mt. Langdon (on the right) with Mt. Parker's cone plain at the head of an alcove beyond, and stops at Upper Bartlett.

Moving on we find ourselves encircled by mountains not easy to keep track of by a novice, even though he has a map open before him. The most conspicuous features are the grandly piled ledges of Hart mountain, on the right, over which the Crawford peaks are heaped together like Ossa upon Pelion. The deep cañon of Nancy's brook withdraws our eyes to the valley, and we see the old Mt. Crawford tavern, just before halting at Bemis station. The venerable Dr. Samuel Bemis, who owned a region measured by a great many square miles, of which this was a part, and who lived near here for half a century, nearly alone, but in a very comfortable manner, is destined to become the chief historical figure of the locality, for his deeds, records and names are identified with the district.

At Upper Bartlett begins one of the steepest railway inclines in the east,—116 feet to the mile, as far as the Gate of the Notch. Two locomotives are used on heavy trains, and you note the sonorous pantings of the laboring machines as, with herculean force, they strain to the task. The speed is nowhere great, yet it is by no means slow, and there is no symptom of stopping. The rhythmic snortings of the iron horse, and the grind of the wheels upon the rails, are echoed from "cliff and scar" in one sullen roar, which adds mightily to the impressiveness of the effect.

Mt. Crawford, with its curious, overhanging pinnacle, like a Canadian *tuque*, is now in full view among the squarer, more forbidding summits across the gorge, which is sinking rapidly beneath our steady, upward progress along the flank of Nancy mountain. The track bends incessantly, cuts a way through promontories, edges around the spurs along a rocky balcony, and leaps cataract-torrents by the help of trusty bridges.

A bewildering array of heights looms up ahead, but presently we separate one vast crag from the rest and keep our eye upon it. A deep ravine intervenes, and the train glides out upon a long bridge, suspended eighty feet in the air. We lean over the rail at the side of the open observation-car and shrink a little at the depth beneath us. From this bridge the glorious alcove down which flows the Mt. Washington river is opened to our view, with dozens of first-rate heights *en echelon* on each side close by Washington in the place of honor at the head. Then we are face to face with the enormous, impending façade of Frankin-stein cliff,—the most majestic escarpment in the mountains,—"a black and castellated pile of precipices," as Samuel Drake calls it. "Thrust out before us, athwart the pass," he exclaims, "a black and castellated pile of precipices shot upward to a dizzy height, and broke off abruptly against the sky. Its bulging sides and regular outlines resembled the clustered towers and frowning battlements of some antique fortress built to command the pass. Gashed, splintered, defaced, it seemed to have withstood for ages the artillery of heaven and the assaults of time. With what solitary grandeur it lifted its mailed front above the forest and seemed even to regard the mountains with disdain! Silent, gloomy, impregnable, it wanted nothing to recall those dark abodes of The Thousand and One Nights, in which malignant genii are imprisoned for thousands of years. This was Frankenstein. We at once accorded it a place as the most suggestive of cliffs. From the other side of the valley the resemblance to a mediæval castle is still more striking. It has a black gorge for a moat, so deep that the head swims when crossing it; and to-day, as we crept over the cat's-cradle of a bridge thrown across for the passage of the railway, and listened to the growling of the torrent, far down beneath, the whole frail structure seemed trembling under us.

"But what a contrast! What a singular freak of nature! At the foot of this grizzly precipice, clothing it with almost superhuman beauty was a plantation of maples and birches, all resplendent in crimson and gold. Never have I seen such masses of color laid on such a background. Below, all was light and splendor; above, all darkness and gloom. Here, the eye fairly revelled in beauty, there, it recoiled in terror. The cliff was like a naked and swarthy Ethiopian up to his knees in roses."

This passed, by a great curve sweeping around it, the real Notch is entered, and the Willey House, 500 feet below, appears at the foot of the hill. We are now high upon Mt. Willey, and crossing the track of the avalanche that swept such devastating tumult into this valley sixty years ago. It is worth while to look backward and watch the shapely and entangled summits recede and regroup themselves. The ponderous, purple-hued front of Willard seems to bar the way ahead, while opposite us the shaggy walls of Webster and Jackson, mottled with autumn colors, scarred with slides and "breaking out" in black blotches of rock, rise sharply up from the Saco cañon, where we look far down into a dense mass of variegated foliage and get glimpses of the bright stream. This is the very chasm itself and we are awed, interested, full of admiration, overwhelmed with an embarrassment of riches in scenery. Then comes a breathless leap across the chasm of Willey brook — a perilous rush along the outskirts of the mountain wall — a gliding from under the dark battlements of Willard — a passage between the stately pillars of the *new* Gate of the Notch — and then with a triumphant blast of the whistle, we emerge into the sunlight and space of the little park at Crawford's station.

CHAPTER XXII.

AT NORTH CONWAY.

I know the shaggy hills about,
The meadows smooth and wide;
The plains that toward the southern sky,
Fenced east and west by mountains lie.

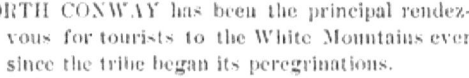NORTH CONWAY has been the principal rendezvous for tourists to the White Mountains ever since the tribe began its peregrinations.

Its extra-broad bottom-lands attracted settlers so early that when the Revolution began there were nearly 300 people in the town (of which this part is the northern edge), who not only offered recruits to the Continental army, but maintained a company of rangers scouting in their own woods. By this time a road had been built northward to Gorham and Lancaster, and upon the close of the war, when the turnpike through the Notch was completed, Conway became an important and busy station.

Those were its best days, but by the time the long trains of freight wagons ceased to roll through its streets, superseded by railways, the town had been adopted by summer boarders and excursionists from the cities, and a new kind of prosperity began. There are four villages within the town, of which North Conway enjoys a preeminence due to its position at the intersection of the Boston and Maine with the Portland and Ogdensburg railroads, or, perhaps yet more, to its relation to the mountains and to the valley-lands of the beautiful Saco.

The village occupies a terrace on the eastern side of the Saco meadows, where the soil is sandy and easily drained. "The green hills guard it on the east, forming a double line of low shaggy summits near the street; and on the west, across the Saco valley, is the long and massive Moat mountain, noble and imposing in its colors and outlines, and the most conspicuous object seen from the village. A little east of north, and about four miles distant, is the crest of the graceful pyramid of Mt. Kearsarge, whose long slopes approach within two miles of the street. To the north-northwest, about sixteen miles distant, is the peak of Mt. Washington, about which several of the other main mountains are clustered. In an opposite direction the valley of the Saco opens to the south, over long stretches of fertile lowlands, banded by the groves that enclose the river. The village is 521 feet above the sea, or 32 feet lower than Centre Harbor. North Conway is the chief summer-resort among the White Mountains, and is occupied by city people from early May until late October. The height of the season is in August, when over 3,000 tourists are sojourning here. During the heated term it is warmer than Bethlehem, but cooler than the villages of the lake-country. Evening gayeties are much patronized, and there are hops, concerts, and readings in the halls of the chief hotels. The adjacent roads are visited, every pleasant day, by riding parties; and rambling pedestrians explore the neighboring forests and

MTS. BARTLETT AND KIARSARGE — NO. CONWAY.

hills, or fish for trout along the falling brooks. It is the beauty and variety of its environs that gives North Conway the foremost rank among the mountain villages, added to the fact that it is at the proper focal distance from Mt. Washington."

The village is hardly more than a community of hotels and boarding-houses,—great and small, antique and modern, elaborate and simple. On the edge of the terrace-bluff, near the station of the Boston and Maine (the station of the other road is on the other side of the village, while the junction of the two roads is half a mile northward) stands the Kearsarge,—an immense hostelry, ranking among the "great" hotels. Another large and older house, from which the White Mountains are visible, as they are not from the Kearsarge, is the Intervale, half a mile northward. Between these two, hotels line the street on either hand, while still others have more remote locations. Style, a rate of expense, and classification of companions, may be found, therefore, to suit every requirement. There is no doubt, however, that among all these houses the *very best* is the —

"Theo," Prue calls out, just here, "whose idea was it that you were reading to me a little while ago about this place being 'at the proper focal distance,' or something of the kind?"

"What I read was written by Mr. Sweetzer; but the idea in that particular phrase is Starr King's. Hand me, if you please, his *White Hills.* Thank you. Now,—let me see,—oh, here it is, on page 175: 'North Conway,' he instructs us, 'lies at the proper focal distance from the hills that enclose it, and from the Mt. Washington range, to command various and rich landscape effects, and this no doubt is the great charm of the place.'

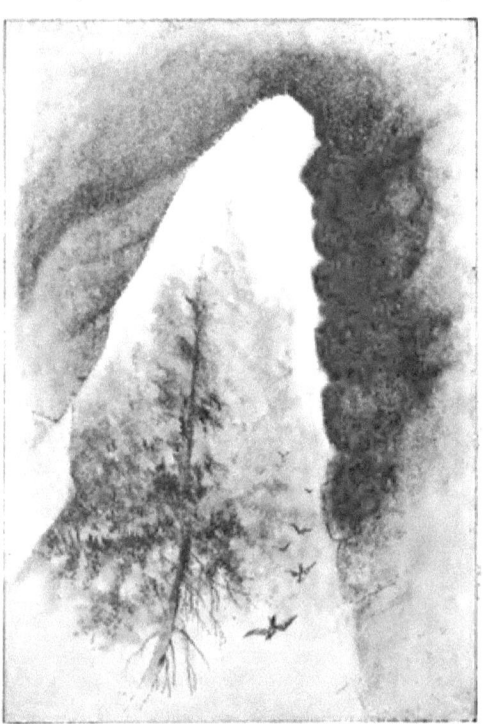

PITMAN'S ARCH—NO. CONWAY.

In another place, he assures us that a most accurate report of the meadow-forms and mountain-guards of the village would give no suggestion of its loveliness, and goes on: 'One always finds, we think, on a return to North Conway, that his recollections of its loveliness were inadequate to the reality. Such profuse and calm beauty sometimes reigns over the whole village, that it seems to be a little quotation from Arcadia, or a suburb of Paradise. Who can tell how it is that the trees here seem of more aristocratic elegance,—

that the shadows are more delicately penciled,— that the curves of
the brooks are more seductive than elsewhere? Why do the nights
seem more tender and less solemn? What has touched the ledgy
rocks with a grace that softens the impression of sublimity and
age? What has made the twilight parks of pine dim with a pensive,
rather than a melancholy, dusk? . . . . The atmosphere and the outlines of the hills seem to lull rather than stimulate. There are no
crags, no pinnacles, no ramparts of rock, no mountain frown or
savageness brought into contrast, at any point, with the general serene
beauty. Kearsarge is a rough and scraggy mountain, when you attempt
to climb it, but its lines ripple off softly to the plain. Mt. Washington does not seem so much to stand up, as to lie out at ease across

THE LEDGES — NO. CONWAY.

the north. The leonine grandeur is there, but it is the lion not erect
but couchant, a little sleepy, stretching out his paws and enjoying the
sun. And tired Chocorua appears as if looking wistfully down into

A land
In which it seemed always afternoon.'"

"Why, that," said my wife, "is pure rhapsody."

"It may be, but it is the honest impression which familiarity with
this spot must make, more or less distinctly, on every sensitive soul.
I could support it by an immense quantity of testimony from all sorts
and conditions of men, and women too, had I the time to bring it
together."

Our first excursion was the regulation drive "around the Ledges" in one of the trim black buckboards that go kiting over Conway's hills from May to October. There are single buggies and landaus, phætons and waggonettes, carryals and gigs, Concord coaches and mountain wagons; but the buckboard has the most fresh air, exercise, and gayety to the mile in it,— and we choose it every time.

The Ledges are two conspicuous knolls of forest-hidden granite

CATHEDRAL LEDGE AND ECHO LAKE — NO. CONWAY.

forming a low saddle-shaped hill at the foot of Moat mountain, on the other side of the Saco, and some three miles distant. Into their hitherward wall the strong current, freshets, and ice-packs of that primeval Saco that once filled all this intervale with the milky meltings of Mt. Washington's glaciers, cut so deeply, that now, in place of the bending slope that originally curved down to the plain, is left only a precipitous face. This front has a total height of 960 feet on the southern or White Horse ledge, and of about 740 on the northern, or Cathedral ledge.

The name of the former is given in recognition of the appearance (in a whitish incrustation) of the forepart of a horse prancing up the face of the ledge, with all the energy he would need to summon were it reality. Mr. Sweetzer sardonically remarks that "newcomers at North Conway are seldom allowed to rest until they have seen, acknowledged, and complimented the equine form of this amorphous spot;" but, as for me, I am forced to confess that I saw this "equine form" very plain at the first glance, without any previous guidance whatever; and I acknowledge this with reluctance, because I detest these chance resemblances which catch the eye and disturb the harmonious whole of a scene, save where, as in the case of the Old Man of the Mountain, a really remarkable contour becomes the predominating interest. I am informed that "all marriageable ladies, maiden or widow, run out to look at it, in consequence of the belief current in New England that if, after seeing a white horse, you count a hundred, the first gentleman you meet will be your future husband!" And, apparently, the poor victim has no way to rid himself of this dreadful spell!

The bold, naked face of the northern crag, in particular, with its rounded, elephantine forehead, streaked and damp, often wears a purplish lustre, as though a draping of rich, gray satin, with rosy reflections in the high lights, were flung over the face of the bluff, so that it is a very striking and beautiful object.

The contiguous ledge takes its name from an arched cavity in its front which you may or may not feel repaid in visiting. Still further north this same protrusion of granite forms Humphrey's ledge, a spur of Mt. Attitash, whence a glorious view is given up and down the Saco. If a person can climb neither Kearsarge nor Willard, he may feel that he has not missed the most beautiful quality of their views after he has looked off Humphrey's ledge.

Just in front of these cliffs lies their mirror,—Echo lake. "The tremendous shadow the cliff flings down," says Drake, "seems lying deep in the bosom of the lake as if perpetually imprinted there. Slender birches, brilliant foliage, were delicately etched upon the surface, like arabesques on polished steel. The water is perfectly transparent and without a ripple. Indeed, the breezes playing around the summit or humming in the tree-tops, seem forbidden to enter this haunt of the Dryads. The lake laps the yellow strand with a light, fluttering movement. The place seems dedicated to Silence itself.

"To destroy this illusion a man came out of a booth and touched off a small cannon. The effect was like knocking at half-a-dozen doors at once. And the silence which followed seemed all the deeper. Then the aged rock was pelted with questions, and made to jeer, laugh, menace and curse by turns, or all at once. How grandly it bore all these petty insolences! How presumptious in us thus to cover its hoary front with obloquy! We could never get the last word. We did not even come off in triumph. How ironically the mountain repeated, 'Who are you?' and 'What am I?' With what energy it at last vociferated 'Go to the devil!' To the Devil's Den we accordingly go."

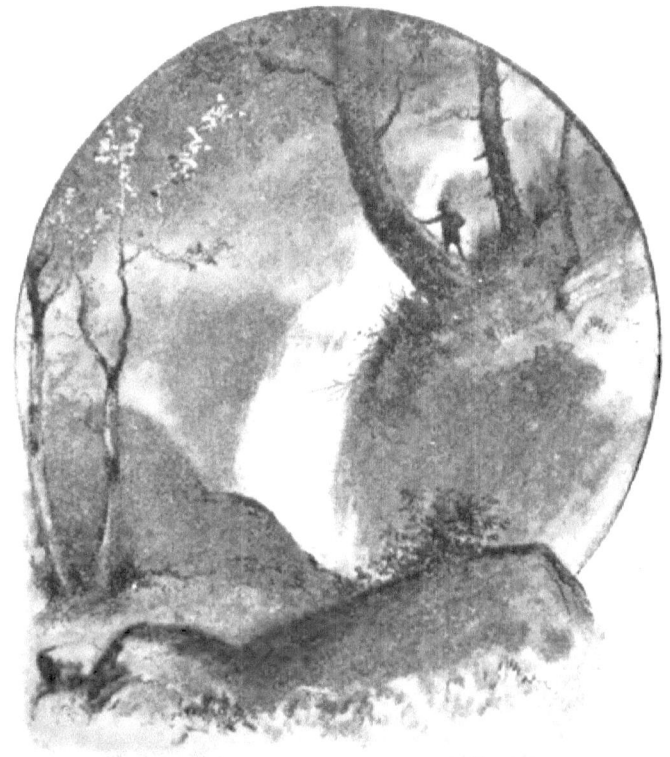

ONE OF NORTH CONWAY'S CASCADES.

This abode of supposed evil is a cavern among fallen fragments, underneath the Cathedral, reminding one of Herbert's remark, "No sooner is a temple built to God but the devil builds a chapel hard by." Not far beyond, a gay torrent comes tumbling down the side of Moat, and hurls itself over the ledge into a series of deeply-rounded basins, called Diana's Baths,— a proof that this is a good sporting region, else why should Diana and her hounds have come here? A plain path strikes up to the top of the ledges, whence you survey all the loveliness of the valley and its eastern wall.

The next morning, Baily and I hired saddle-horses and took a long ride, first to Humphrey's ledge, and then around toward Jackson. When we came back, we found that Prue, instead of gossiping on the porch all day, or playing lawn-tennis on "Sunset bluff," had gone off for a walk by herself toward the Green hills, or Rattle-snake range, directly behind the village. She found an obscure road that crossed the Portland and Ogdensburg tracks near their station, and led into a pine grove filling the hollow beyond, which brought her out, half-a-mile farther on, at the rear of the Artist's Falls Hotel and near the Mineral Spring. Here she might have followed a divergent path up the rocky glen of Artist's brook for three-quarters of a mile to the falls, which have been made famous by so many painters, and which are well worth a visit when the brook is full of water; but instead, she pursued the old wagon-road toward the hills, until she had reached a grassy shoulder where there were some smooth rocks to sit upon. Here the Saco valley was spread out nicely beneath her gaze. Moat mountain, of course, filled all the front of the picture, trees cutting off what lay at its right, but at the left, beyond the dark knoll of The Haystack, rose "the superb crest" of Chocorua,—double-peaked and lofty; and at his left, and beyond him, stretched the blue and crowded summits of Ossipee and the Sandwich mountains.

The air was misty, and she did not think it worth while to take the easy path that leads from the rear of the Artists' Falls House to the top of Middle mountain; but had she done so, and had the air been clear, one of the best views in the neighborhood of Conway would have been her reward. The prospect is, indeed, but little short of that from Mt. Kearsarge itself, for it reaches Sebago lake, near Portland, the Green mountain in Effingham, the Ossipee range, and many heights beyond Chocorua. The noble outlines of Moat rise to the sky on the west, to the right of which the Presidential range sweeps around the north to where Kearsarge obstructs the view.

Among the arrivals at the hotel that evening we were delighted to greet an artist whom we knew very well, and whom before long the world generally will want to know better. Only a few days previous he had made a rapid reconnoisance of the Swift River valley, beyond Albany. This secluded stream lies over behind Moat mountain, and flows eastward from Trypyramid, down through the Albany intervales to the Saco at Conway.

"I have had many and various pleasant rides over the country this summer," he replied to our queries, "but none that equalled that ride of forty miles in a buck-board,—twenty out and twenty back."

"Were you gone only one day?"

"Only one day, but the excursion deserves a week at the least. I started about seven in the morning, with strong indications of rain in the air. The first four or five miles of the road led through the meadow-lands you see out there towards Moat mountain, after which it passed into shady woods, very cool and still,— no noise save now and then the call of a hermit thrush, and a running fire of comments from squirrels that followed us on the walls and fences. At last we came suddenly upon the Swift river, rushing over countless bowlders and making a tremendous racket. No more lonesomeness after that!"

"Is its whole course like that?"

"Pretty much; and how refreshing is the sound of rushing water, on a hot day, as this had turned out to be! It is a drink, by proxy, so to speak."

"How was the road?"

"Excellent,— and the little mare measured the ground so rapidly that she soon took us to Eagle ledge, ten miles from here and about six from Conway,— a frowning wall of jagged rock fully as high as old

A GLIMPSE OF WHITE FACE.

White Horse over there,
In reaching it the road winds
around the southern promontory of
Moat mountain, where the woods were full of
berry-pickers, and openings among the trees would give new and sometimes very odd views of familiar mountains or enchanting bits of meadow. After that it was a constant succession of cliffs, sugar-orchards, and farm-houses in a state of chronic decay."

"More pleasing to you, as an *artist*," I suggest, "than to you or anyone else, as an *owner*."

"Decidedly. As a general rule a house that is picturesque is more or less ruinous. Presently, to go on with my narrative, a louder roar of water warned us of our approach to the falls of Swift river. They didn't amount to much, but in the seasons of freshets must be magnificent. There was a deep, narrow cleft in the rock through which the water was pouring, and I thought it worth a ten-minute sketch."

This he showed us, drawn on a page of his sketch-book in water colors; explaining that the high rocks on top of, and beside the chute, were worn and polished, proving what a volume of water must come down through their interspaces at certain times. The foreground showed the road set between borders of golden-rod and blackberries, the mingled profusion of which produced a most charming effect in black and gold.

"Above the falls we plunged into thick woods, and I was beginning to be discouraged, when suddenly,— and the more effectively by the contrast,— the Albany intervale opened upon my astonished view. It was an oval of meadow-land, something over two miles long and about one in width, as level as a floor and dotted along the road with farm-houses. It was fine!"

VIEW OF ENTRANCE TO ALBANY INTERVALE.

"What mountains were in sight?" asked Prue, eager most of all on this point,—

> For I have taught her, with delighted eye
> To gaze upon the mountains, to behold,
> With deep affection, the pure ample sky,
> And clouds along its blue abysses rolled,
> To love the song of waters, and to hear
> The melody of winds with charmed ear.

NOTE.— Luckily I saw this in proof, though *he* didn't mean I should. The idea! As though I had no *enjoyment* in, not to speak of any *appreciation* of, the scenery, and the songs of birds, and that sort of thing, until *he* "taught" me! I hate to "speak right out in meetin'" this way, but I won't *be so misunderstood*,— yes, *misrepresented* by that horrid man, to all the *dear* friends we made up in those *perfectly delightful* mountains. — P.

"Mountains? Oh, lots of 'em. You remember when you were on Lake Winnipesaukee all those big peaks northward,— Chocorua, Passaconaway, Paugus, White-face and the others?"

"What a question! of course we do."

"Well, I was right behind them, and close at their base, but I would never have recognized them. They form one side of the wall around this delightful spot; and then comes in Hedgehog (swinging round toward the north, you know), Tremont, and others, clear around to Moat mountain and Haystack, down at the mouth of the river. The river itself, by the the way, was wandering through the

THE PINNACLES.

meadows very uncertainly and quietly, in the weakness of extreme youth, for it is born just above. Now that a railroad is building from Bartlett, it won't be long before the place will be a popular point with the tourists, and the road will find their passenger-traffic a bigger item than their lumber-carrying. In the fall it ought to be especially attractive, for fully half the timber is hard wood. The swamp maples were brilliant crimson even when I was there, and the whole valley must now be like a great Japanese punch-bowl for color."

That night there was a terrific storm, but it lulled soon after midnight, and the morning broke clear and still. Our first look was towards Kearsarge, which we meant to climb; and as I saw it I quoted those lines in *Lucile*:—

> And high over our head
> The wrecks of combat of Titans were spread.
> Red granite and quartz, in the alchemic sun
> Fused their splendors of crimson and crystal in one;
> And deep in the moss gleamed the delicate shells,
> And the dew lingered fresh in the heavy harebells;
> The large violet burned; the campanula blue;
> And Autumn's own flower, the saffron, peer'd through
> The wild rhododendrons and thick sassafras,
> And fragrant with thyme was the delicate grass;
> And high up, and higher, and highest of all,
> The secular phantom of snow!

"Snow,— really?" Prue cried, going to the window.

"Only a thin dusting. It will melt away in an hour or two."

The ascent of Kearsarge (or Pequawket, as I wish the people would consent to call it), is not a difficult matter. You are driven from the hotel to a farm house at its base, some three miles distant, where you can hire saddle-horses for the ascent, or can walk up a path which is in excellent condition, though pretty steep in some places. Hundreds of persons tramp over it every season. The distance to the top is nearly three miles, and an hour and a half is usually allotted to the task.

Every feature of this "queenly" peak, whose perfect cone is one of the most satisfying outlines New Hampshire's mountains can show, was distinctly visible in the well-washed air of that morning, as we rode toward the mountain. Each separate tree seemed visible, and we could see the windows in the little house on the summit, and the the shadow-line under the eaves, though it was more than 2,500 feet above us. The road wound between substantial stone walls and past neat houses — how neat! — through Kearsarge Village scattered along a brook whose furrowed rocks, bearing witness to terrific spring-freshets, were now almost bare. Beyond the picturesque little hotels a farm-house stood against the lowest slope of the mountain, where our driver put us down and agreed to meet us again in four hours. Behind the house was an orchard, and behind the orchard a narrow lane entered by a wicket gate. The lane led us to a pasture lot, across which the trail, much gullied-out by rains, conducted us to another gate at the margin of the woods; and having entered them we were fairly started on our climb.

This wood consisted wholly of small second-growth, damp with last night's rain and redolent with the pleasant odor of sweet fern. Ferns of all kind, indeed, were exceedingly abundant, and had been turned to a rich, warm brown in all open spaces, where the frost could get at them. Two or three hundred feet up we surmounted a fine shoulder, whence a noble view down the valley was given; but we only glanced at it, and then set ourselves to a very stiff pull, wasting no breath in talk, but cheered by the chippering of some tardy warblers just starting southward, and taking notes from this high outlook as to their route ahead.

"I suppose," says Prue, with a deep breath between each word, "they — mean — to take — the — air-line."

One lazy little titmouse said *dee-dee* to us, as though too indolent this slumberous morning to give the first half of his song. At the top of this stiff pull came a level space where we sat down to get our breath in the midst of strawberries,— not the wild, but a cultured fruit, indicating that some wayfarer had sat here on a June day, and having refreshed himself on strawberries, had thrown some aside (no doubt he thought it waste) to take root and perpetuate his memory in the grateful minds of his followers. He must have been a good man, since

> Only the actions of the just
> Shall rise and blossom in the dust.

Our next outlook was gained just below the Spring, which is half way to the top, they say; and here the Ossipee range shone plainly above a long line of distant highlands in the south, while westward the rude bulk of Carrigain towered chieftain of the Pemigewasset wilds. We took but a swallow at the spring, into whose clear depths a fine bottle-green frog went diving, for it is a mistake to drink much on such a tramp; and then strode on, the blood playing like a trip-hammer in the back of the head, until, 500 feet higher, we could again begin to look out of the woods, and catch enticing glimpses of sharp Chocorua over the bristling crest of Moat's long bulwark. On again! Soon the forest is left behind and the whitish conglomerate * of the top of the mountain is underfoot. In its crevices only stunted spruce and red cedar, flattened down (perhaps by the weight of snow) out of the way of the wind, can exist, save where, here and there, a better-rooted and sturdier tree manages to keep its foothold; but there is a plentitude of huckleberry bushes and hardy plants. Among this timber-line shrubbery a most inquisitive kinglet came to make our acquaintance, and shriek his *zee zee zee* at us in the sharpest, thinnest, sauciest tone I ever heard an animal utter. I haven't mentioned half the birds (chiefly sparrows, woodpeckers, and titmouses, of various kinds) that we saw and heard, nor the ubiquitous and querulous squirrels always in sight.

---

* The lower parts of Kearsarge are composed of common and trachytic granites, with occasional limited areas of slate. The upper 2,000 feet consists of an igneous felsite, full of rounded pebbles and angular fragments of slate. This fiery flood of molten rock was thrown out before the Helderberg period, in the same eruption that formed the ridge of Moat mountain. The geographical position of Kearsarge is in the towns of Chatham and Bartlett, about four miles from the Maine boundary.—HUNTINGTON.

The rock was bare nearly everywhere over the top of the mountain, and most curiously gnarled and compounded. It lay in ledges which the path surmounted so steeply that it was like going up a vast ruined stairway. Within the allotted time we arrived at the small house on the summit, which replaces the more pretentious hostelry destroyed some years ago, where we were welcomed by a solemn young man, who was both proprietor and cook in this lone restaurant, 3,000 feet above Beacon hilltop.

Buying a bottle of ginger ale and some sandwiches and cookies, made by his wife at the foot of the mountain, we rested while we consumed them. Then we went out prepared to enjoy the view. It *was* enjoyable,— more pleasing, I think, than even that from Mount Washington. Over that kingly height, which ordinarily, of course, is in plain view, hung massive bundles of struggling vapor, cutting off all the northern peaks down to a certain limit marked by a line as straight and level as the horizon of the sea. The bases of the northern peaks, together with all the valleys and foothills from Mount Pleasant around to Wildcat, were in deep shadow, and dull indigo in color, becoming purple on the lower slopes, where the red of the colored leaves shone through. The clouds overhead in that quarter, had gathered thick and gray-white, streaked by horizontal folds of a dark blue, or, higher up, of a pure sepia tone. Now and then there would be a break, and some portentous head would frown through, but in general the Presidential group was hidden from us.

At Washington's left, where the Pemigewasset peaks were tumbling aloft, the sky was full of great cumuli, shining white as marble palaces in the azure, dappling the nearer hills with queerly shaped shadows, and casting the splendid outlines of innumerable tall mountains toward the west into solid masses of dark purplish blue. Lafayette was just visible,— white plumes of cloud waving about his chapeau.

Farther south, Whiteface, Passaconaway, Chocorua, and the rest of the Sandwich chieftains stood out sharp and clear against a fleecy sky; and to their left, between masculine Chocorua and feminine Ossipee, a vista opened across the basin of Lake Winnipesaukee.

Southward, the vision swept a whole quadrant of broken hills, none lofty enough to cut the horizon more than do the tossing waves at sea, but showing, nearer at hand, the ample sweep of the Saco, with its sinuous current, prairie-like savannas, its richly colored terraces and sloping boundary-hills. The sides of the latter, and of our own mountain and all the foothills near by, were carpeted with a Persian pattern of foliage,— the dark coniferous trees in masses separated by lines and clumps of brilliant hard-wood trees, which were richly toned even in shadow; but where the sunlight struck through they glowed like the patches of wild crimson poppies you see in May on the verdant plains of southern California. All down the centre of this gay picture ran the smooth meadows, dotted with gipsy encampments of elms and maples, exceedingly green in the sunlight, while here and there glistening spaces or ribbons showed where a pond slept or a river wandered. The nearer hillsides were fairly ablaze with color,—not in solid masses of flame; that would have been too much; but in innumerable points of carmine, orange and yellow, evenly scattered among white-and-green birches and the richly dark spruce and pine. One can trace the waters of the Saco almost continuously from its source to its mouth, but no part of it is so lovely as those exquisite green intervales at Conway, encircled by the autumnal hillsides.

There are ponds by the score, each reflecting the clouds or flashing the sunlight. Sebago seems quite near, and a strong glass discerns the smoke of Portland and the glimmer of light upon the sails in Casco bay. The ocean itself is readily visible in a proper light; and, farthest of all, Monadnock, 100 miles distant, straight south, sketches

MT. WASHINGTON, FROM CONWAY MEADOWS.

a faint blue crescent upon the horizon. Eastward, Maine stretches away comparatively level, yet not monotonously so, the foreground spangled with irregular lakelets and embroidered with streams and shadowy glens, and the horizon notched with pale blue summits. The loftier groups toward the Rangeley lakes are hidden from sight. In Ticknor's *Guide* an elaborate description of all that is to be seen from this peak is written out, supplemented by a panoramic sketch.

Toward sunset that evening, we left the hotel and sauntered down the road to the covered bridge. "The sky was serene and beautiful. The sun shone with a soft and elegant lustre, such as seems peculiar to that delightful weather which, from the 20th of September to the 20th of October, so often elicits from the mouths of mankind the epithet of charming. Mildness tempered the heat and serenity hushed the world into universal quiet."

The hither end of this bridge has always been a favorite lounging place with Conway lovers. The village itself looks well from here, grouped upon the terrace, ensconced, in trees and sheltered under the rude and hirsute strength of Middle mountain. But the view up the river toward the White Hills is the main attraction to this spot.

The Saco winds toward you in a double curve. The bank upon your right is a bluff, the top of which is an emerald-turfed meadow. The further bank is low, and bordered by a thick line of maples and alders, overhanging the water and reflected in its placid surface. On the right, the meadow-level is narrow,—the terrace crowned with woods that in the middle quite reach the bend of the river in shapely copses. Light-leaved birches form the front of this bushy line, but behind them stands a dark and stately rank of spruces. Thus on each side beautiful banks of trees shut in the view toward the centre, whence comes most gracefully the dimpled river; and across this opening, far above its foothill spurs, is erected the massive pointed arch of Washington, isolated from its neighbors, grand and lonely.

This is the picture sketched in the accompanying illustration; but at best, that can only show the fine composition and effects of light and shade. You cannot see how blue were the sky and the river; how rich the green of the meadow-grass and fresher foliage; how splendid the sunlight and shadow on the noble background of crags and summits, nor how the fiery torches of the maple boughs, waving here and there among the verdant leaves of shrubbery, or conical masses of hemlock and pine, served as points of brilliance accentuating and glorifying the sketch. This wonderful and delicate display of color, nothing less than the brush and palette of a master hand could show. The best of wood-cuts can only *suggest* the beauty it holds.

The air was flooded with sunshine when we looked out next morning, and tingled upon our cheeks like a tonic as we walked rapidly down to the station. In this exhilarating way, therefore, we bade good-by to the mountains.

With eyes satisfied for the present, and carrying away a rich store of food for memory, we rushed southward, giving farewell glances to many and many a familiar peak and notch,—" the wavy lines of far-receding hills."

Then came the knightly vigor and mailed strength of Chocorua, towering right beside us for final admiration; the mirror-plates of Ossipee and Silver lakes; and the pretty villages scattered in the valleys that seem so green and spacious to us after the narrow and rocky defiles; the clustered peaks of Ossipee, the lone hill in Effingham, the symmetrical cone of Copple Crown,—and so good-by to the White Hills!

CHAPTER XXIII.

Homeward by the North Shore.

<blockquote>
The sea is calling, calling,
Along the hollow shore.
I know each nook in the rocky strand,
And the crimson weeds on the golden sand,
And the worn old cliff where the sea-pinks cling,
And the winding caves where the echoes ring.— ANON.
</blockquote>

NOW a new interest lay ahead,— glimpses of old colonial seaports and coast scenery, and reminiscences of that Pilgrim history in which every American must feel the keenest interest; for we were going homeward along the Eastern Division, or coast line of railroad, extending from Portsmouth to Boston.

"It is perfectly natural," remarks Baily, "that all these places along the northern shore of Massachusetts should become, as they are doing, the haunt of a constantly increasing throng of pilgrims."

"Of course it is. There is scarcely a headland, a reef, an island, a hill, and certainly not one of the older towns, on the coast between Boston and Portland, which is not linked with some noteworthy incident in our history, or about which poetry has not thrown some of its own peculiar charm. There is not a town on this seaboard but was the home of ancestors for a time of all who are of New England descent; not an old graveyard but we find in it stones marking their last resting-places."

"Yes," Prue assents; "and here, too, have lived and written the masters of our literature, and I believe that before long, the scenes of many of the poems of Whittier, Longfellow or Celia Thaxter; of the romances of Hawthorne, the river-voyages of Thoreau, and quantities of other stories, and travels, and essays written under these mossy roofs, will be as eagerly searched for, and regarded with as much interest, as are now the spots described in Wordsworth's *Excursion* or in Scott's *Lady of the Lake*."

The principal charm of this coast to many, however, will not be its historical associations, but the rare beauty of its scenery. There are other parts of our great seaboard which surpass this in grandeur,— as at Mount Desert or Grand Manan; and possibly in loveliness, as in eastern Long Island; but there is no part where so many of the elements of beauty are found in perfect combination. Here, richly cultivated fields and green lawns slope down to the water's edge, and picturesque cottages crown every knoll; while close at hand may rise a rugged hill, clothed as it has been for centuries with pine, its base torn and rent into a thousand fantastic shapes by the ever-restless sea. Nestled at the foot of some sheltered cove you come upon a quaint fisherman's hamlet, and on the other side of the point may be a city's wharves. Beaches of unsurpassed beauty are broken by cliffs, where one can sit unwearied for hours and watch the breaking waves. And all along the coast there rises a range of hills from whose tops are most enchanting views, in which sea and land, city and village, meadow and forest, blend in a picture of indescribable beauty.

"The interest and profit of a holiday spent upon the eastern shore of New England will be greatly increased if one has some previous knowledge, however slight, of the local history of the places to be visited. To obtain this will not be difficult, as nearly every place has a a library, in which half-an-hour judiciously spent will enable one to obtain a general outline of the history, together with the most important events connected with the place. It is wise also, in every place, to make the first visit to the top of some hill, securing if possible, the services of an intelligent person to point out the various objects of interest. Of the value of a fortnight's excursion of this kind in this part of our country it is difficult to speak too highly."

At Portsmouth, then, (whose hotel accommodations are the envy of its neighbors), we halted, long enough to take a long drive and a sail over to the Isles of Shoals, and a trip to York beach (a description of which has already been given,—Chap. V.), by the new branch railroad, some ten miles long, which now runs to the beach from this city.

Pring, in 1603, Champlain, in 1605, and Smith, in 1614, all reconnoitered this bay, and the latter attached his name to what are now called the Isles of Shoals. They properly describe the river-mouth as a bay obstructed by large islands and indenting the rocky shores with many inlets. On one of these islands is now the Kittery navy-yard; on another, constituting the ancient town of Newcastle, the great Wentworth Hotel, looking southward across Little harbor to the mainland cape which divides the bay from the open sea. This is Odiorne's point, and here, in 1623, John Mason, representing the Laconia Commercial Company, built the first house in New Hampshire, the foundations of which may still be traced. A few years later, the company chose a site for its "great house" on an eminence farther up the river, marked on the maps since Smith's voyage as Strawberry hill or Strawberry bank, now in the southern part of the city. This was in 1631. There dwelt Capt. Walter Neale, the first governor, a soldier of fortune, who discovered the White Mountains and named them the Chrystal Hills. There originated the enterprise which developed Portsmouth and the valleys of the upper Merrimac, Piscataqua and Saco. It was not a religious but a money-making community, and hence the picture of the earliest civilization here has a brightness that does not belong to that of its Pilgrim neighbors.

Explorations soon showed that the dream of gold and precious stones, or even of mines of baser metals, had been a "baseless fabric," but commerce widened, and with wealth grew its pomp and circumstance. Many stately relics still remain of these busy old merchant days which preceded the Revolution (the first overt act of rebellion against the crown was committed here in seizing the powder stored in Fort William and Henry, in December of 1774,— the powder whose opportune arrival saved us at the battle of Bunker Hill), and put to shame newer and perhaps more costly houses. Whatever direction the rambler takes through Portsmouth's streets,— so beautifully shaded with the mighty elms and maples the fathers planted,— he will come upon notable houses, some of which, like the Ladd, Warner and Langdon mansions, are among the finest existing specimens of our colonial architecture.

The most remarkable of them all is the Wentworth mansion at Little harbor, about two miles from the centre of the city,— a pleasant walk or an even more delightful boating excursion. It is a curious, rambling old place, built by the last colonial governor, Benning Wentworth, in 1750, for a refuge from the turmoil (and gossip, perchance) of the busy town. The house itself is substantially as when the old governor left it. The old front door, now disused, opens into a surprisingly small entry in which are still the racks for the muskets of the governor's guard. At the right, and on a lower plane, is the council chamber,— an imposing room with an elaborate wooden mantel, the carving of which is said to have required a year's labor. Several notable portraits adorn the walls, one by Copley. Beyond, is the billiard room, in which stands an ancient spinnet, strangely suggestive of the revelry that ceased long ago; and revelry *did* go on, for the Wentworths were a wild lot, and this one, as everybody knows, graced a banquet on the night of his birthday by marrying Martha Hilton, his maid-servant, who, by the way, was quite as good, or better than he, in all save polish of manners. Both Whittier and Longfellow have woven the incident into poems, but neither author could save the censure of Lady Wentworth's descendants, on the score of too free "poetic license." When the old governor died, his wife married a younger Wentworth, and with her husband entertained Washington when, in 1789, he made a sort of triumphal progress through these colonies. That is the last memorable festivity the old house saw. Its rooms and furniture are now cared for, and a fee of twenty-five cents is charged to visitors as a contribution toward the expense of this worthy guardianship.

The gay influences of which I have spoken are seen in the appearance of the town. It is as venerable and quiet as any of these seaports, whose best days came to an end when the Embargo act of 1812 put a

Old Wentworth house

stop to their marine enterprises; yet its broad and open streets, and its hundreds of fine old mansions do not carry with their age decay or mould, but elegance and traditions of good cheer. "This, with her well-preserved colonial architecture and long descended household furniture, china and silver, and the gentility befitting such inheritances, as well as that which comes from breeding and ancestry, make up the chief charm of Portsmouth. . . . The completed and restful look of everything make one grateful for the fate which has left it undevastated by improvements." It must not be supposed that Portsmouth is dilapitated or at all behind the age in feeling, however. The time-worn streets are lighted by electricity; the ancient mansions are furnished with modern appliances for comfort; over their mossy gables are strung telephone wires, and the minds of their occupants are wide-awake. Yet the past has always been respected, so that no wanton change, or brash parvenuism disturbs either the self-satisfaction of the older citizens, or that unity of appearance with historic interest which is so charming to strangers.

One of the most delightful walks is down to the scene of the first landing at Odiorne's point, where that family has a homestead dating back to 1660, and then over to Newcastle, on Great island, concerning which Mr. John Albee has lately written a rambling history full of antiquarian enthusiasm.

A mile from Newcastle village stands the The Wentworth, one of largest and finest summer hotels on the eastern coast. "It stands on a bluff overlooking the sea and the whole surrounding country. On the west may be seen the Pawtuckaway mountains, in Nottingham, Saddle-back mountain, in Deerfield, 'The Blue hills of Strafford,' and on the north, in a clear atmosphere, the White Mountains. In the foreground are the three bridges connecting the island with the mainland and the quaint old city of Portsmouth, with its environs and harbor full of little islets, twenty in number. On the north are the navy yard, Kittery Foreside, and Mount Agamenticus, the throne of the great sagamore, Passaconoway, known in legend as St. Aspenquid. On the northeast you look down on the mouth of the 'gay Piscataqua,' and the compact village of Newcastle on its south bank flanked by Fort Constitution and the antique Walbach martello tower, said to have been built in one night in anticipation of an English invasion.

"On the other side of the river are Kittery point, the home of Sir William Pepperell, Gerrish's island (which contains the cairn of the royal Champernowne), and the long broken coast of Maine. East is the Atlantic ocean and the Isles of Shoals, six miles distant. Looking southeast you see Ipswich bay, enclosed by the long, slender arm of Cape Ann. In the bend of Ipswich bay are the Rye and Hampton beaches, six and ten miles distant. Coming nearer are Odiorne's and Frost's points. Between the hotel and these two points

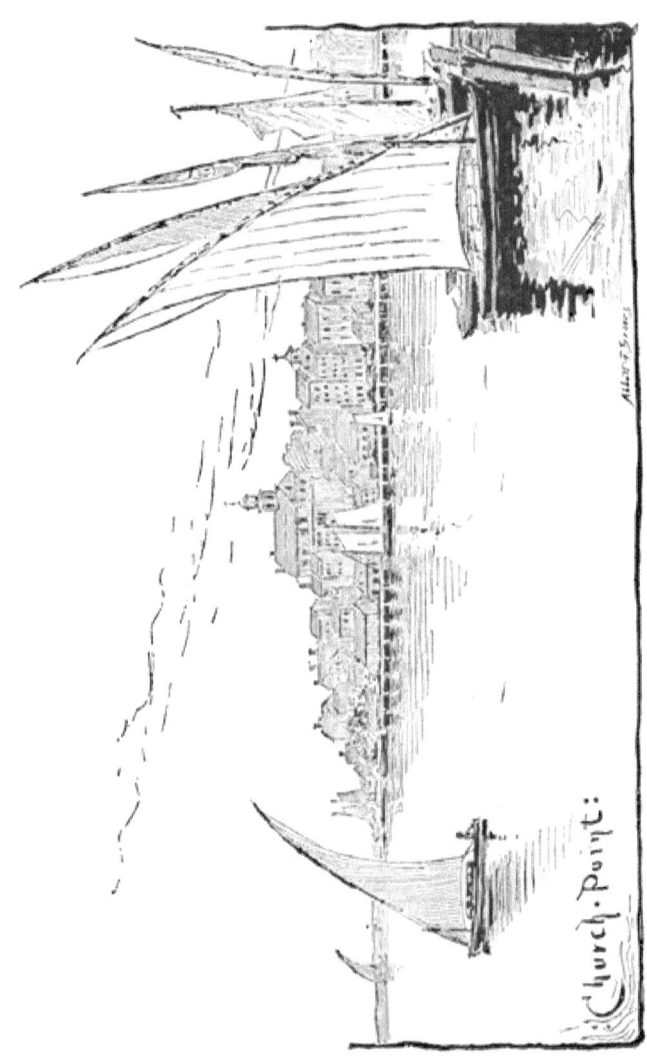

is Little harbor, forming an inland lake suited to fishing, boating, and bathing. On the southwest and west is a wooded country, through which runs the beautiful Sagamore creek, emptying into Little harbor directly opposite the hotel. On the shores of this creek are many picturesque old houses, among them the noted Martine mansion, the Lear Hermitage, and at its mouth the famous Wentworth house."

On Kittery point stands "the queer old Fort McClary, a nondescript structure, half wood, half stone, and many-angled; something between a block house and a Martello tower." A little distance eastward of it is the mansion of Sir William Pepperell, and his tomb. Sir William was a trader and the son of a trader; a militia colonel, rich, prosperous, a man of probity and sagacity, and the central human figure in these parts, in the first half of the 18th century. In the French war of 1745, he was selected, in spite of the fact that the governor of the province, the doughty old Benning Wentworth, might have gone, to lead that famous expedition against the citadel of Louisburg. Vaughn and Portsmouth did most of the practical work of gaining the victory, but Pepperell got the lion's share of the credit and the first knighthood issued to an American. Besides his own mansion, there are several others in Kittery associated with his name or fame: the Bray house, built in 1660; the Sparhawk house; the Cutts house, of tragical history; and others. Indeed, it has been said that in his prime he could travel from here to the Saco and always sleep under his own roof. Francis Campernowne is another name of noble descent, identified with early history at Kittery; and the boat-ride around the point and along the shores to Spruce creek, which leads up to York, is a delightful experience for the student of colonial annals.

Of one little incident whose sequel we have already learned (Chapter V.), a word ought to be said. In September, 1775, two British ships of war, the *Scarborough* and the *Canceaux*, were in Portsmouth harbor, and ready to carry away Gov. John Wentworth. They were also ready to burn the city; but "the fascinating Mary Sparhawk, the Tory belle of Kittery, captivated the heart of the *Canceaux'* commander, Captain Mowatt, and changed his fell purpose." She thought Portland would do just as well to sack as Portsmouth; and so he sailed away to that port, and burned 400 houses. Thus Mr. Albee tells the story; and it is very likely that the gallant captain wanted pretty Polly Sparhawk to believe her influence so effective; but in reality, the memory of his insult on Munjoy hill, must have been more potent than regard for either Portsmouth or the belle of Kittery.

From Jaffrey point and other headlands of the shore at Portsmouth, the Isles of Shoals, only six miles away, show plainly their low outline. "Often, however," remarks Mr. Albee, "the mirage elevates them, and then they resemble the chalk cliffs of the English channel; sometimes changing to the battlements and towers of a feudal city, then fading away, as if raised and dispelled by enchantment. Every day brings some change in their appearance. Though anchored, they seem to have the mobility of the sky and the water. One day they are on the farthest horizon-line; another they are but a step. . . . They are our weather-glass; and we judge of the day or the morrow, whether to fish or plant, according to their monitions."

Perhaps no part of the coast less needs to be written about, yet an account of this district would be incomplete without including so old and popular a resting-place for tourists. Time was, years ago, when the islands had a large population and commercial importance. The security which they offered from the Indians made them very early the resort of fishermen; and by the middle of the 17th century they were the home of a large and busy community. These were a wild and lawless set, however, and no women shared their home until after 1650, when a more settled civilization took the place of fishing encampments. Star island had a town called Gosport, containing 400 inhabitants, prior to 1700, and the records of this fishing outpost contain some curious reading. At the outbreak of the Revolution the people were ordered off the islands, as it was feared they might give aid to the British. A few only returned at the close of the war, and for many year's past very few persons have lived there the year around, yet in summer the islands often fairly swarm with humanity, and a humanity of a style far removed from the simple fisherfolk of old.

COTTAGE AT JAFFREY POINT.

A little steamer runs back and forth three or four times a day, during the pleasure season, between the islands and Portsmouth, a distance of twelve miles. The northernmost of the group is Duck island, which is almost unapproachable, and tenanted by seafowl. Two miles to the southward, Appledore lifts up its huge

> Ribs of rock . . . round which
> The nightmared ocean murmurs and yearns,
> Welters, and swashes, and tosses, and turns.

It is the largest of the islands, being a mile in length, and seventy-five feet above the sea at it highest point. A stone's throw away is Haley's or Smuttynose, to which are joined at low tide Malaga and Cedar islands. A short distance to the westward of the latter is Star, its summit still crowned with the little granite church around which were once gathered the houses of Gosport. Still farther westward are Londoner's, with its solitary house and tiny sand beach, and finally, White's island, where the lighthouse stands, and which has gained immortal fame as the home of a little girl who became one of our sweetest poets,— Mrs. Celia Thaxter.

It were vain to attempt to describe the varied charms which these barren rocks have for those who love the ocean; to tell of the countless rifts and chasms into which the sea has rent the shore, or to point out the solitary rock on which, to one looking over the broad expanse of the deep, there comes such a strange exhilaration and fullness of enjoyment. But it is an experience for a lifetime to stand on such a spot during an easterly gale, and watch

> The mad Atlantic,
> When surge on surge would heap enorme,—
> Cliffs of emerald topped with snow,
> That lifted and lifted and then let go
> A great white avalanche of thunder.

It is not until you are close to it that any landing is visible upon Appledore, and then the steamer turns into a miniature harbor and lands at a little wharf in front of a big hotel and a group of cottages, where a confidential jollity reigns as the sentiment of the place, due to the close way in which everybody is thrown together on this lonely island. The northern part of Appledore, Charles Dudley Warner describes as an interesting place to wander. "There are no trees, but the plateau is far from barren. The gray rocks crop out among the bayberry and huckleberry bushes, and the wild rose, very large and brilliant in color, fairly illuminates the landscape, massing its great bushes. Amid the chaotic desert of broken rocks further south are little valleys of deep green grass, gay with roses. On the savage precipices at the end, one may sit in view of an extensive sweep of coast with a few hills, and of other rocky islands, sails, and ocean-going steamers. Here are many nooks and hidden corners to dream in and make love in, the soft air being favorable to that soft-hearted occupation."

A little steamboat does the duty of ferry-boat between the islands, and is always available for a short excursion. By it you go to Star island where there is a bigger hotel, even, than that on Appledore. It was from a ledge at the southern end of this island that Miss Underhill was swept away in 1848 by an unexpected wave; and the hotel is surrounded by relics of Gosport.

A certain bright morning found us back from the Isles of Shoals and resuming our trip.

The first station south of Portsmouth is Greenland, — a small, fruit-raising centre, near which stands Breakfast hill, where a terrific battle with the Indians once occured.

"I reckon it was because of that icy mountain that Greenland was given its name," is Baily's somewhat ambiguous observation.

"Why? — What icy mountain?"

"Breakfast hill."

"Why *icy?* I persist."

"'Cold day when they got left.' Cold — icy mountain. See?"

"No, I don't. That's miserable, my friend. Try again."

"By the way," Prue interrupts, "*who* 'got left'— Indians or whites?"

Baily is disgusted and declines to answer. The questioner turns to me.

"I don't know,— I forget," she forces me to acknowledge.

"Strikes me you're as weak in your facts as Mr. Baily is feeble in his wit."

This crushing retort enforces silence until the Hamptons come into view. Through this town runs that stream of which Whittier wrote his stirring poem *The Wreck of Rivermouth*. This river, or inlet, separates Salisbury beach, south of it, from Hampton beach. The latter beach is divided by Boar's Head, a noble bluff some seventy feet high, jutting far out into the ocean. To the north, beyond Little Boar's Head, a lesser bluff, lies the far-famed Rye beach, for many years the most frequented of all the beaches on the eastern shore. Its attractions, in addition to the bathing and the sea-views, consist principally of the pine-woods lining the shore and the beautiful country inland. The upper limit of this beach is Straw's point, which is near Portsmouth. From these headlands, on which cottages have been built and roads laid out, remarkably fine pictures up and down the coast are revealed:—

>And fair are the sunny isles in view
> East of the grisly Head of the Boar;
>And Agamenticus lifts its blue
> Disk of a cloud the woodlands o'er;
>And southerly, when the tide is down,
>'Twixt white sea-waves and sand-hills brown,
>The beach-birds dance and the gray gulls wheel
>Over a floor of burnished steel.

Stages run from Greenland and North Hampton stations to Rye beach, connecting with principal trains. Hampton "is now a quiet and pleasant land of peace and plenty, abounding in gray old colonial mansions and traversed by broad level roads." Hampton Falls is an ancient village, north of the station, in which lived the venerable Dr. Langdon, and here, in 1737, the governors and legislatures of Massachusetts and New Hampshire met, surrounded by military guards and all the pomp and circumstance possible, to confer upon the question of the boundary. They failed to agree and referred the matter to the king. His orders were intended to be carried out; but, in fact, it is only within two or three years that the precise limits of Massachusetts in this region have been settled. In early times Hampton river saw much West Indian and local commerce, ship-building and cod-fishing.

The extensive salt-marshes, where now huge stacks of hay dot the wide expanse like an immense encampment of Indians on the plains, were the attraction in the early settlement of this region, since these marshes afforded the hay which there was not clearing enough to cultivate upon upland meadows. One of the old customs of the place survives in Salisbury, which occupies the dry land between the Hampton salt-marshes and the Merrimac river, and is full of pleasant traditions. This custom has led the people of the vicinity during the last two cen-

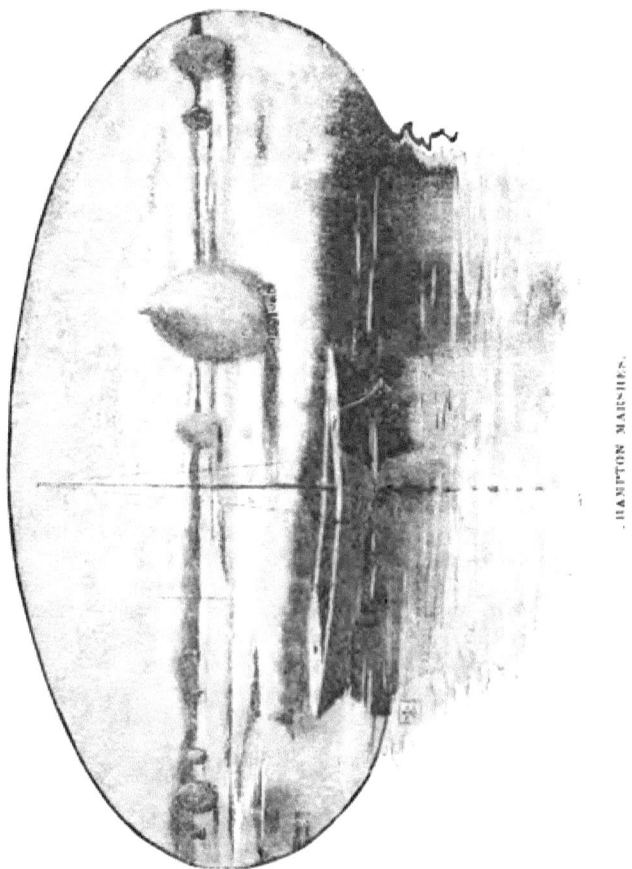

HAMPTON MARSHES.

turies to gather in August for a picnic on Salisbury beach, whose six miles of sand is skirted with cottages and hotels, and where is the scene of Whittier's *Tent on The Beach*. This gathering has of late years assumed enormous proportions, as many as 25,000 persons sometimes coming together and listening to speeches,—chiefly political. A branch-railway from Salisbury runs north to the busy, yet graceful, factory village of Amesbury, ensconced in hills overlooking the Merrimac, where Mr. Whittier lives, and to which there are many allusions in the poet's verses. It has been well said that his poems might serve as a guide to Essex county; and the best commentary upon them from this point of view will be found in an illustrated article by George M. White in *Harper's Magazine* for February, 1883.

Crossing the long and lofty bridge that spans the Merrimac, we find ourselves at Newburyport, and once more in Massachusetts.

"The pleasantest and easiest way to see Newburyport, and its parent town, Newbury, is to take a carriage, as many of the points of interest are some distance from the centre of the city. High street, which runs for about six miles on the ridge along the river, parallel with the shore, impresses one from the first by the noble trees which shade it, its great width, and the succession of old houses which line it on each side for a great part of the way. There is very little variety in the architecture. They are generally three stories high, the upper being lower-studded than the others, with the door in the middle, opening into a wide hall which runs through the centre of the house. The prevailing color is white; and they are all set back some distance from the sidewalk, with well kept door-yards." The size of these old houses is amazing. Each one would do for a hotel, if the spacious rooms were each cut up into *suites;* and the difference between the means and cost of building in those days and this, as well as the changed sentiment in regard to home-life and domestic economy generally, are suggested to every visitor.

On the right-hand side, just south of State street, is the house of the late Caleb Cushing. Soon after passing the Oldtown church, at the foot of a short lane on the left, is what is known as "the old garrison house," on the doubtful supposition that it was erected for that purpose during the Indian wars. The older part is a striking bit of architecture, what you might see in almost any old English town, but almost unique in this country. Beyond this lane there are fine views of the sea and coast, while near at hand

> Long and low, with dwarf trees crowned,
> Plum Island lies, like a whale aground.

Passing the Lower Green, the burying-ground of the first settlers above can be seen in a field on the right, where a few stones are still visible above the grass.

Up the river, one should visit the old ship-yards, now deserted and grass-grown, furnishing picture-subjects that an etcher would love to try his hand at. A mile further the quaint and beautiful chain-bridge is reached. This, the first bridge of the kind in the United States, was built in 1792, and crosses to Deer island, where is the summer residence of the novelist, Mrs. Harriet Prescott Spofford. Mr. Parton, the historian, and his wife, "Fanny Fern," live not far away; the castle-like farmhouse of Sir Edward Thornton is in sight; while Ben: Perley Poore has the quaintest old "chateau," in the country, a short distance farther on. I think nothing could be more entertaining in the way of river scenery than the drive up the bank of the Merrimac, even as far as to Haverhill.

Another part of the city of great interest to the sight-seer, is the suburb Belleville, where the eccentric Lord Timothy Dexter used to live; the same who wrote the book in which all the punctuation marks were put in a lump at the end, to be distributed by the reader as he pleased.

These are all scenes and memorials of a peaceful history. The first settlers came in 1635, led by a minister named Parker, who had won fame at Oxford by his writings. They sailed up Parker river, and landed near where the bridge now crosses. This became the farming centre of Newbury, but at once there began to grow up, near the mouth of the Merrimac, a settlement devoted to fishing and maritime industries, which in 1764 was separately organized as Newburyport. It soon became one of the most important of New England's seaports, and built so many ships that in 1792 alone, ninety vessels left its stocks. From here sailed the first privateer commissioned by the American republic, fitted out by that great merchant, Nathaniel Tracy, in whose quandam mansion the Public Library is now domiciled. During the Revolutionary struggle Mr. Tracy sent out at his own cost no less than 47 ships of the same character, mounting 340 guns, and manned by 4,418 men. A thousand citizens, at least, were lost or captured at sea, and the town's war-expenses amounted to $2,500,000. With natural pride the citizens boast that their grandfathers destroyed tea in the Market square before the Mohawks threw it into Boston harbor.

"But the Revolution, and the drain of men for the Essex County regiments, checked the prosperity of the place, and in 1788 only three vessels were built. President Dwight says of the village in 1796, 'Indeed, an air of wealth, taste, and elegance is spread over this beautiful spot, with a cheerfulness and brilliancy to which I know no rival.' Washington, Lafayette, Talleyrand, Louis Philippe of France, and other famous men were entertained here by the aristocratic families. An extensive foreign commerce was firmly established, and in 1807 the tonnage of the port was over 30,000. The Embargo fell with crushing force upon this maritime industry, and the great fire of 1811, which swept away sixteen acres from the most densely built quarter, checked the prosperity of the town, and reduced its population to 6,388. Its valuation in 1810 was about the same as in 1870. The town grew slowly, and its Merrimac-built ships were famous throughout the world for fleetness, strength, and symmetry, and were made in large numbers until the decline of American commerce." (*Sweetzer*.) Of late years the cotton-mills, the shoe-manufactories, and the ship-yards (now, however, closed) have restored to the town something of its ancient activity.

We greatly enjoyed driving about Newburyport, and spent two days in doing so very pleasantly, for we had a letter of introduction which furnished us with the most amiable of guides and companions. But to Baily the town wore an especially joyous look, for here he met,— whom do you think? The lady from Washington who had been the bright particular star of our little rainy-day party at Phillips, away down in Maine. I had felt — though I had pooh-poohed Prue's voluble assertions to the same effect — that our bachelor had been hard hit, as the saying is, by that young lady. I knew he had written to her, and that the letter cost him nearly a whole day's thought and pretty nearly a whole night's work, which was an entirely new manifestation of unreadiness in him; and I knew he had had at least one letter in return, which fact he begged me to conceal from Prue,— another novel development in his give-and-take good humor. And when we accidentally learned that she was here in Newburyport, and, a few moments afterward, by pure chance, met her in the street, discovering an acquaintance between her and our guide so that we were all thrown together, I no longer doubted my friend's sentiments.

That evening he detained me, as we were about to say good-night, and begged me to take a stroll with him and a cigar — you may be sure it was a good one! — before going to bed. I let him talk to suit himself, and it was not long before he came round to the subject nearest his heart and made a clean breast of the matter. I didn't attempt to discourage him,— had no wish nor any reason to dissipate by a word the sweet delusions with which he was pleasing himself in regard to this young lady, who was a fine girl to be sure, but yet, to my eyes, was not superhuman in qualities nor wholly unique in loveliness. Nor did he know, what I had happened to learn (but kept to myself), that the young lady had been the recipient of a legacy which placed her far above any need for service in the Treasury, or any where else, for pay, hereafter; so that his love was as instinctive and unselfish as that of Pyramus and Thisbe, or of any other fond pair, who ever yearned and dreamed, and came out of the clouds at last to find a firm footing together upon a smiling earth, and so " were happy ever afterward."

Well, Prue and I prolonged our stay a whole day more on Baily's account, and helped his courtship (unspoken, of course, as yet) all we could. I suppose Prue would have liked nothing better than to play mock-dueña for a month. But one day was all *I* could stand, and so the next morning we set off again on our travels homeward.

Newburyport left behind, the train carries us out across immense salt-marshes, whose hundreds — perhaps thousands — of haystacks, perched upon small piles, lifting them just out of reach of the tide, stand like an enormous encampment of Indians upon a prairie. The varying colors which at every season, but especially in the autumn, overspread these spacious grassy flatlands, are always changing and beautifully relieve the monotony which might otherwise condemn them. These marshes are in Rowley and are traversed by the winding and sluggish currents of the Rowley and Parker rivers. The people who settled the uplands along their borders happened to include several fullers, and they soon set up a small mill in which was made the first cloth manufactured on this continent by English people, or perhaps, by any European.

Next comes Ipswich, the ancient *Agawam* of which colonial history has so much to say, and where now is a village packed with reminiscences. All the early voyagers were greatly pleased with the place, which the Indians had selected before them as a favorite farming ground. "This place," says John Smith in 1614, "might content a right curious judgment. Heere are many rising hilles; and on their tops and descents many corne fields and delightfull groues."

It very narrowly escaped being the first landing place of the *Mayflower*, which sailed to Plymouth instead, only because there happened to be rough water on the bar. The first settlement was therefore deferred until 1633, when John Winthrop, Jr., bought the whole township of the Indians. The next year the Rev. Nathaniel Ward went there as pastor, and soon after wrote that famous tract called *The Simple Cobler of Agawam in America*, which was one of the earliest real estate advertisements issued in this country. Several of the men who succeeded to his pulpit were noted for authorship,—among the rest, William Hubbard. Near the station stands, perhaps, the oldest house in town. It is said to have been the garrison house, and also to have been, for a short time, the residence of Governor Endicott. It is well worth a visit. Passing up Market street the first object of interest is the house in the cellar of which the three regicide judges were hid from British officers. The church on the Green is built on the site of the one where Whitefield had his famous encounter with the devil, whom the stalwart preacher chased from corner to corner of the church, into the belfry and out upon the steeple, from which Satan was obliged at last to take a flying leap. Ascending Town hill at the head of the street, whence a very remarkable view of sea, dune-marked shore and rolling meadows is obtained, and passing along the ridge, the ancient grave-yard is reached, where an hour can be whiled away among the crumbling and curious stones that marked the dead-and-gone celebrities of Agawam. One stone goes back to 1647. Crossing Choate's bridge,—anybody will tell you the story of its building a century ago, and how the people meant to hang Choate if it fell down—you reach the Baker house, reputed the oldest in town; and then may climb the hill where an Indian maiden sat so long that her ghost is thought to be there still, awaiting the return of her lost sailor-lover.

> He never came back! Yet faithful still,
> She watched from the hill-top her life away;
> And the townsfolk christened it Heartbreak hill,
> And it bears the name to this very day.

There are legends about the bar, also; and many points along the coast where now summer hotels, cottages, and camping parties, make the beaches populous with merry-makers.

Essex and Wenham stations are parts of old Agawam, and in each there is material enough for a whole book of pleasant reminiscences. Then comes Beverly, with a more modern air, and a little later we dodge into a short tunnel and out again under the roof of the Salem station.

"I suppose no one ever comes to Salem for the first time," Prue observes, as we saunter down the crooked main street, "without thinking, first of all, of the witchcraft; and that is unfortunate, because that panic lasted only a little while, and did not begin in Salem, but up in Danvers, and a great many people outside of this one town were engaged in it."

"Very true. Why, even down in Virginia they treated some old people abominably — even put them to death — on the same charge."

"For that matter half the world believes in witchcraft still," Baily adds. "But are we going to Gallows hill, where they hanged some of the poor wretches in 1692, and out to old Salem Village to see the houses and other relics of the panic?"

"Not I, for one!" exclaimed our lady. "The sooner it is forgotten the better. Let's walk about the town — it is really a beautiful and busy old place, they say — and then run down to Marblehead."

"Agreed."

To this harbor, in September of 1628, came the vessel bringing Governor John Endicott and his company, to join the few families under Roger Conant who had retreated to Naumkeag, as the locality was called, from the inhospitable shores of Cape Ann. (The Pilgrims seem to have had the most singular success in hitting for their first residences upon precisely the worst situations to be found along the whole coast). The next summer a large number of colonists arrived, the best known of whom was Francis Higginson; and the year following came Governor Winthrop. The town grew steadily and spread peacefully into the neighboring country, but little of startling incident belongs to its story up to those fatal days of 1692, which have lent to it such sad celebrity. Almost the only notable circumstance earlier than the witchcraft frenzy, was the expulsion of Roger Williams. The tiny church in which he preached during his brief ministry can still be seen behind Plummer Hall; and the house where he lived stands on the corner of Essex and North streets. As some of the official proceedings in the witch trials of 1692 took place before Judge Jonathan Carver, who was its occupant at that time, it has since been known as "the witch-house." Leaving these gruesome times, and that darkened locality, we seek along the water-front traces of Salem's subsequent prosperity, for it was as a maritime place that she steadily grew in numbers and importance. All that she saw of war was one Sunday morning in February, 1775, when General Leslie marched over North bridge in his unsuccessful attempt to seize some cannon belonging to the citizens. She sent many men into the Continental ranks, however, while her fishermen and sailors became the flower of the navy.

At the close of the war, the East India trade was opened, and Salem flourished exceedingly until the ruin of 1812 overtook her commerce. It was during this time of great fleets and fabulous profits, when her merchants were princes, in truth, and Salem captains were swaggering in every port of the world, advertising Yankee shrewdness, pluck, and ingenuity,— it was then that these fine large houses were built, and these elegant gardens were planted that are the admiration of visitors to-day. To go down to Derby wharf and wander about the warehouses and the old custom house, recalling the scenes with which the century was ushered in there, is to get as near to the romance of commerce as is possible in this country; and perhaps, in general, there is more romance to the acre, in and about "peaceful" Salem, than anywhere else on the continent. Fortunately, too, so many books and magazine articles and stories have been written dealing with the old town and its history, that no one need burrow in the dust of mouldering buildings or records to acquaint himself with either of them.

"How natural it is, then," remarks Prue, "that the greatest romancer of our country should have been bred here."

She was speaking, of course, of Nathaniel Hawthorne, whose birthplace on Union street we saw, and whose nook in the custom house, where he wrote *The Scarlet Letter* and so much more, was shown to us. But scores of other novelists and historians, warriors, politicians, and great teachers, have been sons of Salem, and its society now is singularly intellectual and aristocratic. Such institutions as Plummer Hall and its libraries; the Peabody Institute and Academy; the East India Marine Hall and Museum — the latter especially interesting — and the various schools of high degree, are testimonials to this regard for learning and refinement, past and present.

Salem, though likely to be thought of chiefly in connection with its past, is by no means dead. It has some 30,000 inhabitants and active business interests. These are mainly in the line of leather production and shoemaking, and have drawn into the outskirts of the city a large population of foreigners.

After we got through with our glance at Salem — and it was merely a glance — Madame Prue was in haste to go to Marblehead; but I, on the contrary, desired the party to follow me on a run down to Cape Ann and back. This Prue agreed to do if I would go with her to Marblehead later; but when Baily was consulted, he told us with a timid air, quite different from his ordinary self-assurance, that he must beg to be excused, as he had engaged to go to Newburyport that evening and stay through the next day.

"There's some sort of a party on hand for this evening, you know, and tomorrow,—well—I believe there's to be a boating-picnic; and Miss—"

Yes, yes. "And Miss—" That would be all the tune now.

"Good-by, good-by,—old fellow," I said, and seized his hand, wrung it for an instant and turned aside with something that sounded like a sob.

"Farewell, farewell, dear friend. We'll never see thee more. Heaven bless you—ah!" And pressing her handkerchief to her o'erflowing eyes the gentle Prue drooped silently away.

"Well, of all the idiots I know," cried Baily, "you stand at the head. What do you mean by this infernal nonsense! Can't a man go to see his girl without being cried over as if he were going to be hanged?"

"Of course he can," Prue retorts, whirling round, her face sparkling with merriment, "if he will be above-board about it, and not sneak off as though he were ashamed of himself. Do you suppose that young lady, or any other, would feel flattered at hearing you apologize for wishing to spend some hours in her society? You're a goose!"

"I suppose I must be, as I am the next thing to a perfect duck," is Baily's repartee, as he boldly stands beside the little lady.

Thus we raised his spirits and sent him off rejoicing to his lady-love, while we took the train to Gloucester and Rockport.

This road branches from the main line at Beverly, an eastern suburb of Salem, devoted to leather and shoemaking on land and yachting on the water; in winter you may see dozens of crack sailing and steam-yachts hibernating alongside the railroad bridge. Turning seaward the road follows the coast, giving frequent views of the sea, for about seventeen miles, a little north of east, to the barren, surf-beaten rocks at the end of Cape Ann. For the first half of this distance the shore is indented by numberless small coves, whose out-jutting promontories, each crowned with one or more red-roofed cottages, give it a singular attractiveness. But beyond the mouth of Gloucester harbor its character suddenly changes; and there are few places more suggestive of storm, shipwreck and death, than the rock-bound desolate shore from Eastern point to the end of the cape. A range of hills, rising often sheer from the water's edge, extends from Beverly to Rockport, the foot of the last, Pigeon hill, being washed by the ocean. At first these hills are densely wooded; but on the cape itself they are strewn for the most part with huge bowlders, between which, here and there, a stray pine finds scant room to grow, giving a sense of barrenness and desolation quite in harmony with the savage, storm-beaten shore. A turnpike, built through this rocky wilderness with great ingenuity and solidity, runs close to the water the whole way, affording, now glimpses of the sea, now wide panoramas in which water and land are mingled, until at length, at the uppermost point, the sea in all its magnificence holds undisputed sway over every sense.

A little way beyond Beverly is the station Beverly Farms, which is justly regarded as one of the most attractive spots for a summer residence upon the whole coast. It is never overrun by a promiscuous swarm of visitors, as the land is almost entirely held by a few wealthy proprietors, who are constantly adding to the beauty of the shore by cultivation of its natural advantages and the building of most inviting looking houses. The beach is somewhat sheltered by Great Misery island, over which can be seen Baker's twin light-houses. Manchester-by-the-Sea, a little way beyond, is of the same character. William Black was entertained there during his American visit, and has incorporated an account of the place in his *Green Pastures and Piccadilly*. He speaks of it, in one reference, as "a small, scattered, picturesque watering-place, overlooking Massachusetts bay, the Swiss-looking cottages of wood dotted down anywhere on the high rocks above the strand," with many more words lending a romantic color to the place, such as we are accustomed to hear bestowed upon scenes of beauty in foreign lands, but that sound unreal, though none the less true, when applied to a home-locality. Beverly Farms, Manchester and Magnolia, the next community beyond, are the summer residence of many people of wealth in New England, not only, but boast among them a great many names of national repute; and it is not too much to say that no other piece of coast approaches this in the double charm of natural beauty and artistic cultivation. An indication of the kind of people who dwell there appears in the fact that the railway finds it profitable to run several fast trains a day, each way, to which are attached parlor cars, each seat in which is rented by the season to a regular passenger.

Magnolia takes its name from the abundance of magnolia trees in the woods,— a plant very uncommon elsewhere in New England. This part of the shore is growing in favor with the public, and is less exclusive than its southward neighbors. There are several hotels on the Point, which is some two miles from the station. Kettle and Knowlton's coves are pretty nooks in the granite coast-wall; and just beyond the latter is that remarkable break in the rocks called Rafe's chasm, where the surf makes a magnificent display in stormy weather.

As these woods and rocks are full of poets and painters, verses and pictures innumerable have been made in their glorification. "How charming the Manchester shore is, and how the people who own all these pretty houses," exclaims one enthusiast, "must hate to leave their perches on the rocks above the sea! Magnolia point used to be, once upon a time, the nearest approach to a French sketching town of which this shore could boast. Our easels by the roadside blew over as often as if we had been in Normandy, and, to my mind, the sea was much bluer and the sun brighter. I never can enter the wood by the little station without remembering the kind friends, the clever set, who used to sit on the platform here in October, with bundles of canvas, waiting regretfully for the Boston train."

Picturesque in many ways, and especially about its wharves, yet expressing a wholly different sentiment, is Gloucester,— a city of 25,000 people at the head of a noble harbor, and the foremost fishing-port in the world. Whatever else it may do or appear to be, Gloucester, first and last, is *fish*: cod, halibut, mackerel,— mackerel, halibut, cod,— fresh, salted, dried, and smoked. Her fleets haunt the distant sea-banks, and her men serve in navies and the merchant-marine all round the world. If I should begin to tell such stories as you may hear upon her wharves, or on the decks of her beautiful schooners, or within the comfortable homes of her innumerable captains, there would be no ending. I must just say, therefore, to every and any inlander, that he

OLD WHARVES AT GLOUCESTER.

will never regret a visit to Gloucester, nor find dull the reading of her annals and the study of her adventurous trade.

Beyond Gloucester the railroad climbs over a dreadful stretch of almost naked rocks to the odd little seaport of Rockport, whose tiny harbor is one of the most sketchable on all this picturesque coast. Rockport is famous for its quarries of granite which are a little outside of the village, and reached by a branch of the railway. How well-worth seeing these quarries are, to anyone with artistic appreciation, you can judge from the illustrations accompanying a brightly descriptive article upon them in *Harper's Magazine* for March, 1885.

A little north of Rockport, beyond the great quarries, is Pigeon Cove, at the foot of Pigeon hill, whose green slopes are in striking contrast to the other rock-strewn hills of the cape. About fifty acres of land lying between this village and the northeastern end of the cape have been laid with streets and avenues in every direction. Many summer cottages and boarding-houses have been built, and the place attracts crowds of visitors and summer residents. The woods afford fine opportunities for rambling, while the ocean views are superb. Standing on the extremity of Halibut point, one could almost fancy himself on the deck of a ship far out at sea, but for the enormous waves, that, even on a calm summer's day, break at his feet. This is the very end of Cape Ann, thrust boldly out against the ocean; and it is covered thick with historical incidents belonging to the time of the earliest voyagers and colonists, to whom it was a landmark. Fine old traditions are rooted in the crevices of its rocks, and many a poem has been inspired there,— Whittier's *Swan Song of Parson Avery*, for one.

Following the wagon road around to the northern shore of the cape, and passing under the beautiful willow arch, the pedestrian reaches Lanesville, a part of Gloucester, and the home of fishermen and stone workers. Bay View is the bluff near by, where there are some noble summer residences and whence a fine and extensive view oceanward is given. The next point of interest is Annisquam, a quaint village built around the coves that form its harbors. To students it has lately become well known as the seat of a seaside school of natural history, which grew out of the fact that the United States Fish Commission made Gloucester its summer station for several years,— a matter of great value not only to the town, but to the fisheries-interest of the whole country.

Of all the suburbs of Salem, none is more interesting than antique Marblehead, which once was the second settlement in New England in wealth and extent of its commerce. It was hard for us to realize this fact, as we wandered about the charmingly irregular streets of this most picturesque of all our sea-shore places; though every few steps brought us in sight of some stately relic of the fortunate past. Save for yachts and a few coasters, the spacious harbor is now deserted; yet a century ago it was always crowded with merchantmen and fishing vessels, the wharves and water front were thronged with buyers and sellers, and noisy with seamen in foreign garb and "full of strange oaths."

In its history and in its antiquated appearance lies the attraction of Marblehead to the traveller,— and no one who has ever heard the name can lack curiosity to visit the place, or, having gone there, can fail to feel abundantly rewarded. I have time here for only a hint of this history and picturesqueness, culled from that bright pamphlet by an anonymous writer, entitled *Eastern Ramblings*, from which I have freely quoted in this chapter. Anyone can easily find more detailed information.

The first thing which strikes the stranger is the utter unsuitableness of the locality as a town-site,— a mere mass of granite knolls and ledges. But the town grew there accidentally, with reference to the fine harbor. "From the very beginning of the settlement of Massachusetts bay these rocks had been a place where fishermen had been accustomed to land and dry their fish; but it was not till the beginning of the last century, that, under the influence of their pastor, John Barnard, the townspeople began the business of exporting fish. From this time the commerce grew rapidly, until the fleet of merchantmen and fishermen numbered several hundred vessels. Then the wealthy merchants built those houses, of which the Hooper and Lee mansions are the finest specimens left. The latter, now occupied by two banks, with its noble hall and grand staircase, its wainscotted parlor and richly carved chimney-piece, enables one to catch a glimpse, as it were, of the state in which the merchant princes of those old colonial days lived. In the events leading to the Revolution, Marblehead took a prominent part. Her townsmen, under the lead of Elbridge Gerry, to whose wise counsels and ready pen some of the most important of the early Revolutionary measures were due, were eager and defiant in their determination to resist British tyranny to the bitter end. Nor should Boston ever forget, that, in the time of her greatest trial, it was from Marblehead that she received the most sympathy and aid. A Marblehead captain, John Manly, first hoisted the American flag; and, according to John Adams, a mortar taken by him, drove the British out of Boston. Another, Commodore Tucker, 'captured more British vessels, guns, and seamen than any other captain in the service.' One of the bravest exploits of the whole war was that of James Mugford, who, just released from a British ship by the entreaties of his newly married wife, captured a powder-ship and carried her to Boston at the critical moment when the ammunition of our army was nearly exhausted. On his return in his fishing smack he was beset by boats from the British fleet, and fell, mortally wounded, after successfully repelling their attacks. A monument has lately been erected to his memory. Colonel Glover's regiment, composed wholly of Marblehead men, and known as the Marine regiment, was no less effective on land. Had they not manned the boats on the night of the eventful retreat from Long Island, it is doubtful if Washington could have saved his army, nor would he have won the battle of Trenton had not the same brave men ferried the troops across the half-frozen Delaware on that bitter cold December night. In the war of 1812 nearly one fifth of her whole population were serving either in the army or in the navy. Possibly some of the oldest inhabitants may still remember the day when the rocks were covered with those anxious men and women watching the fight between the Chesapeake and the Shannon. . . . In the war of the Rebellion the same spirit was shown, the three Marblehead companies being the first to report in Boston on the call for troops, after that signal gun was fired at Fort Sumpter, and she is said to have furnished more men, in proportion to her size, than any other place in the north.

"To-day, the chief business carried on in the town is shoemaking, the fisheries being almost wholly abandoned. Though one misses the active bustle and strange sights of a thriving seaport, yet a ramble through these quiet streets will give one much to enjoy. The irregularity of the ledges on which the old town is built, lends even to ordinary houses a peculiar quaintness; and the streets are picturesque in a degree unusual in a New England town. Add to this an unrivalled sea-view from almost every point, and you will understand the charm which Marblehead has for all who know it. Not far from the entrance to the little harbor is the old well,—all that is now left of the Fountain Inn, with which is connected the one romance of this matter-of-fact old town. . . .

"A short distance from the site of the inn is the house where 'poor Floyd Ireson,' the hero of Marblehead's tragicomedy, ended his blighted life. Whittier's ballad tells his sad story, with a poetic license which is now resented by his former townsmen; and it is doubtful if the visitor to Oakum bay will get a civil answer if he asks a neighbor to point out the injured skipper's cottage.

"A pebbly beach — the scene of Hawthorne's essay, *Footprints on the Seashore*, and Longfellow's poem *A Fire of Driftwood* — connects Marblehead neck to the mainland. This part of the town was for many years a resort for summer visitors, who lived in camps or rude huts; now, red-roofed cottages and summer hotels have almost wholly taken their place, and the holiday camping parties will soon be seen no more. A walk or a ride around The Neck gives many fine views, together with the sight of some grand rocks. . . . The Eastern Yacht Club have their club-house on The Neck, and on Thursday evenings throughout the summer, music and dancing enliven the scene.

"The oldest church in the places is St. Michael's, built in 1714, and remaining substantially unchanged to this day. Its curious roof and the brass chandelier, presented to the church in 1732, are worthy of note."

From Marblehead we did not return to Salem, but went by that line of railroad which runs along the shore through the pretty summering hamlets, Devereux, Clifton, Beach Bluff and Phillips Beach, where natty modern cottages line the shore and solid old farmhouses are seen inland. This road rejoins the main line at Swampscott, which is a large and flourishing community in summer, and in winter, when the almost numberless boarding houses are closed, a very quiet one. Down at Blaney's beach, however, which is the shore-front of Swampscott, there remains a great deal of the primitive and quaint appearance acquired before the locality became fashionable; and this, to many persons, is the most entertaining part of the whole gay region. "The boats come in, the fishermen jump into the water and draw them up on the beach, just as their fathers and grandfathers did, day after day, for generations back. In the cottage doors stand the women, whilst the children play about their feet and watch for the return of the boats, as they stood when the first boats went out. Behind this hamlet the hill rises quite precipitously; and after somewhat of a scramble, you find yourself in pine woods, from beneath whose branches you look across the bay to Nahant."

In 1629, five colonists of Salem struck out for themselves and chose the plain which we enter upon as soon as we pass Swampscott. The Saugus river makes its way to the sea here, and the settlement was called after it until 1637, when it was formally named Lynn, after Lynn Regis, in England. (An ancient village, still called Saugus, lies a few miles inland, and is reached by the roundabout "Saugus Branch" of the railroad). Lynn was distinguished at an early day for two things — its historian, William Wood, and its iron foundry (started about 1642), where were made the dies for the pine-tree shillings; where in 1654 was built the first fire-engine for Boston; and where the scythe was invented and first manufactured. The origin of the shoe-trade, which is now Lynn's almost exclusive industry, was the coming to the town in 1750 of a Welshman named John Dagyr, whose enterprise and skill were such that he speedily attained to wide celebrity. "Rising from the heart of the city, to the height of 185 feet, is High Rock. The view from the top can hardly be surpassed in beauty by any upon the coast. On the right lie Boston, Chelsea, and the harbor, made, as Wood says, 'by a great company of islands whose high cliffs shoulder out the boisterous seas.' Directly in front is Nahant, with its ribbon of sand connecting it with the mainland, and far beyond on the horizon can be seen the low line of the south shore. Farther to the north is the pretty village of Swampscott, half hidden amid the trees; and over the pines lies Marblehead. Salem and the Gloucester shore bound the view in that direction. Inland, the eye sweeps over an almost boundless extent of city and country, field and forest, Mts. Wachuset and Monadnoc and other lesser hills being visible. . . . At the foot of this hill lived, for half a century, the once famous fortune-teller, Moll Pitcher. Her cabin, which is still standing, though removed from its original place, was the resort chiefly of sailors, most of whom followed her advice implicitly. Many a time, it is said, ships have been unable to obtain crews on account of her warnings. Besides climbing this rock, the visitor to Lynn should not fail to go through Ocean street to Swampscott,— a street lined with pleasant residences, across the lawns of which can be obtained most inviting glimpses of the ocean."

Lynn is the last station on our long list. Already Bunker Hill monument and the State House dome are within sight. We rush like the sea-wind across the Mystic meadows, and through the back-yards of Chelsea and Somerville. Then, while we gather up our packages, and look at one another with glances which try to tell how grand an excursion we have had and yet (so contradictory is human nature) how good it will seem to get home, we rattle noisily over the Charles River bridges and come to a standstill in the railroad station on Causeway street, in dear old Boston.

We had telegraphed the time of our intended arrival, and Patrick was waiting at the depot when the punctual train drew up. He had a carriage ready, and, keeping Baily with us for one more day, at least, we were soon jarring noisily over the paving stones,— how different from the yanking lurch of the buckboard in the Maine woods, or the easy swing of the Glen coach, or the smooth roll of wheels around Lancaster and Conway, Portsmouth or Lynn!

"You oughtn't to complain!" growled Baily; "you're in *Boston* — what more can you ask, short of Paradise!"

We very properly paid no attention to such a remark as that. New Yorkers can sometimes make themselves intensely unpleasant, and nothing is more disagreeable than an exhibition of envy. No person born and bred in Boston, and expecting to go to heaven by a special rapid transit from this most Christian city, need pay the slightest attention to such wrong-headed insinuations. Besides, we had just turned the corner and were in our own familiar street. Prue leaned forward and uttered a little ejaculation of surprise.

"One would think we were giving a party,— just look at the house!"

Evidently a fire had been built in every grate, and the gas lighted in every burner of all the rooms.

"I was thinkin' ye'd like to see it lookin' cheerful-like when yez came home," says Bridget, her honest face welcoming us in a blaze of red hall-light, and with a smile as expansive as her white apron.

"Well, I *am* glad to get back!" cried Prue, taking a little run through the parlors before darting up stairs to lay aside her wraps.

Then Bridget disappeared, giving me a chance to extinguish a dozen or so of her kindly but wasteful burners, while Baily, tossing aside his overcoat, sang jauntily,—

Be it ever so costly,
There's no place like home.

But it seemed to me, as his tone lingered and softened on the last word, that he had more in his mind than simply a bit of badinage.

Then Prue came down, and, with happy eyes, led the way to our bright dining-room, where, when we had sat down, Baily must first of all command us to fill our glasses to the brim; and next, rising, he must make a little speech, giving unheard-of credit to Prue for all our pleasure and its happy outcome. This done, with a gallant bow he leaned forward and touched the rim of her glass and mine with his. "Health and happinss to you, dear Madame Prue — and to you, sir — and next year may you come to be *my* guest!"

"Can you not say *ours*," ventured my wife, pausing an instant with an arch glance across the sparkling wine.

"I certainly mean to try!" Baily retorted bravely, and so we drank a double toast all round,— yea, a triple one, for you, dear reader, were not forgotten.

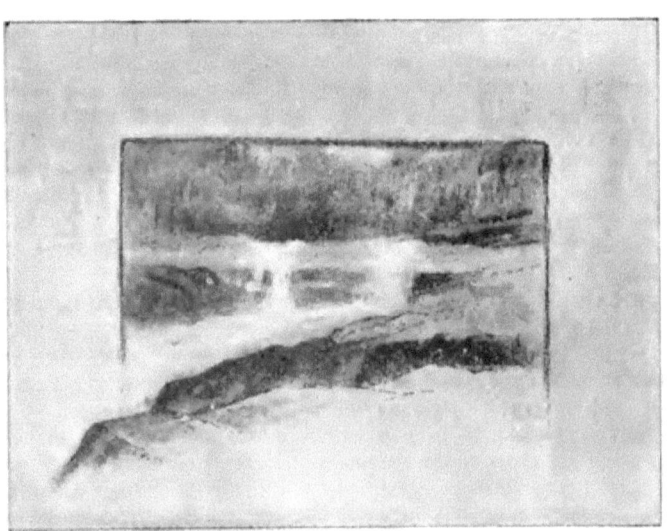

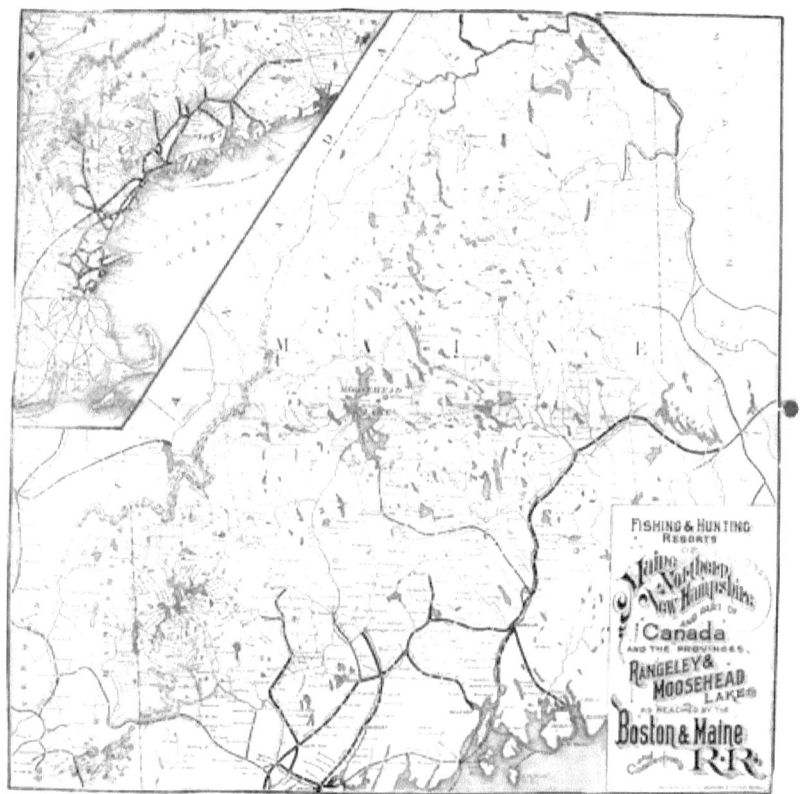

www.ingramcontent.com/pod-product-compliance
Lightning Source LLC
Chambersburg PA
CBHW032115230426
43672CB00009B/1745